How To Tutor

Books by Samuel L. Blumenfeld

HOW TO START YOUR OWN PRIVATE SCHOOL — AND
WHY YOU NEED ONE

THE NEW ILLITERATES

HOW TO TUTOR

HOW TO TUTOR

Samuel L. Blumenfeld

Arlington House

New Rochelle, N.Y.

Library of Congress Catalog Card Number 73-10834

Manufactured in the United States of America

Library of Congress Cataloging in Publication Data

Blumenfeld, Samuel L.
    How to tutor.

    1. Tutors and tutoring. 2. Education, Primary
I. Title.
LC41.B58   372.1'39'4   73-10834
ISBN 0-87000-212-0

FOR
Janet and Claude,
Suzy and Nini

Contents

Preface

The need for tutors today is greater than ever. The reason for this is quite obvious. Public education is mass education, and there are hundreds of thousands of children who need individual, one-to-one attention if they are to achieve any real success in their schoolwork. The mass educational setting is simply not conducive to good work for many slow-learning children. In addition, public school instruction is deficient in so many ways, that millions of children of average intelligence are not learning what they should. This fact has been confirmed over and over again by the many educators who have written books about the problem. The public schools have begun to recognize their deficiencies in recent years and the result has been a proliferation of student tutoring programs in which older students tutor younger students. In fact, these volunteer-tutor programs have become an integral part of the mass educational process and have been expanded to include volunteers from all sections of the community. The National School Volunteer Program estimated in 1973 that there were as many as two million volunteers tutoring about five million children in three thousand programs.

However, there is no way of knowing the effectiveness of these tutoring programs. Most of them have been instituted to help the student tutors as much as the children being tutored. Thus it is hard to know if a student tutor is doing the kind of instructional job which requires a higher degree of skill and knowledge than he might possess. In addition, there is no way of knowing whether the instructional methods being used by these student tutors are sound or not. As for the non-student volunteers, William L. Smith, director of the U.S. Office of Education's Division of School Programs, pointed out at a 1970 Right-to-Read conference that there is "little or no empirical evidence to show that volunteers make a significant difference in progress and achievement of individual pupils, particularly those in the inner-city." The reason for this, obviously, is that the volunteer tutors are instructed to use the same teaching methods as used by the professional teachers, but on a one-to-one basis. Hence, the lack of real progress among the pupils, and hence the need for this book, which provides a sound program of instruction in the three basic subjects of primary education: reading, writing, and arithmetic.

Most parents wait until their child is having difficulty at school before they think of providing some remedial or tutorial instruction. Sometimes the child is already so far behind, so confused, so frustrated by the experience of not learning in the first two grades, that the remedial program must be a long and difficult one. However, proper tutoring at the preschool level or in the first and second grades, as a preventive measure, can make sure that the child has the basic foundation on which he can build his school achievement. Too many children do not get this foundation in the first two grades of public school, and as a result, get into deeper and deeper trouble as they try to advance on a shaky or non-existent foundation without a thorough knowledge of the basics.

The purpose of this book is to provide the tutor with an instructional program which will provide the child with the proper foundation of fundamental knowledge and skills by which he can further enlarge this knowledge and develop these skills. It can be used by anyone interested in tutoring children: student tutors, parents, retired teachers, and housewives with some college or professional background, who would like to earn extra money by tutoring in their homes. It can even be used to tutor adult illiterates in the basics.

Reading, of course, is the big problem in today's public schools. The incredible pedagogical confusion which exists among primary school educators concerning reading instruction is the basic cause of the high degree of reading disability among school children. In my book, *The New Illiterates*, I wrote at length about this problem, its causes and its remedies. The reading instruction program in this tutoring book has been devised specifically to provide tutors with a way of circumventing the confusion that now besets primary and elementary school educators regarding this subject.

There is no reason why any American child need suffer, even though he must be exposed to the current deficiencies and malpractice in elementary school instruction. Tutoring in the basics at home by parents, or by a paid tutor, can insure that the child will be spared the agony of frustration and confusion which beset many children exposed to the uncertainties of their teachers. This book, therefore, can and should be used with preschool, first-grade, and second-grade children as a preventive program to spare the child later need for remedial instruction. It can also be used with pupils in higher grades who lack a strong foundation in the basics.

It cannot be stressed too much that instructional competence depends basically on the soundness of the instructional methods used. Unfortunately, the public schools have become the arena for pedagogical debate and experimentation in which the children are freely used as guinea pigs. The result is that many children are exposed to unsound teaching methods which leave their mark on the children's minds. Some children never recover from the damage done in these classrooms.

It is interesting that John Holt, in his popular book, *How Children Fail*, could write, "The unbelievable incompetence of some of the kids sometimes drives me wild." Yet he made virtually no attempt to investigate the instructional methods to which these children had been exposed to see if, perhaps, the genesis of their incompetence could be found in the incompetence of the methods used by their teachers. Yet Holt's observations were made during the late fifties and early sixties, when elementary reading instruction in our schools bordered on the insane. Today, the situation has improved a little, but the instructional incompetence is still not to be believed. It is the opinion of this writer that the present constitution of our educational system not only makes this incompetence possible, but also inevitable. This is all the more reason why tutoring can be of such great importance in saving thousands of children in distress. Confirmation of this can be found in the March 1971 issue of the *Reading Teacher*, in which

Frank Vellutino, Director of the Albany Study Center for Learning Disabilities, wrote:

> Surveys and statistics notwithstanding, the magnitude of the [reading] problem is well appreciated by school administrators and teachers who must live with it daily. Reading specialists in particular are overwhelmed by the many children requiring remediation. The number of youngsters, however, who need assistance far exceeds the number of trained professionals available.

Thus, the need for private tutors is both obvious and urgent.

Acknowledgments

In gathering the knowledge necessary to create this book, I was fortunate to have at my disposal two great depositories of educational literature, namely the Boston Public Library and the Monroe C. Gutman Library of the Harvard Graduate School of Education. I am indebted to Malcolm C. Hamilton, head of public services of the latter institution, for making its facilities available to me.

The reading primer is derived from the research I did for my previous book on the reading problem. The writing primer is the result of extensive research on that subject in educational journals and textbooks. There is little available in print for the layman on that subject. The arithmetic primer required considerable research in the history of both arithmetic and mathematics and an inspection of both the old out-of-print arithmetic textbooks and the new elementary mathematics textbooks. By comparing the old arithmetic with the new math, I hope I have been able to come up with something better than either as far as an approach to beginning arithmetic is concerned.

My thanks is also due to Master Douglas McElwain for posing for the picture used in the handwriting primer and to David Hildt of the National School Volunteer Program for supplying me with the materials used by that program. I am also grateful to James W. Jackson of the Southern Educational Communications Association for arranging a tour of primary classrooms in several private schools in Columbia, South Carolina. The enlightening discussions I had with teachers and headmasters turned out to be extremely helpful in confirming what my research had indicated. Finally, my thanks must go to David Franke, Senior Editor of Arlington House, who suggested the need for such a book on the three R's and made its writing possible.

S. L. B.

Boston

May 1973

Part One

How to Qualify as a Tutor

The art of tutoring is as old as education itself. In the early days, before the Industrial Revolution, before there was such a thing as mass education, children were taught the basic educational skills by tutors, or in very small school houses. The wealthy hired tutors not only to instruct their children in the necessary skills of reading and writing, but also to provide a proper moral upbringing. The hiring of a tutor was considered a very important business. John Locke, the English philosopher and educator, writing in the 17th century, described the difficult problem of finding a good tutor who, he insisted, should have "sobriety, temperence, tenderness, diligence, and discretion," qualities he considered as "hardly to be found united in persons that are to be had for ordinary salaries nor easily to be found anywhere." He explained further:

> The great difficulty will be where to find a proper person. For those of small age, parts, and virtue are unfit for this employment; and those that have greater will hardly be got to undertake such a charge. You must therefore look out early and en-

quire everywhere, for the world has people of all sorts. . . . If you find it difficult to meet with such a tutor as we desire, you are not to wonder. I only can say, spare no care nor cost to get such an one. All things are to be had that way, and I dare assure you that if you can get a good one, you will never repent the charge but will always have the satisfaction to think it the money of all other the best laid out.

Of course, the kind of tutors John Locke wrote about (the tutors who served the aristocracy of preindustrial times) are not the kind needed today. The tutoring we need is of a much more limited kind, resembling the situation of a person who gives piano lessons. Yet, even tutors on this limited scale must have certain qualities which make them successful in their tutoring. If you intend to tutor children you should be fond of children, have enormous patience, be affectionate, and understand the young mind: its eagerness, its curiosity, its tendency to wander from the difficult problems at hand, and its resistance to required effort. So, it does take considerable skill to teach a child. The three most important ingredients of good tutoring, however, are patience, an understanding of the young mind, and a knowledge of the subject you are teaching.

Children also have very strong egos. Their desire to succeed is very great, and success in learning is important to their self-esteem. Therefore, they must be taught in very gradual steps, so that success is assured by the simplicity of what is taught. Never show impatience if the child does not catch on. There may be something in the way you are presenting the subject, or some distraction on the part of the child, or some slowness in the child's ability to understand what you are driving at. Perhaps the child has not fully digested the previous lesson. It may even be necessary to go one step backward before you can take the next two steps forward.

The child's self-esteem is as fragile as his constitution. You would not expect him to carry a heavier weight than his physical strength permitted. Likewise, you must not expect him to understand something too complex for his young mind to grasp. And you must not expect him to learn easily or well if the methods you use are illogical, confusing, or poorly thought-out. We teach the complex by breaking it down into smaller, simpler parts. That is the method we have used in the program of instruction in this book. We start with the simplest and most elementary parts, make sure the child learns them, and proceed from there. In each section of the book you will find more precise instruction for the subject to be taught.

Who is qualified to be a tutor? Anyone willing and able to do the job can tutor. If you are a parent with a high school education, you are eminently qualified to teach the basic program in this book to your own child—provided you have the time and patience to do so. If you are a high school or college student you may also qualify if you can follow the instructions in this book, relate well to children, and understand their learning problems. Retired teachers, of course, make excellent tutors, adapting their years of schoolroom experience to the tutoring situation. And finally, there is that large category of married women with college educations who, for one reason or another, do not pursue full-time careers, but have the time, the energy, and the desire to offer tutoring services at home for a few hours a day. For such women, tutoring can indeed be an excellent way of supplementing the family income as well as performing a valuable, needed service for the community. If you charge five dollars an hour and tutor four children a day, that will provide you with one hundred dollars for a five-day week. That one hundred dollars can be used to pay a lot of bills. Of course, you must declare that income on your income tax return, but you can also deduct all the expenses involved in earning that money. Such expenses would include advertising, materials, books, pencils, paper, blackboards, phone calls, postage, and other expenses incurred in earning that money, including, incidentally, the cost of this book. If you set aside a small room in your house for tutoring, you can deduct all the costs of maintaining that room, namely electricity, heat, and a portion of your total rent.

It is not necessary to have had formal teaching experience to become a good tutor. If you have enjoyed reading to children and answering their questions, then you should enjoy tutoring. With the proper instructional materials, anyone who enjoys children can become a good tutor.

How do you find children who need tutoring? In a small community, word of mouth is the best way. A small sign in front of your house, a short classified advertisement in the local paper, or a notice on the bulletin board of a laundromat or supermarket are some of the ways to make your services known to the community. Also, if you have done schoolteaching in the past, your friends in the school system (teachers, advisors, administrators) might be of some help in locating children who need tutoring. You might even type up a promotional letter explaining that you specialize in tutoring preschoolers. Have it multilithed and mail it out to families and schools in the area. You might make your services known to women's clubs, or parent-teacher associations in the area. And, of course, there are the "yellow pages."

How much to charge depends on how great the demand is for your time and the parents' ability to pay. An hourly fee of between three and ten dollars can be charged. You might start at the lowest practical fee until your tutoring skills are perfected and your reputation established. By then you should have more requests for your services than you can handle. You might then be justified in charging a higher fee. If you find that you can successfully tutor more than one child at a time, you might still charge the same fee but increase your income by tutoring more than one child in one hour.

The Art of Tutoring

The art of tutoring, like any other art, is learned in the doing. To be really good at it requires some special personality traits, skills, and sensitivity. The one-to-one relationship brings you into direct, personal contact with the pupil. There is always some tension, some anxiety in a relationship of that proximity. The way you relieve that tension and anxiety is to make the child feel that he or she is liked. You might start out by saying something nice about the child's appearance. You should also let the child know that he is in for an interesting time, that both of you are going to enjoy the hour you spend together. If you are tutoring in your home, choose a well-lighted, bright part of the house for the instruction area. Treat the child with courtesy, helping him (or her) off with his (or her) coat. Show that you are glad to see him. All of this is to make the child receptive to your instruction and to put him at ease.

Since you both will be sitting together, have two chairs and a table on which you can spread out the instructional materials. You should also have an upright blackboard. You might sometimes find it easier to explain things by the use of such a blackboard in conjunction with side-by-side instruction. Be flexible. The instructional materials in this book can be used with as much flexibility as the situation requires. See what works and see what doesn't. Each child is different, and you will find that an approach that works with one child may not work with another. The most important point to remember is that each child is an individual and that you will have to work with him in order to find the approach that suits him best. Each child brings to the tutoring experience a different amount of knowledge, a different attitude toward learning, and a different attitude toward the tutor. The expert tutor knows how to adapt himself to the personality of the child.

In the tutoring situation the child is relieved of the problem of competing with others in the classroom. But at the same time, he wants to make a good impression with the tutor. Anyone who comes for instruction, whether it be a child or an adult, is sensitive to the fact that he is inferior to the instructor in the area of knowledge in which he is to be instructed. The child who does not know how to read may not think of himself as an illiterate, but he does know that he lacks a skill which every child slightly older than him already has. He is sensitive about his intelligence and his ability to learn. He badly wants to succeed and can be easily disappointed if he falters. Therefore, it is important to pace your instruction according to the child's ability to learn. It is also important to give him a pat on the back when he learns well. In feeling out the child's abilities and general understanding, be patient, affectionate, and maintain a sense of humor. Never scold, never show anger, never show impatience.

Plan each lesson in advance. Know the material you are going to cover. Get to the instruction once the child has settled down. Do not waste time. Get the child absorbed in the learning process so that he does not have a chance to be distracted. After you explain something to him, have him do it, write it, or read it. This gives him a chance to absorb what he has been taught and to use his hands and fingers or express his thoughts verbally. If, during the lesson the child seems overly restless and inattentive, try to find out the cause. Are you going too fast or too slow? Is your approach too dry? Perhaps a short break for a drink of water might be helpful.

In order to maintain the appropriate pace of instruction, you will have to be sensitive to the child's rate of learning. It is better to give him a little more of what you think he can learn than less. By giving him more, you don't give him a chance to be bored. In addition, by giving the child a little more to learn than his present capacity, he becomes accustomed to the process of exerting mental effort. This is important, for although we should try to make learning as interesting, exciting, and as pleasant as possible, there is no escaping the fact that learning requires mental effort—mental work—and the sooner the child becomes accustomed to the process of mental work, the sooner he will understand, appreciate and enjoy the whole process of intellectual mastery. Therefore, maintain a pace that requires the child to exert some mental effort. However, do not require efforts which are clearly beyond his capacity. Reading, writing, and arithmetic require the child to master a good deal of symbolic abstraction. Such mastery does not occur effortlessly. But once the mind is put to work, it begins to expand its capacity to handle even greater abstractions.

The mind works in a very remarkable way. It has the power to integrate a great deal of new knowledge with what it already knows, and the result is a greatly expanded understanding. The mind seems to have a limitless ability to absorb knowledge over a long period of time, and this ability expands with use—just as a muscle will grow larger if it is required to lift heavier loads.

Muscle building by weight lifting is probably a perfect example of a similar process which goes on in the brain, namely, the expansion of capacity through greater exertion and use. If a weight-lifter lifts the same light weight a thousand times, it will not expand his muscle. He can only achieve this by lifting a much heavier weight to the limits of his capacity. To go beyond his present limit requires an exertion that is painful but necessary if his capacity is to grow to meet greater demands.

The brain's capacity expands in the same way. It requires mental exertion of a comparable intensity to reach a higher level of ability. No one likes mental exertion any more than he likes physical exertion, and this is true of adults as well as children. But such exertion, unfortunately, is necessary if the child is to achieve any degree of mastery of the subject matter at hand. Thus, the child should be led slowly, patiently and gradually to understand how he must exert mental effort to acquire the skills and knowledge necessary for him to advance scholastically. Of course, like the muscles of the body, the brain becomes tired and requires periods of rest and recuperation—especially after great exertion. The tutor should be able to sense when the child's mind is tired and that he can learn no more during that period.

The tutor can be greatly instrumental in teaching the child the most efficient ways of using his mind by guiding its use step by step. The instruction in this book has been designed to give the child a sense of order in what is being learned. The approach has been to reduce the complex to its simplest parts, so that the child can be led to grasp simple concepts before moving on to the more difficult. Once the child sees the logic behind the symbolic systems he must work with, he has taken a giant step toward intellectual development. Most of the "work" in mental exertion consists of understanding concepts. The rest consists of either pure rote memory, or repeated use of concepts until they become automatic responses.

Teaching a child the basic skills of reading, writing, and calculation is like teaching him how to swim or play the piano. The skills to be learned require lots of practice. There is not much difference between mastering a physical skill and mastering a mental skill. Both require effort and practice. Both use up energy. Both have to be taught in an organized, logical way. Both can be made exciting or dull, depending on the approach of the teacher. But the process of mastering a physical or mental skill is an exciting one for the student, for he looks forward to mastery with great anticipation. Swimming and playing the piano will afford him many years of enjoyment and pleasure. Reading, writing, and calculation will afford him years of enjoyment and rewarding activity, increasing his capacity to earn money and providing the kind of life for himself that he will want. Thus, in teaching any basic skill to a youngster, one must see it in terms of long-range, life-long use. One must see it as contributing to the child's future adult happiness. To be concerned simply with the child's present enjoyment of what he is doing is to shortchange him in the future. His ability to master a skill will contribute greatly to his own self-esteem, his own sense of self-worth, and his ability to make his way in the world with confidence. That is why it is worth taking the time to make sure that the child masters the basic skills.

A good tutor can easily earn the everlasting gratitude of a youngster who is having trouble learning in a crowded classroom where his special needs and problems are ignored. But it takes time to identify the pupil's learning difficulty. You do this first by finding out what the pupil actually knows. Some children are afraid to admit that they don't know what they think they should. They don't want to appear stupid. The fear of being thought stupid or of actually *being* stupid is very real, and is in itself a learning handicap. The child must get rid of this fear, and the tutor can help him remove this fear by showing him that he can learn.

Children who cannot learn via the deficient instruction in school classrooms tend to blame themselves for not learning. They are in no position to question the instructional methods being used by their teachers. Thus, if they fail to learn they think it is because of their own deficiency, not the instructor's. The schools tend to reinforce this view by insisting that there is something wrong with the child, not the instructional methods. Books have been written listing all the things wrong with children who cannot learn to read via the prevalent methods being used in the classrooms of America. There are, fortunately, a few books listing the things wrong with the methods, not the children. In *The New Illiterates* I analyzed the teaching methods which have been used to teach millions of children how to read, and I showed how deficient these methods were. I also showed how tenaciously so many educators have clung to these methods (despite tremendous criticism) and how detrimental they were to the children exposed to them.

It is, of course, possible to undo the damage done by faulty teaching methods, but it can be an extremely difficult task. Any bad habits learned in the first and second grades are very hard to displace with good ones. In some cases it is impossible. Some children simply cannot unlearn these bad habits. That is why it is so important to start the child off on a sound footing with sound instruction.

The fear of failing is the greatest handicap to learning, and a child gets this fear only when he begins to see that he cannot cope with the material being given him in the classroom. As a tutor, you need never arouse the fear of failing for the simple reason that you are free to use any method which will enable the child to learn the concepts and skills he is being taught. If the child is normal and has an adequate vocabulary, he can learn all of the basics with no problem at all. If the child comes to you because he is having difficulties in the classroom, try to get to the heart of the problem. To do so you must find out the following: the methods to which the child has been exposed in the classroom, how much he has learned, what he knows and what he doesn't know, and if the child is physically normal as far as eyesight and hearing are concerned.

It is important to have this preliminary information about the child if you are to tutor him successfully. You can find out what methods he has been exposed to by visiting the school he attends or has attended, by talking to the teachers he has had, and by examining the textbooks used. In the Appendix to *The New Illiterates*, I listed and evaluated the most widely used reading instruction programs in this country. Check that list to see if the child has been taught by one of the methods evaluated. If he has been exposed to one of the deficient methods, you will have to devise a way to overcome the bad habits learned.

The instructional materials in this book start from the beginning. They start with the assumption that the child has not as yet been instructed in these subjects. But they can also be used with children who have already been taught something. That is why it is important to find out how much the child knows. You can pace your instruction accordingly. Before taking on the child, you should question the parent sufficiently, so that you have an idea of how to proceed. Here is a suggested list of questions which will elicit the information you should have:

What is the child's age?

What schools has he attended?

What grade is he in?

What textbooks is he using in school?

Has he had any instruction at home in the subjects to be tutored?

What instructional methods has the child been exposed to in school and at home?

What are his present skills?

Does the child have any specific learning problem which the tutor should be aware of?

Does the child have normal hearing and eyesight?

With that basic information, you will be in a much better position to tutor the pupil successfully.

Why Tutoring Can Succeed Where Classroom Teaching Does Not

Perhaps the most important advantage tutoring has over the classroom situation is that the tutor can much better guide the attention of his pupil than can the classroom teacher. He can direct the pupil's attention to the particular idea or knowledge to be mastered. In a large classroom a child's attention can easily wander. There are a hundred potential distractions around him. Focusing attention requires the effort of self-control, an effort which many children fail to make. The tutor helps the child focus his attention by being right there beside him. He does this mainly through dialogue, by talking directly to the pupil and eliciting responses. In this way the tutor can assess immediately whether the child is grasping the concepts being taught. Conversely, it might take weeks in the classroom before the teacher could discover whether the pupil has learned what he was supposed to learn. If the pupil is particularly clever in hiding his ignorance, or if the teacher is indifferent to a child's understanding of the subject, the child's ignorance may never be discovered. Some children manage to get through high school completely ignorant of concepts they should have learned in the early grades—concepts which teachers in later grades assume the child knows. Children are often too embarrassed to admit that they lack fundamental knowledge in some subject areas. They pretend to know when they really don't.

These hazards are eliminated in tutoring. The tutor keeps a close tab on what the child knows and he does not proceed further until the child firmly grasps the ideas and knowledge he must have in order to go on. Why is the classroom situation so non-conducive to learning? Distractions, fear of appearing ridiculous in the competitive situation, lack of teacher attention, and the teacher's tendency to want to control and manipulate a whole class rather than understand the individual student are among the principal reasons. The teacher must teach as if all students learn alike when it is obvious they do not. In a classroom where children are deadly afraid of appearing stupid, they tend to give the answers they think the teacher wants to hear. They do not think in terms of what is objectively correct, but what will please the teacher.

In tutoring, the teacher must not be interested in merely eliciting so-called right answers, but in seeing that the pupil understands the concepts being taught. The interaction between tutor and pupil is so close and so dynamic, that the tutor can sense when a child has grasped a concept and when he hasn't. If the child doesn't fully understand what he is being taught, the tutor does not mark the child wrong, or score him a failure. He simply continues to work with the child until the child *does* grasp the concept to be learned. The classroom teacher, however, because of the distance between him and the pupil, has no way of knowing whether the child has learned anything. He can only find out by way of a test given a day, a week, or a month later—if at all. The child sees the test as an arbitrary judgment of his intelligence. If he fails, he feels stupid and incompetent.

In tutoring, this entire process of measuring intelligence is avoided. The child simply does not proceed to anything more complex until the tutor is satisfied that the child has mastered the material taught up to any given point. This is why tutoring can be so effective. The tutor works directly with the mind of his pupil and can sense when the pupil is learning and when he is not. When the pupil is not learning, the tutor can immediately find out why, make whatever adjustments are necessary, or explain things in different, more comprehensible terms until the pupil learns. The moment of learning comes when the pupil integrates in his own mind the concepts or knowledge the tutor imparts. The tutor can see if the pupil understands what he is learning by a process very much like instant replay. Sometimes understanding does not come all at once, but in bits and pieces. Eventually the bits and pieces fall into place and become a comprehensible whole. This is the learning process, and the tutor becomes intimately aware of how it works by seeing it operate in the child right next to him.

In this process the child's motivation is directed not merely toward pleasing the teacher, but to pleasing himself and proving to himself that he can master a skill, understand a concept, and also absorb knowledge. The pupil, of course, wants the tutor's approval, but the tutor must be clever enough to make the child feel that important sense of satisfaction which comes from mastery of the subject rather than from the tutor's praise alone. Satisfaction with self is far more important in building self-esteem and self-confidence than teacher approval. The former comes with a pleasing knowledge that one knows how to use one's mind; the latter, merely from an acknowledgement of good behavior.

John Holt contends that children fail in the classroom "because they are afraid, bored, and confused." He explains:

> They are afraid, above all else, of failing, of disappointing or displeasing the many anxious adults around them, whose limitless hopes and expectations for them hang over their heads like a cloud.
> They are bored because the things they are given and told to do in school are so trivial, so dull, and make such limited and narrow demands on the wide spectrum of their intelligence, capabilities, and talents.
> They are confused because most of the torrent of words that pours over them in school makes little or no sense. It often flatly contradicts other things they have been told, and hardly ever has any relation to what they really know—to the rough model of reality that they carry around in their minds.

The tutor can eliminate all three causes of failure. First, he can eliminate the fear of failure by simply proceeding according to the child's own learning pace; by making sure that the child understands the concepts imparted to him, by sensing when the child is having difficulty, and by sometimes taking one step backwards in order to take the next two steps forward. The tutor's sensitivity to a child's learning behavior permits him not only to catch the child when he is not learning but, through an intimate, constant dialogue between tutor and pupil, permits the child to catch himself as he begins to understand how the learning process takes place. All learning is inner dialogue, and the tutor-pupil dialogue is an externalization of this process. That, alone, makes tutoring a superior learning experience *because the learning process is learned*, as well as the subject matter.

The tutor can also eliminate boredom by making the process of intellectual mastery as exciting and exhilarating as it actually is. Nothing is more satisfying to the human being than intellectual mastery, for the simple reason that the mind is man's special tool for survival, his most distinguishing feature when compared to the other species. His mind is what has made him superior to other species. Therefore, when the mind masters a skill it provides deep psychic satisfaction to its owner—a metaphysical and existential satisfaction related to his special place in the universal scheme of things. When a child masters an elementary intellectual skill, he derives a real feeling of efficacy, competence, and independence—all of which increase his self-esteem and self-confidence. In a tutoring situation, the pupil is too busy mastering a skill to get bored.

The tutor can also eliminate the confusion that besets children in today's classroom. If his instructional methods are consistent, rational, and sound, there will be no confusion. The instruction in this book has been prepared to eliminate the kind of contradictory, senseless instruction which is so much a part of modern elementary pedagogy. We have written this book specifically to make it possible for the child to circumvent the confusion to which he will be exposed in the classroom. Since tutoring, at this time in our educational history, can only supplement the classroom, we realize that children will be exposed to our contemporary pedagogical confusion no matter what they learn from a tutor. However, the tutor can so fortify the child with good learning habits, with an understanding of basic concepts, with a mastery of elementary skills, that no amount of classroom confusion will hamper the child's continued progress.

Thus, we see in tutoring an essential alternative to the classroom situation, an alternative more and more parents will turn to as more and more qualified tutors offer their services to a public which desperately needs them.

Part Two

Reading

Reading is the most important single skill a child will learn during his entire school career, for on the ability to read depends the development of everything else. In fact, reading is the beginning of real intellectual development, and if the child is not taught to read properly, his entire intellectual development will be handicapped. The reason for this is quite simple. Language is the vehicle of thought. We formulate all our concepts in terms of words. If we restricted our thinking and learning only to the words we heard and spoke, our intellectual development would not be very great. The written word, however, is the depository of all humanity's complex thinking, and an individual must have easy access to the world of written language to be able to increase his own intellectual development. Thus, the facility with which a person reads can influence the degree of his intellectual growth. If a child is taught to read via methods which make reading disagreeable to him, he will turn away from the written word entirely and deprive himself of man's principle means of intellectual development. This has occurred quite frequently among our functional illiterates, who have been taught to read by such deficient methods that they have found reading to be too difficult and painful a task to perform.

The extent to which reading instruction has become deficient in our schools has been the subject of many important books, from *Why Johnny Can't Read*, by Rudolf Flesch (published in 1955), to my own book, *The New Illiterates*, published in 1973. That the problem should still persist is an indication of the obstacles that institutions sometimes place in the way of real progress. Thus the need for this book, which circumvents these institutional obstacles.

To better understand what is involved in teaching a child or an adult to read our written language, it would be useful to quickly review the history of writing. The first writings of primitive man were not inscriptive representations of spoken language. They were pictures representing ideas of a religious character. The spoken language was used to interpret the pictures, and we can assume that the interpretations varied from reader to reader and generation to generation. Undoubtedly traditions grew up around the interpretations so that there evolved a very close relationship between the picture and what was said about it.

This earliest form of writing is known as pictography or ideography. Pictography evolved into hieroglyphics, which was an attempt by way of picture symbols, ideographs, or characters, to depict spoken language more accurately. As civilization became more complex and the need for recording history, religious doctrines, court procedures, and commercial transactions became more urgent, hieroglyphics more and more corresponded to spoken language. Some characters represented whole words, others represented parts of words. Anyone who wanted to write had to learn the meanings of thousands of characters and symbols. However, since hieroglyphics were of pictographic or ideographic origin, they tended to incorporate many of the inaccuracies and ambiguities inherent in such a writing system. Eventually some hieroglyphics went so far as to include phonetic clues to the actual spoken words they represented. But the hieroglyphics still had to be learned by memory, character by character, and it was a laborious, tedious task. Only scholars and priests became expert users of hieroglyphics.

Finally, because the need was so urgent, someone invented a way of *directly representing spoken language* in as accurate a manner as possible, doing away entirely with the hieroglyphic system. He studied the sounds of the spoken language, isolated them, and designated symbols, or letters, to stand for each. This set of sound symbols was called the alphabet, after the names of the first two letters in the system, alpha and beta.

The superiority of the alphabetic method of writing was clearly demonstrated, and all civilized nations in the Western world eventually adopted this method of writing. The advantages of the alphabetic method over hieroglyphics were obvious. It permitted a greater precision in the recording of spoken language and therefore a greater precision in conveying thought. It required much less reliance on pure memory. It was much easier and faster to learn than hieroglyphics. Whereas before, only scholars and priests (who spent years learning the meanings of thousands of hierogylyphic symbols) were able to become expert readers and writers, now it was possible for anyone of average intelligence and with a little instruction to learn how to read. After the invention of the alphabet, learning to read consisted of mastering the sound-symbol system and acquiring a facility to translate a running inscription into the spoken language it represented.

It should be noted that pictography was not at all a representation of spoken language, even though spoken language was used to interpret picture writing. The evolution of pictography into hieroglyphics, however, indicated that men saw the need to represent spoken language in a writing system and were getting closer and closer to the sound-symbol idea. However, it was the inventor of the alphabet who realized that hieroglyphics, with its encrusted mystical traditions, had to be discarded entirely if a purely secular and practical sound-symbol system was to come into being. So he started from scratch, isolating the sounds of the spoken language and creating a set of symbols to represent them. Thus, writing was liberated from the stifling traditions and superstitions of hieroglyphic writing, with its enormous difficulties, its religious and occult symbolism, and its association with an elite class of temple scholars and priests.

It is interesting to note that the first alphabet was invented by a Phoenician as a commercial tool, and that its first use was in recording commercial transactions. The developing international commerce of man in an era of primitive capitalism gave birth to alphabetic writing. Yet, because the alphabet was such an ingenious invention, men later attributed its origins to divine inspiration.

The break with the hieroglyphic tradition was important for the advance of civilization. It took mysticism and occult symbolism out of writing. It removed writing from the exclusive domain of the scholar-priest class. It made writing easier and reading faster and more accurate. This was most important for the intellectual development of man, and the Greeks, who were the first to use alphabetic writing for intellectual purposes, put mankind on the road to modern civilization. Because it was now so easy to write, men could record their thoughts which other men could then read with accuracy. This greatly facilitated the recording of ideas and the transfer of ideas from one mind to another. Thus, the alphabet accelerated intellectual exchange, and with it came an accelerated intellectual growth.

It is important to realize that all thinking is conducted in terms of the spoken language. Our thinking is internal dialogue, while our discussions with our fellow men are external dialogues. All thinkers and scientists express their ideas in terms of spoken words which are then transcribed into sound-symbols on paper. These written words are then translated back into spoken words by the reader.

There are some people who believe that written language, because it is more carefully expressed and stylistically polished, can no longer be considered the same as spoken language. This may be true from a stylistic point of view. But from the practical and functional point of view involving the process of transcribing spoken words into their sound-symbol representations, there is no difference whatever between the spoken and written languages. All writing must be articulated back into spoken language in order to be understood—whether it is done by so-called silent reading, in which the inner voice speaks to the individual, or by reading aloud. Thinking is internalized dialogue, and reading is listening to the thoughts of someone else.

Thus, the ability to read consists of translating written words accurately back into their spoken counterparts. The ability to write consists of transcribing spoken words into written sound-symbols. The alphabet provides us with the set of sound symbols to be used in this two-way process.

How old should a child be before he is ready to learn to read?

Old enough to understand what you are doing. As soon as a child has developed a sufficient speaking skill he should be ready to learn how to read. A child's vocabulary indicates to what extent he has picked up the spoken language used around him. Deaf children can be taught to read without having heard a word of the spoken language. Thus, if a child can jabber away intelligibly, he has already expanded the use of his mind considerably and is ready to learn to read.

The child's speaking vocabulary, in fact, is a very good indicator of his intelligence. Listen to the child very carefully. Use a cassette recorder to record his conversation. Make an inventory of his speaking vocabulary. You will be surprised how many words he uses. You can further test his vocabulary by pointing to parts of his anatomy and asking him to name them, or to objects in the room. You can discuss concepts with him to test his understanding of abstraction. The child's mind expands its knowledge about life all around him on the order of a geometric progression. He uses one-, two-, and three-syllable words every day. Obviously, a mind which is aware of so much around him, with a capacity which is expanding daily, is ready to learn how to read. And every child looks forward to learning how to read. It represents to him a tremendous step forward.

When starting out, you tell the child that he is going to learn how to read. Before he can, however, you tell him that he must learn the alphabet. It is the first necessary step on the road to reading. You explain what the alphabet is: a set of sound-symbols. You explain the meaning of a sound-symbol system. Thus, he will understand that learning to read is a process which takes time. This is the intelligent approach. A child who has learned to speak several thousand words all by himself is involved in a continuous learning process and is quite an intelligent human being, and you should acknowledge this intelligence by explaining to the child, in terms he can understand, how he is going to be taught to read. Indicate to the child that you understand how intelligent he is: "Think of all the words you have learned all by yourself," you might tell him. "You must be a very smart young man." You are not flattering him, you are not lying to him. You are telling him the truth. A child of four or five who has learned to speak several thousand words all by himself is demonstrating the natural intelligence he was born with, a natural intelligence which, in normal children, is so strong and assertive that it permits learning to take place with little conscious effort. But one should not fall into the trap of believing that no conscious effort is made in learning the first speaking vocabulary. Children make very real efforts to correlate what they see and what they hear with what they say. However, the method they use is trial and error, with the correct responses being confirmed by everyday experience and use.

Obviously, if you are going to teach anyone to read written English, which is an alphabetic system of writing, you must teach him the sound-symbol system used in written English. In addition, you must give him enough practice in using that system so that he can read any writing he sees with complete ease and understanding.

There is only one problem with the English writing system. Because of the fact that we use twenty-six letters to represent about forty-four speech sounds, and because English has been enriched by the invasions of other languages, our writing system has a large number of irregularities and inconsistencies. Therefore, it must be taught in as orderly and logical a way as possible, starting with the most regular aspects of the sound-symbol system and progressing into the most irregular. Since even the irregularities become regular once they are learned (regular in the sense that they never change once learned) there really is no great problem in learning to read English writing. If the approach is logical and well organized, any child can learn to read English with no great problem. This has been proven by centuries of experience with millions of children. Unfortunately, in our country, where our alphabetic writing system has been taught hieroglyphically for the last forty years, our children have had incredible reading problems. The problems have arisen only because of faulty teaching methods. There is nothing wrong with the children. There is a great deal wrong with reading instruction as presently practiced in our schools. Again, I refer the reader to my own book, *The New Illiterates*, and I quote one line from *Why Johnny Can't Read* which is almost as true today as it was when written in 1955:

> The teaching of reading—all over the United States, in all the schools, and in all the textbooks—is totally wrong and flies in the face of all logic and common sense.

In 1973, one would have to revise that to read:

The teaching of reading—all over the United States, in *most* of the schools, and in *most* of the textbooks—is for the most part wrong and flies in the face of all logic and common sense.

The schools are in a period of transition—from the hieroglyphic method back to the alphabetic one. Eventually, however, it will be seen, as it was seen by the inventor of the alphabet, that hieroglyphic methodology will have to be discarded in its entirety before the teaching of reading can once more become logical and sensible. How long this will take is anyone's guess—perhaps another ten years. We have prepared this book for the tutor who does not want to wait ten years, and for the pupil who ought not to be subjected to today's instructional confusion because adults have too great a vested interest in error. No child need be deprived of learning how to read his alphabetic writing system alphabetically. This primer was written for his benefit.

Teaching a child to read an alphabetic writing system is not a difficult task, but it does require three basic elements: time, patience, and organization. Since learning how to read consists of first learning to master the English sound-symbol system, it will take time to achieve such mastery. How much time? How long would it take an adult to master the Morse code or Pittman shorthand with a working proficiency? It would depend on how readily you picked up the skills and how often you practiced them.

For the child, learning the sound-symbol system can have its difficulties. He is not aware that his speech sounds can be isolated and that symbols can be used to represent them. Yet, this is what he must be taught. So we start by first making him aware of what symbols are—especially the alphabet letters. We teach him the alphabet. We also teach him to hear the sounds he makes. We teach him to distinguish one sound from another. Then we teach him to match particular sounds with particular letters, so that when he sees them he also hears them. This is important, for the child should be able to translate into sound what he sees in writing.

There is another aspect to the learning of the sound-symbol system which can be an important part of a child's education. In learning the sound-symbol system, the child is performing an important and difficult intellectual task. He is learning a set of abstract symbols and he is learning the logic whereby these symbols are used. To a child this can be an enormously exciting intellectual revelation. He is learning far more than merely how to read. He is learning about a system of abstract symbols and how they can be logically used for very practical purposes. Thus, he learns about the practical uses of abstraction. This can put him firmly on the road to intellectual development by helping him understand the practical value of an abstract system of symbols—something which will also be useful to him in understanding mathematics.

Therefore, it is important to teach the sound-symbol system in such a manner that the child derives all of the intellectual dividends which mastery of the system can earn him. A child of four, five, or six may not learn all of this in the terms we state it, but he does learn something about logic, order, and their place in the learning process. He learns a great deal about learning while learning.

Most modern reading instruction books do just the opposite. They keep the sound-symbol system either a total secret or pretend that it doesn't exist. They bury the alphabetic principle in a deluge of pictures, stories, and totally irrelevant activities. Then they make of written language something so complicated and difficult, that the child comes to the conclusion that learning to read is simply beyond his poor intellectual means. Other instruction books teach the sound-symbol system in illogical bits and pieces, combining such instruction with hieroglyphic concepts about word recognition. The result is a confusing mess for the young mind.

The instruction in this book teaches the child the sound-symbol system very thoroughly and very systematically. When he has learned it he may well understand why men consider the alphabet the single most important invention of the human mind.

Some teachers think that children do not have the capacity to understand anything as sophisticated as the sound-symbol system. But we know from centuries of experience that children have no trouble learning the alphabet or understanding the concept that letters stand for sounds. This has been so since the days of the ancient Greeks. There is no reason why it should be any different or more difficult in modern America.

So we start first by teaching the child the alphabet: the shapes of the letters and their individual names. We teach him to recognize the twenty-six letters in their capital and small forms in alphabetical order. And we do not rush the child. We take as much time as is needed. As he learns to recognize and name the letters, he also learns to print them and write them. It is important for the child to be able to both name the letter and print it. We are teaching him a sound-symbol system which is to be used to transcribe spoken words as well as to read them. He should start out knowing that it is a two-way process and that he must learn to use the sound-symbol system in both ways.

There are many ways to make learning the alphabet interesting for a child. I suggest using a very direct and intellectual approach. You might tell the child: "We are going to learn the alphabet. Can you tell me what the alphabet is?" The child will probably respond that the alphabet is "letters" or "a, b, c" or something along that order. He may not know what the alphabet is at all. Whatever his answer, you tell him: "The alphabet is a set of sound-symbols." Now that may sound terribly complicated at first, but then when you begin to explain it to the child, you realize that he is quite capable of understanding what you mean.

You first discuss the sounds that he makes with his voice. You tell him that he can make about forty-four different sounds while talking, and that different letters stand for different sounds. You play a game of isolating speech sounds so that he can see what you are driving at. Then you explain what the word *symbol* means: something which stands for something else. You give examples: how a green light on the corner stands for "go." How the red light stands for "stop." How a blinking yellow light stands for "caution, slow down." All of these lights are symbols. Use other symbols the child may be aware of: arrows pointing direction, flags symbolizing nations. The point is to teach the child how something can stand for or represent something else. In the case of the alphabet, the letters stand for speech sounds. However, each letter has a name and he should learn their names before he learns what sounds the letters stand for. You can also explain that the alphabet is a sound-symbol *system,* and you can explain the meaning of the word system by saying that it means a "regular way of doing things so that all the letters work together." Once he learns the regular way of using the sound symbols he will be able to read and write.

Admittedly, this may be a lot for a child to understand. But as he learns the alphabet, the meaning of what you have been telling him will dawn on him, and that moment of understanding on his part will be his first real intellectual insight. It is an exciting occasion for a young mind and one that will give him a tremendous sense of satisfaction.

John Holt, in *How Children Fail*, gives an interesting description of this learning phenomenon and what happens to it in school:

> To a very great degree, school is a place where children learn to be stupid. A dismal thought, but hard to escape. Infants are not stupid. Children of one, two, or even three throw the whole of themselves into everything they do. They embrace life, and devour it; it is why they learn so fast, and are such good company. Listlessness, boredom, apathy—these all come later. Children come to school *curious;* within a few years most of that curiosity is dead, or at least silent. Open a first or third grade to questions, and you will be deluged; fifth graders say nothing. They either have no questions or will not ask them. . . . Curiosity, questions, speculation—these are for outside school, not inside.

We therefore approach the teaching of reading on the premise that the child wants no secrets kept concerning the process he is going to master, even though the information may seem to be, at the moment, beyond his understanding. Children at age four, five and six are forever asking questions. They are very inquisitive, and there is no reason not to give as accurate an answer as one can to any question.

Since the child is constantly surrounded by alphabet letters (on cereal boxes, television, billboards, and in reading materials at home), he will be familiar with them. First find out if he already knows some of the letters by name. If he does, ask him which ones he knows. You might ask him to go through the alphabet with you and point out the ones he can name. In any case, you introduce him to the alphabet in alphabetical order, telling him that once he knows them by name, he and they will be life-long friends, for he will be using them for the rest of his life. We teach him the alphabet in alphabetical order because: (1) it is easier to learn it that way, (2) there is no good reason to do it in any other way, (3) he will have to know the letters alphabetically in order to be able to use a dictionary.

Teaching the Alphabet

You introduce each letter by name. You point to the letter and tell the child, "This letter's name is *ay*." Then you point to *B* and tell him, "This letter's name is *bee*." Teach him several letters at a time. Have him print and write the letters as he learns them. The reason why the names of the letters have been spelled out here in the text is to remind the tutor of the important distinction between the letter names and the letter sounds. For example, the letter *A* has four sounds, and the *ay* (long *a*) sound is only one of them. That sound also happens to be the name of the letter. The sound of the letter *B* is not *bee* but something approaching *buh*. Notice how impossible it is to give the sound of some consonants without adding a vowel element. In your own mind, however, the distinction between the letter sound and the letter name should be quite clear. The name is important, because the names are a means of identifying the letters, just as the names of individuals are used for that purpose. However, many people tend to confuse the letter names with the letter sounds because of their close similarity in English. In Greek, the letter names (*alpha, beta, gamma*) are quite distinctive and there is no way of confusing them with the letter sounds. However, in the transfer of the alphabet from Greece to Rome, these distinctive names were lost and new names quite similar to the letter sounds were adopted. The Latin alphabet, of course, became our own.

However, there is no reason to confuse the child. He is learning the letter names and their individual shapes so that he can identify them and know one from the other, just as he knows his friends by their names. Remember also that our letter names contain an element of each letter's sound, so that the letter names will be important reminders of the letter sounds when we get to that phase. Before we get to that phase, however, the child should know this much: the names and shapes of the twenty-six letters and the fact that the letters stand for speech sounds.

In teaching your child the letters, teach him to print or draw them in capital and lower-case forms. When he starts to learn the letter sounds, he can start learning to write cursively. The primer on writing can be used in conjunction with the reading primer for this purpose. Such printing and writing practice makes the child learn the shapes of the letters more thoroughly. Also, he must get used to the idea that reading and writing are inseparable skills. One goes with the other. When you learn the Morse code you learn how to send messages as well as receive them. When a stenographer learns shorthand, she learns how to take dictation as well as read it back. It is the same with the alphabet. The inventor meant it to serve as a way of writing or putting down the spoken word on paper as well as a way of reading or translating back into speech the written words on paper. Thus, reading and writing, or decoding and encoding as the linguists prefer to call it, are two parts of one skill, and should be learned simultaneously. The learning of one reinforces the other. In addition, it teaches the child that the alphabet is to be used as a means of conveying his thoughts in writing to others as well as a way of reading the thoughts of others. It is important that he be an active sender of messages as well as a receiver. He is a talker and listener, not just a listener, and he should be able to transcribe his talk into written words with ease. Thus, we start writing from the very beginning.

There are a number of pleasant and playful ways in which the child can be taught to recognize different letters. He can cut letters out of magazine and newspaper advertisements and paste them on the blank pages of an artist's pad—each page devoted to a particular letter. This can be his own personal alphabet book, and hunting for new letters to add to his collection can teach him to recognize the letter shapes more quickly. If he asks about words, point to the different letters in the words and tell him that he will be able to read the words after he is taught the letter names and then their sounds. Tell him, "You will be able to read any word you see after you know all the letters and their sounds."

A child is quite capable of understanding that learning is an orderly process and continues in logical steps. When you proceed in this way, you are teaching the child something about the learning process, which is as important to know as what he is being taught in that process. It develops an orderly approach to learning which he will be able to apply in all his future schoolwork.

No pictures should be used in conjunction with teaching the alphabet. The picture the child should be looking at is the *letter itself*, not an apple, or a ball, or an elephant. Pictures are a dis-

traction which can only delay learning the sound-symbol principle. We make this point because shortly after the child knows the
letters, he will be taught to identify them with speech sounds, and
this is very crucial. A letter is a symbol of a sound. It is not the
symbol of anything else. The letter is supposed to stimulate his
mouth, lips and tongue to shape themselves into particular
sounds. It is not supposed to make him think of an apple or an
elephant. He must translate groups of letters into speech, and he
will do this more readily the better he associates the letters with
sounds.

You may ask, how can the child learn the letter names without
some sort of picture to remind him of it, such as a bumble-bee for
B, etc. If the child is taught the letters in alphabetical order, he
learns them through constant repetition. This learning will be reinforced in the letter-sound phase, in which he uses the letters
constantly. Also, the alphabet song is an excellent way to teach
the letter names. It is purely a sound approach and requires no
pictures as intermediaries.

Teaching the Letter Sounds

Assuming that the child has learned the alphabet, we are now
ready to teach him the letter sounds. His knowledge of the alphabet does not have to be letter perfect before we move on to this
next phase, for the simple reason that the child will learn the
letters better as he uses them. However, be sure that he knows the
alphabet well enough to proceed to the next phase.

When you are ready to teach the letter sounds, you tell the
child: "Now we are going to learn the sounds each letter stands for
so that you can put the letters to work for you. You will be able to
put the letters together to make words, and you will be able to
read words by knowing the sounds the letters stand for." This is
the essence of what you want to convey to the child: that letters
stand for sounds, and that the letters in a written word tell you
how to say it.

In teaching the child the letter sounds, we must always
remember that the alphabet was originally invented by an adult
for use by adults. It was easy enough at that time to teach an
adult to isolate the distinct sounds of the language and indicate

which letter represented which sound. And obviously, the alphabet was invented by a man who spoke clearly and heard clearly and could distinguish between the fine differences of speech sounds, between the *t* and the *d*, between *s* and *z*, *m* and *n*, *b* and *p*. But a child's attunement to speech sounds is quite different. His words run into one another, and he may talk child-talk or baby-talk. So the approach must be scaled down to the child's ability to grasp the knowledge you wish to impart. *Take as much time as you need to do the job.* There is no rush. A four-, five-, or six-year old has all the time in the world in which to learn how to read. What is important is not how fast he learns but how thoroughly and accurately. Remember, there are no shortcuts to mastery. When the child learned his own speaking vocabulary, he set no time limit on how many new words he had to learn per day. He learned as he went along. In learning to understand an abstract set of sound symbols and how they are used, we must expect that some children will learn all this faster than others. It does not matter how fast a child learns to master this set of abstractions. The important thing is that he can and will master it if given the proper instruction and enough time in which to do it.

As we have pointed out, the alphabet is perhaps the greatest single intellectual invention of man. The sound-symbol system is an exciting piece of work, exciting to learn when you know that it is going to open up the entire world of literature to you and permit you to express your own thoughts in a durable, lasting way. How do you convey such intellectual excitement to the young mind? By being excited about it yourself. "Did you know that every word you speak can be put down on paper?" you tell the child. That's exciting. "And that's what you are going to learn to do—to put down on paper every sound you make with your voice."

By telling the child this, you've established the concept in his mind of being able to represent speech sounds on paper. This is the association you want to establish in his mind—that letters on paper stand for sounds which he can make with his voice, and that the sounds he makes can be put down on paper by way of letters representing them.

The following sequence of instruction has been devised to accomplish what we want: an orderly understanding of the relationship between letters and speech sounds; an ability on the part of the child to hear the differences in spoken words, and to translate them into written symbols.

Before proceeding into lesson one, however, a short word about the special problem our written language poses. While our written language is about eighty-five percent consistent in its sound-symbol correspondences, there are enough irregularities to warrant a very careful step-by-step procedure to minimize possible confusion. Since the child's own speaking vocabulary has a large number of irregularly spelled words, we can make use of only a few of them in the early stages of instruction. That is why the child should be told that he is learning *how* to read, and that he will be considered a reader when he can read and write any word in his speaking vocabulary.

In the course of learning the sound-symbol system, however, the child will learn a lot of new words simply because these words fall into the most common and regular spelling patterns and best illustrate the alphabetic principle. They will represent a considerable expansion of his own vocabulary. After the child has shown that he can read these words, it is not necessary to spend too much time on their meaning just yet, since he will not be using these words in his own speaking vocabulary for a while. Emphasis on comprehension and meaning should not begin until *after* the child has mastered the entire sound-symbol system and can read and write with ease every word in his own speaking vocabulary. When this is done, the emphasis can then be shifted to the comprehension of new words, the general expansion of the child's vocabulary, and the general appreciation of literature.

The plan of instruction is quite simple, based on the special characteristics of our sound-symbol system. We have forty-four sounds in our language, twenty-one of which are vowel sounds. Since there are only six vowel letters in our alphabet (*a, e, i, o, u,* and part-time *y*) which must represent twenty-one vowel sounds, most of the difficult work in learning to read is in mastering the vowel-symbol correspondences. They are best learned in spelling family groups. Se we begin with the five short vowels in combination with the consonants. The spelling patterns in these short vowel groups are the simplest and most regular in our written language. They are easy to learn and they teach the child the basic principles of the sound-symbol system. From there we move into the various consonant blends of our language. Finally, we learn the rest of the vowel sound-symbol correspondences with all of the important irregularities, such as silent letters, archaic spelling patterns, irregular spellings.

By the time the child has completed his final lesson he should be able to read any word he encounters. He may mispronounce some of the words he has never heard. But this is understandable. It should never be forgotten that the written language is merely a shadow of the spoken language and that the spoken language is one's basic guide to the pronunciation of the written word, regardless of spelling. In most cases the written word provides sufficient indication of stress and accent. But in multisyllabic words, the reader's knowledge of the spoken language becomes an indispensable requisite for correct pronunciation. The dictionary, of course, helps us determine how an unknown word is pronounced. However, a child learns it better by hearing it spoken. Thus, *pronounce all the words clearly.*

A Note on How to Use the Instruction

It should be noted that the division of the instruction into numbered lessons is for the sake of convenience and to provide a guide to the proper sequence of skill acquisition. The tutor can cover as many lessons as he feels the pupil can absorb in any one session. If the tutor feels that he has gone too fast, he can always go back a lesson. Each lesson represents additional material to be mastered or a review of what has already been learned. The instructions in each lesson are not to be considered rigid and inflexible. They should be used as a suggested guide to teaching the material in each lesson. The tutor may discover a more effective way to convey the same material to the pupil according to the pupil's particular response. We wish to encourage the tutor to use his imagination, experience, and judgment in making the material of each lesson understandable to the pupil. Do not be rigid and inflexible in your approach. If the pupil responds easily and readily to the instruction as given by the text, that is good. But if he doesn't, that does not mean that the child is stupid or even slow. It may mean that he cannot quite grasp the concept being taught, and that the instruction is not clear to him. In that case try a slightly different approach, or go back to the point where he does understand and try again.

Above all, always maintain a spirit of patience, good humor, and a willingness to find the right path to the child's understanding. Each one of us learns in a slightly different way. The tutor's job is to find out how each pupil learns best. That is the essence of tutoring: to tailor the method to suit the child. Since no single book of instruction can possibly be made to suit every child, the tutor must use his special insights into a particular pupil's learning behavior to modify or bend that instruction to suit the child. However, this book makes clear that the only road to reading proficiency is through a thorough mastery of the sound-symbol system. This is the goal the tutor must always keep in mind when modifying the instruction. This goal must not be abandoned, no matter how slow the child may be in catching on to the sound-symbol principle. Once the child grasps the principle, his progress will be rapid. Remember, there is no reason to place arbitrary time limits on learning. The child will learn if you take the time and have the patience.

Lesson 1: Start by telling the child that you are now going to teach him the sounds the letters stand for. "Let's start with the first sound. Now listen to the sound I make." Make a short *a* sound. "Did you hear that sound?" Make it again, and ask the child to repeat it after you. "That sound is not a word all by itself, but you hear it and say it often in many words. Can you say it again?" After the child repeats the short *a* sound and hears you repeat it, print the letter *a* on the blackboard or on the sheet of paper in front of the child. "The letter *a* stands for the sound you just made. It is called the short *a* sound. Now I am going to say five words with that sound in it, words that you use every day: *am, an, as, at, ax.*" Print them in lower case letters under the *a* in a straight line across, and say them again. Give examples of how each word is used in a spoken sentence, so that the pupil understands that they are words. A word is a unit of speech that has meaning. "The short *a* sound all by itself doesn't mean anything. But a sound that means something is a word. *Am, an, as, at, ax* are all words because they have meaning.

"Now each of these words has two letters in it. Can you name the letters?" Have the child spell each word, saying the word after he spells it. "Now if the words each have two letters, and each letter stands for a sound, how many sounds do you think each word has?" Repeat the word *am* slowly. Write and say the short *a* sound; then write and say the word *am* just below it. "Do you hear the difference between ă and *am*? When we say *am* we add another sound to the ă. What is the sound we added to the ă in the word *am*?" Say the *m* sound. "Did you hear it? Can you say it?" After the child says the *m* sound tell him that the letter *m* stands for the *m* sound. "So if we want to write the word *am* we must write *a-m*, because these are the letters that stand for those sounds."

Repeat the procedure for *an, as, at, ax.* In this instance teach the *s* as soft *s*. Just as the vowel letters represent more than one sound, some consonants also have variant sounds. But at this stage, we are teaching only the sounds used in the words presented to the child. Have the child print these words, say them, spell them, and write them. Make sure he understands that each word has two sounds and that he can match the right sound with the right letter. Point out how the name of each letter, except *A* in this instance, gives him a hint of the sound each letter stands for. Exaggerate the sounds so the child can hear them distinctly and learn to recognize them when heard.

When you are convinced that the child knows these letter sounds thoroughly, tell him that there are two kinds of letters in the alphabet—vowels and consonants. *A* is a vowel and *m, n, s, t,* and *x* are consonants. The other vowels are *e, i, o,* and *u.* All the rest are consonants. Explain that the vowels are the most powerful letters in the alphabet, because you can't have a word without one. Consonants must always have vowels with them. They can never stand alone. You needn't elaborate at this point. Suffice it merely to establish the fact that there are two classes of letters: vowels and consonants.

By now the child has learned a great deal. He is beginning to hear words with a greater awareness of their different sounds, and he has seen how these different sounds are represented on paper by alphabet letters. He sees that the letters on paper are printed or written from left to right in the same sequence as they are spoken. The five words can also be printed on cards and flashed to the pupil in short drills to help him develop quick written-word-spoken-word association.

Lesson 2: Review all of the material taught in lesson one. When that is done, arrange the words *am, an, as, at, ax* on top of the page or blackboard and tell the child that you are going to make some new words for him. Directly under *am* write *Sam*, under *an* write *man*, under *as*, *has*, under *at*, *sat* and under *ax*, *tax*. It should look as follows:

am   an   as   at   ax

Sam   man   has   sat   tax

Thus, we've used the consonants the child already knows, added the *h*, and expanded our written vocabulary to ten words. (All of these words are in the child's speaking vocabulary. If he is unfamiliar with the word *tax*, explain it.) Ask the child to listen to each three-letter word and to see if he can hear the three sounds in each word. Start with the short *a* as the first sound, expand it to *am* by adding the second sound *m*, expand it to *Sam* by adding the third sound *S* as the beginning of the word. Explain that we use a capital *S* in the word *Sam* because it is a proper name and all proper names begin with capital letters. Repeat this procedure with the other words. With the word *has* identify the sound the letter *h* stands for. Now tell the child that he knows enough written words so that he can read his first sentences. Write:

Sam has an ax.   Sam sat.

Tell the child that a sentence begins with a capital letter, whether the first word is a name or not, and that it ends with a period.

By now the child should begin to understand the principle behind word building, how each letter's power is used in writing words. Review the consonant sounds: *m, n, s, t, x, h*. Now use the *h* to create *ham* under *Sam*, *hat* under *sat*. Write the sentence: *Sam has ham.* See if the child can read it. When the child is thoroughly acquainted with these twelve words, can write them, read them, and spell them, introduce the consonant *d* by changing *man* to *Dan* and *Sam* to *dam*, explaining what a dam is. Point out that *Dan* is written with a capital *D* because it is a proper name. Introduce the consonant *w* by adding *wax* under *tax*.

Also drill all the words on flash cards to help develop quick response.

Lesson 3: Review and consolidate what the child has learned up to now. He has been introduced to the following consonants: *m, n, s, t, x, h, d,* and *w.* He can read the following words:

am	an	as	at	ax
Sam	man	has	sat	tax
ham	Dan		hat	wax
dam				

Dictate the following sentences to the child and see how well he can write them out. Tell him to make sure that the first word in his sentence starts with a capital letter and that the sentence ends with a period:

Sam has ham.

Dan sat.

Dan has wax.

Sam has an ax.

Lesson 4: Ask the child if he can hear the difference between the words *an* and *and.* Give some examples of the use of *and* in such phrases as you *and* I, he *and* she, mother *and* father, knife *and* fork, etc. Ask the child if he can hear the additional sound at the end of *and.* Write *and* for the child and ask him to spell it. Ask him to name the letter which stands for the sound at the end of the word. Point out how the two consonant sounds, *nd,* blend together. Write: *Sam and Dan, man and ham, tax and wax.* Let the child read them. Now write the word *and* and put the letter *h* in front of it, and ask the child if he can figure out what new word you have written: *hand.* Put an *s* in front of *and* and explain how it becomes *sand.* Introduce the consonant *l* by adding it to *and* to make *land.* Ask the child if he can identify the sound the *l* stands for. Now you can play a game and see how many sentences the child can write with all the words he now can read:

am	an	as	at	ax	and
Sam	man	has	sat	tax	hand
ham	Dan		hat	wax	land
dam					sand

Here are a few suggested sentences. Explain that when a sentence is in the form of a question, we put a question mark at the end of it instead of a period:

Dan has an ax.

Has Dan an ax?

Sam has ham.

Has Sam ham?

Dan has land and sand.

Has Dan sand?

Sam sat.

Dan sat.

Introduce the following new words and show the child how they relate to the words he already knows: *tan, mat, Nat, Max.* Define the words he is unfamiliar with.

The child has already learned the sound of the letter *d* with the words *Dan, and,* etc. Now introduce him to the word *ad,* defining it as in "want ad," and show him how by using the consonant letter sounds he already knows he should be able to read such words as *dad, had, lad, sad, Tad.* Make up practice sentences if you feel the child needs additional work in learning these new words. Also, use short flash-card drills to develop and reinforce automatic written-word-spoken-word response.

By now the child has learned the sound-symbol correspondences of the short vowel a and the consonants d, h, l, m, n, s, t, w, x, and the consonant blend nd. The child by now has grasped how the sound-symbol principle works or he is in the process of doing so. Some children catch on faster than others. If he does not catch on as yet, there is no reason to be concerned. The sound-symbol principle will be demonstrated over and over again in the lessons to follow, and at some point he will grasp it. Also, do not be concerned if the child cannot complete all the material in one lesson during one session. Take as much time for any one lesson as is necessary to complete the material. If, on the other hand, the child progresses rapidly through the lesson, you may go onto the next without waiting.

Lesson 5: In this lesson we will introduce the child to most of the other consonant letter sounds. Use as much time as is necessary to cover this material. Remember, the division of the instruction into lessons has nothing to do with time. It is simply a convenient way to provide a logical and orderly sequence of skill acquisition. Therefore, the material in any one lesson may be covered in as many sessions as may be necessary.

Introduce the child to the consonant b. Ask the child, "What is this letter?" When he gives you its name tell him that now he is going to learn what its sound is. Write the words: *bad, ban, bat, band* in a line. Say the words and ask the child if he can identify the sound which the letter b stands for at the beginning of these words. If the child has trouble isolating the "buh" sound, say it for him. Simply ask him if he hears the b sound when you say the words. *The sound he hears is the sound the letter stands for.* If he can reproduce that sound in isolation it is an indication that he is learning the sounds quickly. If not, say the sound for him and continue the lesson. Then write *dab, lab, nab, tab* in a line, say them and ask the child if he can identify the sound the letter b stands for at the end of the words. Define the words when discussing them.

This same general procedure should be followed in teaching the sounds of the other consonant letters as they are introduced. Take as much time as is needed in teaching the sound of each letter. Introduce consonant c with the words: *cab, cad, can, cat*. Ask the child to identify the sound at the beginning of these words which the c stands for. Next, introduce consonant f with the words: *fab, fad, fan, fat.* In teaching these words, take time to explain what they mean. *Fab* is the name of a household detergent for which he may have seen commercials on television. If his mother has a box of *Fab* at home, he will be able to read its name. A *fad*, you can explain, is a style or hobby that many people are interested in for a short time. Give the example of the hoola-hoop fad. This word is obviously not in the child's speaking vocabulary, and he may not entirely understand its meaning. But he should be able to read it on the basis of what he knows about letters and the sounds they stand for. Words like *fad* should be treated almost like nonsense syllables. Their value at this point is in giving the child practice in learning the letter sounds. At this point, meaning is secondary to the technical skill of reading—translating sound-symbols into speech. Words like *fan* and *fat* are in the child's speaking vocabulary and he will enjoy seeing what they look like in their written counterparts.

Introduce consonant *g* with the words: *gab, gag, gas.* Define the words. With the word *gag* the child has the opportunity to learn the *g* sound in initial and final positions. It should be noted that in addition to learning the letter sounds, the child is also expanding his vocabulary. Make the discussion of each new word as interesting as possible. Next, introduce consonant *j* with: *jab, jam, Jan.* Then introduce consonant *p* with the words: *pad, Pam, pan, pat.* Explain that the reason why *Pam* has a capital *P* is because it is a proper name. Next, introduce consonant *r* with: *ram, ran, rat.* Following this, introduce consonant *v* with the words: *Van* and *vat.* Explain that *Van* is a name, but that the word *van* is a truck. Then introduce consonant *y* with: *yam, yap.* With the word *yap* teach the child the *p* sound in the final position, since this is the first word he has had ending with *p*. Finally, introduce *z* with: *zag.*

With the completion of this material, the child will have learned the sound-symbol correspondences of consonants *b, c, d, f, g, h, j, l, m, n, p, r, s, t, v, w, x, y, z.* Do not be concerned if the child's knowledge of every letter sound is not perfect. He will get plenty of practice in learning the letter sounds as we take up the other vowels.

These lessons can be made additionally interesting by making the learning of the new words exciting. With the knowledge the child already has, the world of alphabet letters and words is beginning to make a little more sense to him. He will probably look more carefully at the cereal boxes on the breakfast table or the signs around him to see what words he can recognize.

Lesson 6: Review. The child has now covered the short *a* sound in combination with consonants: *b, c, d, f, g, h, j, l, m, n, p, r, s, t, v, w, x, y, z,* plus the final consonant blend *nd.* His reading vocabulary now includes the following lists of rhyming words:

ad	am	an	and	as
bad	dam	ban	band	gas
cad	ham	can	hand	has
dad	jam	Dan	land	
fad	Pam	fan	sand	
had	ram	Jan		
lad	Sam	man		
mad	yam	pan		
pad		ran		
sad		tan		
Tad		Van		

at	ax	cab	gag	yap
bat	Max	dab	zag	
cat	tax	Fab		
fat	wax	gab		
hat		jab		
mat		lab		
Nat		nab		
pat		tab		
rat				
sat				
vat				

The above lists can be expanded to include the following rhyming words, which can be learned by the child with the skills he already has:

cap	bag	Al
gap	hag	Cal
lap	lag	gal
map	nag	Hal
nap	rag	pal
rap	sag	Sal
sap	tag	Val
tap	wag	

All these words can also be arranged alphabetically to illustrate more graphically to the child the sounds of the consonants in the initial position:

ad	bad	cab	dab	Fab
Al	bag	cad	dad	fad
am	ban	Cal	dam	fan
an	band	cap	Dan	fat
and	bat	cat		
as				
at				
ax				

gab	had	jab	lab	mad
gag	fag	jam	lad	man
gal	Hal	Jan	lag	map
gap	ham		land	mat
gas	hand		lap	Max
	has			
	hat			

nab	pad	rag	sad	tab
nag	pal	ram	sag	Tad
nap	Pam	ran	Sal	tag
Nat	pat	rap	Sam	tan
		rat	sand	tap
			sap	tax
			sat	

Val	wag	yam	zag
van	wax	yap	
vat			

If the child needs additional practice with these words, an endless number of simple sentences can be made from them. The child will get plenty of additional practice with the consonant sounds while learning the other vowel sounds. Therefore do not linger too long on these exercises if the child in your judgment has mastered the material sufficiently to move on.

Lesson 7: Explain to the child that so far he has learned only regular words, and that now he is going to learn an irregular word. Explain that some written words are not pronounced exactly as they are spelled. The reason for this is that many years ago the word was pronounced differently. The pronunciation has changed but not the spelling. One such word is *was*. Write the word *was*. Show how it is spelled to rhyme with *as* and *has*, but that it is pronounced *was (woz)*. Do not write "woz" for the child since he is not yet familiar with the short *o*.* Merely write *was* but pronounce it as it should be pronounced. This inconsistency will not trouble the child. It should be explained in a simple matter-of-fact way without any fuss. It should be noted that the only inconsistency is in the sound of the vowel *a*, not the other two letters. Also, this irregular word will relieve the monotony of the short *a* words. Here are a few suggested sentences illustrating the meaning of the word and its spelling:

> Pam was mad.
>
> Jan was as mad as Pam.
>
> Val was fat.
>
> Tad was as fat as Val.
>
> Dan was bad.
>
> Sam was as bad as Dan.

Lesson 8: Review the two *s* sounds. Explain that sometimes the *s* stands for a harder sound and sometimes a softer sound, as in

*In some parts of the country *was* is pronounced *wuz* rather than *woz*.

these words: *gas, has, sad, as, sand, was.* See if the child can distinguish between the two *s* sounds. He can only tell which sound to say by hearing in his mind the word as it is spoken. But the *s* stands for both sounds.

Lesson 9: Introduce the *ck* consonant combination ending. Teach the words: *back, hack, Jack, lack, Mack, pack, rack, sack, tack.* Ask the child to identify the sound the *ck* stands for. Explain that sometimes two letters will stand for one sound.

Lessen 10: Introduce the short *e.* Explain that the letter *e,* like *a,* is a vowel. Accustom the pupil to recognize the short *e* sound as distinguished from the short *a.* Start with the word *Ed.* Compare *Ed* with *ad.* Then expand *Ed* into *bed, fed, led, Ned, red, Ted, wed.* Introduce the word *egg,* pointing out that the double *g* sounds the same as a single *g.* From *egg* expand into *beg, keg, leg, Meg, Peg.* Take the word *keg* and have the child identify the sound the letter *k* stands for, since this is the first word he has had beginning with *k.* As for the spelling inconsistency between *egg* and *beg,* this should pose no problem. The child does not expect perfect consistency. In fact, the reason why he will be able to understand and master the sound-symbol system is because it does have a very high degree of consistency. The basic consistency between written symbols and spoken sounds is the great abstract lesson he is learning, one that gives him great intellectual satisfaction. So the exceptions that prove the rule should neither be ignored nor overly stressed but merely pointed out. *By pointing out the occasional exceptions and irregularities, the basic consistency of everything else is reinforced.*

Next take the word *and* and change it to *end.* Emphasize the difference in sound between *and* and *end.* Ask the child to say the two words and have him write them down from dictation. Now expand *end* into *bend, lend, mend, send, tend.* Show how *bat* can be changed into *bet; mat* to *met; pat* to *pet; sat* to *set; vat* to *vet; ban* to *Ben; Dan* to *den; man* to *men; tan* to *ten.* Go through the following list of words with the child:

web	Ed	deck	egg	bell	gem
	bed	heck	beg	cell	hem
	fed	neck	keg	dell	
	led	peck	leg	fell	
	Ned		Meg	hell	
	red		peg	sell	
	Ted			tell	
	wed			well	
				yell	

Ben	bend	pep	yes	bet	Rex
den	lend			get	Tex
Jen	mend			let	vex
Ken	send			met	
Len	tend			net	
men				pet	
pen				set	
ten				vet	
yen				wet	
				yet	

Lesson 10a: Review the words *bell, cell, dell,* etc., and point out that the double *l* stands for the same sound as a single *l.*

Lesson 10b: Consonant *c* as *s* sound. Explain that *c* stands for both a *k* and an *s* sound. Illustrate with the words *cat* and *cell.* Have the child look at the words, listen to the sounds, and identify the sounds the letter *c* stands for.

Lesson 10c: The consonant *g* sound as in *gem.* Explain that the letter *g* stands for both the *g* in *gem* and the *g* in *get.* Most of the time, however, it will stand for the *g* sound as in *get.*

Lesson 10d: Explain that so far the pupil has learned three ways in which the *k* sound is written; *Ken, cat,* de*ck,* *keg,* *can,* Ja*ck.* Tell the child, however, that only by practice will he learn to spell each word correctly.

Lesson 11: Review. The name game. Since many simple names illustrate the short *a* and short *e* sounds in a variety of consonant combinations, a game can be devised in which the child makes a list of friends whom he would invite to his birthday party. He can choose from: *Pam, Sam, Dan, Jan, Nat, Van, Pat, Max, Tad, Hal, Sal, Val, Al, Ned, Ed, Meg, Peg, Jen, Ken, Len, Jack, Mack.* Let him practice such simple combinations as:

Jack and Dan.	Pam and Mack.
Meg and Peg.	Ned and Nat.
Van and Sam.	Jen and Len.
Max and Ed.	

Names are also good for dictation purposes and spelling tests.

Lesson 12: Many sentences can be made from the words already learned. These sentences are for the purpose of helping the child master the sound-symbol system. No story interpretation is needed or even desirable at this point. The child should be totally absorbed in the challenging job of mastering the sound-symbol system. The sentences are quite obvious in meaning, and you can think up many more:

Jack has let Mack get wet.

Pam had ham and an egg.

Jen fed Al an egg.

Rex can sell ham.

Can Ken yell well?

Yes, Ken can yell well.

Make up other sentences if you feel that additional work is necessary before moving on to the short *i*.

Lesson 13: The short *i*. Begin with the words: *if, in, is, it, ill.* Explain that the letter *i*, like *a* and *e*, is a vowel. Compare *a* as in *at*, *e* as in *Ed*, and *i* as in *it*. Let the child hear the differences. Let him say all three short vowel sounds. Use *Al, el,* and *ill* to illustrate the three sounds. Then expand *if, in, is, it, ill* as follows:

if	in	is	it	ill
	bin	his	bit	Bill
	fin	sis	fit	dill
	pin		hit	fill
	sin		kit	gill
	tin		lit	hill
	win		mitt	Jill
			pit	kill
			quit	mill
			sit	pill
			wit	quill
				rill
				sill
				till
				will

After the child demonstrates his ability to read the above, further expand the short *i* words to include the following:

fib	dick	bid	big	dim	dip	hiss	Dix
rib	hick	did	dig	him	hip	kiss	fix
	kick	hid	fig	Jim	Kip	miss	mix
	lick	kid	gig	Kim	lip		nix
	Mick	lid	jig	rim	nip		pix
	Nick	mid	Mig	Tim	pip		six
	pick	rid	pig	vim	quip		
	quick	Sid	rig		rip		
	Rick		wig		sip		
	sick		zig		tip		
	tick				zip		
	wick						

Lesson 13a: Introduce the consonant *q* and explain how it is always followed by a *u* as in: *quit, quill, quip, quick.* In teaching these words, see if the child can identify the sound the *qu* stands for.

Lesson 13b: Explain that the double *s* as in *kiss* stands for the same sound as a single hard *s* as in *gas.*

Lesson 14: Review. Suggested practice sentences:

Bill is ill.

Kim is ill and Nick fed Kim an egg.

Rick bit his lip.

Fix it.

Mix it.

Quit it.

Will Bill win?

Will Jill kiss Bill?

Make up other sentences if more practice is needed.

Lesson 15: Introduce the name *Phil.* Explain that *ph* together stands for the same sound as *f.* Explain that *Phil* and *fill* are pronounced exactly alike. Acquaint the child with the idea that often two different words that sound alike are spelled differently. Expand *Phil* into *Philip* and ask the child to read his first two-syllable word.

Lesson 16: Introduce the word *a.* Tell the child that the letter *a* alone in a sentence stands for the word *a*, as in *a bed, a map, a cat, a hill,* etc.

Lesson 17: Introduce the word *the,* as in *the hat, the cat, the sand,* etc. Let the child listen to the *th* sound so that he can identify it and make the proper sound-symbol association. Take the words *at, in,* and *is* and make them into *that, thin,* and *this.* Note that *thin* has a harder *th* than *the.* The child should pronounce a word as his knowledge of the spoken language indicates. All of these words are in his speaking vocabulary and he should have no trouble pronouncing them as they are spoken. See if the child can say the sound the *th* stands for by itself. If he can't, say it for him. Also add *th* to *em* to make *them.* Show him how the *th* sound is also found at the ends of words like *with, bath, path.* Have him learn to read the following words:

```
the     bath     Beth     with
that    math
them    path
thin
this
than
```

Have the pupil practice with the following sentences and others you might make up:

```
That thin cat has that fat rat.

This cat has that hen.

The cat fell in the bath and got wet.

Beth sat with Bill.

Will Jill sit with Beth?
```

Lesson 18: The short *o.* Begin with the words *on* and *ox.* Let the child hear the distinction between short *a,* short *e,* short *i,* and short *o.* Let him see and hear the difference between *an, in* and *on; ax, ex,* and *ox.* Expand *ox* into *box* and *fox.* Expand *on* into *Don* and *Ron.* Further expand your short *o* words to include the following:

Bob	cock	cod	*of*	cog
cob	dock	God	*off*	*dog*
gob	hock	mod		fog
mob	lock	nod		hog
rob	mock	rod		log
sob	pock	sod		
	rock	Tod		
	sock			
	tock			

mom	on	cop	cot	ox
Tom	Don	hop	dot	box
	Ron	mop	got	fox
	son	top	hot	pox
	ton		jot	sox
	won		lot	
			not	
			pot	
			rot	
			tot	

Lesson 18a: Irregular pronunciations. There are a number of words within the short *o* spelling families which are not pronounced as the pupil might expect. Point out that these words are pronounced as they are spoken. They include the following: *of, off, dog, son, ton, won.*

Here are a few practice sentences in which these words are used. Again, these exceptions to the rule confirm the consistency of everything else:

Ron is the son of Bill.

Don won his dog.

The dog got off the log.

The dog did not sit on the rock.

Don won a ton of ham.

The dog got on and off the cot.

Don got a hotdog.

Note the two-syllable word, *hotdog*. Explain to the child that many two-syllable words are made up of two one-syllable words put together. Tell the child that he will learn more about syllables later on. (See lesson 27.)

Lesson 19: Introduce the apostrophe *s: Bill's dog. Dan's cat. Pam's hat.* The apostrophe means possession. Here are some practice sentences:

Rick has Tim's dog.

Peg's cat is sick.

That is Don's pig.

Lesson 20: The short *u* sound. Review the short *a*, short *e*, short *i*, and short *o* sounds. Tell the pupil that now he is going to learn the short *u* sound which is found in many common words. Say the short *u* sound and write the words *us* and *up*. Compare the initial sounds of *as*, *is*, and *us*. Expand *us* into *bus*, *fuss*, *pus*. Expand *up* into *pup* and *cup*. Have the pupil learn to read the following short *u* words:

cub	bud	bug	cull	gum	bun
dub	dud	dug	dull	hum	fun
hub	mud	hug	*full*	mum	gun
pub		jug	gull	sum	nun
rub		mug	hull	yum	pun
sub		rug	*pull*		run
tub		tug			sun

up	us	but	lux	duz
cup	bus	cut		
pup	fuss	gut		
	Gus	nut		
	muss	*put*		
	pus	rut		

Lesson 20a: Point out the irregular pronunciation of the words *full, pull,* and *put.* Numerous sentences for practice reading can be made up from the words the child already knows. Include irregular words in the sentences. Here are some suggestions. You can make up many more:

The dog dug in the mud and had fun.

Tom's dad is a cop and has a gun.

Can Jack pull the big log?

The red jug is full and Gus has it.

The cat fell in the tub.

Was it a big cat?

Lesson 21: Introduce the *sh* sound. Explain how as in *th,* two consonant letters stand for one sound. Teach the following *sh* words:

ash	mesh	dish	gosh	gush
bash		fish		hush
cash		wish		lush
dash				mush
gash				rush
lash				*push*
mash				
rash				
sash				
wash				

shack	shed	shin	shock	shun
		ship	shop	shut
			shot	

Irregular pronunciations: *wash* rhymes with *gosh. Push* is pronounced as the spoken word indicates.

Lesson 22: Introduce the *ch* sound. This is another single consonant sound written with two consonant letters. Such a consonant sound designated by two letters is know as a consonant digraph, as illustrated in the following words:

chap	check	chick	chop	chuck	rich	much
chat	chess	chill		chug		such
	Chet	chin		chum		
	chex	chip				

Lesson 23: Introduce the *wh* sound (another consonant digraph) which is a single consonant sound represented by two letters, as in the words below:

what	when	whim
		whip

Irregular pronunciation: *what* rhymes with *hot*.

Lesson 24: General review. We have covered the five short vowel sounds, *a, e, i, o, u,* all of the consonant sounds, and *ch, ph, sh, wh, qu,* and *nd.* Now would be a good time to see how well your pupil has mastered this much of the sound-symbol system and to give him general practice with what he already knows. You can do this by having him read a series of sentences which you can make up, or by reading mixed word lists, or by giving spelling tests. You can test him with the following word combinations which can also be quite amusing because they resemble tongue-twisters:

bad	fad	fat	dad	ban	rib
bed	fed	fit	did	Ben	rob
bid			dud	bin	rub
bud				bun	

Nat	get	let	band	pep
net	got	lit	bend	pip
nit	gut	lot	bond	pop
not				pup
nut				

pan	pat	lack	pack	deck	hack
pen	pet	lick	peck	Dick	heck
pin	pit	lock	pick	dock	hick
pun	pot	luck	pock	duck	hock
			puck		

sack	bag	bat	Dan	fan
sick	beg	bet	den	fin
sock	big	bit	din	fun
suck	bog	but		
	bug			

tack	mash	ship	shot
tick	mesh	shop	shut
tock	mish		
tuck	mosh		
	mush		

In having mastered this much of the sound-symbol system successfully, the pupil will be eager to master the rest. He has seen how new knowledge builds consistently and logically on what he already knows and how it all makes sense, how it all fits together in a comprehensible system. Words are no longer a mystery to him. He can't as yet read them all, but he already can read many of them and has had the thrill of figuring out and recognizing words he has been speaking and seeing all around him. He knows that eventually he will be able to read all words with the same ease he now reads those he already knows.

Lesson 25: Adding *s* or *es* to words to make them plural or change tense. The child changes verb tenses and makes plurals in his speech all the time without technically being aware of what he is doing. We want him now to recognize that sound change on paper. First ask him if he can hear the difference between the words *hat* and *hats* and tell you what that difference means. Repeat this with a number of words. Do the same with a few verbs: *win, wins; run, runs*. Write them out:

hat	hats	cup	cups
bed	beds	kiss	kisses
win	wins	cat	cats
run	runs	box	boxes
yell	yells	hand	hands
bell	bells	egg	eggs

Explain why with two-syllable words like *kisses* and *boxes* we add an *es* instead of simply an *s*. Indicate the two syllables by writing *kisses* as *kiss-es*. Make up practice sentences using plurals and tense changes, such as:

Bill has ten boxes of eggs.

Dick has six cats.

Rick picks six kids.

Lesson 26: Contractions. Take the phrases *is not, can not, has not, had not, did not, it is,* and *let us* and show how they can be contracted in writing to resemble their spoken counterparts:

is not	isn't	it is	it's
can not	can't	let us	let's
has not	hasn't	did not	didn't
had not	hadn't		

Suggested practice sentences:

Is Bill sad? Bill isn't sad.

Can Ken run? Ken can't run.

Is this Peg's dog? This isn't Peg's dog.

It's Jill's dog.

Let's run.

Has Peg a cat? Peg hasn't a cat.

Did Jill's dog run? Jill's dog didn't run.

Lesson 27: Two-syllable words. There are a good many simple two-syllable words made up of two regular short-vowel pronunciation units or two one-syllable short-vowel words. See how many your pupil can read on his own. Help him if necessary. The point is to show how two syllables are put together to make one word. Discuss the meaning of the words he does not know. After he can read them, use them in a few simple sentences with other words he knows. The exercise is to advance his mastery of the sound-symbol system as used in writing and reading multisyllabic words. Show him how to divide a word into syllables in order to be able to figure it out and read it. Define a syllable as a speech unit with one vowel sound, with or without consonants. For example, the word *a* is a one-syllable word without any consonants, while *wish* is a one-syllable word with three consonants.

hotdog	hot-dog	helmet	hel-met
boxtop	box-top	velvet	vel-vet
zigzag	zig-zag	tomcat	tom-cat
catnip	cat-nip	gallop	gal-lop
ticket	tick-et	lesson	les-son

napkin	nap-kin	lentil	len-til
tidbit	tid-bit	pencil	pen-cil
habit	hab-it	comet	com-et
rapid	rap-id	puppet	pup-pet
gallon	gal-lon	upset	up-set
candid	can-did	mimic	mim-ic
basket	bas-ket	public	pub-lic
tonic	ton-ic	suntan	sun-tan
magic	mag-ic	sudden	sud-den
unfit	un-fit	hatbox	hat-box
goblin	gob-lin	sunset	sun-set
robin	rob-in	hatrack	hat-rack
chapel	chap-el	bashful	bash-ful
picnic	pic-nic	dental	den-tal
kidnap	kid-nap	until	un-til
linen	lin-en	vomit	vom-it
visit	vis-it	husband	hus-band
rabbit	rab-bit	wagon	wag-on
nitwit	nit-wit	exit	ex-it
vivid	viv-id	Philip	Phil-ip
civil	civ-il	rivet	riv-et
Nixon	Nix-on	within	with-in

Suggested practice sentences:

Jill has a picnic basket full of hotdogs.

Jack has put on his dad's ten-gallon hat.

Bill's mascot is a rabbit.

A magic goblin sat in the wagon.

Philip has a hotrod.

Peg can mimic a puppet.

The next series of lessons is devoted to final consonant blends with regular short vowels in one-syllable words. This will teach the child to recognize the written symbols for two consonant sounds blended together at the ends of words. Some of the words are not in the child's vocabulary and may be difficult. In that case, do not dwell on them, but concentrate on the words the child already uses. The purpose of these lessons is not to teach vocabulary but to teach sound-symbol correspondences. Once the child has mastered the latter, emphasis can be shifted to vocabulary. Before proceeding, however, please read the instructions following lesson 63.

Lesson 28: Review of the double consonant endings *bb, gg, ll, ff, ss, tt*. The child has already been taught that double consonants stand for the same sound as single consonants. The following mixed word list has been prepared for quick review:

bell	Matt	doll	fill
hill	well	muff	puff
ebb	add	kill	less
cuff	Webb	fell	dull
hull	mill	kiss	tiff
egg	Jeff	will	hiss
lass	yell	miff	sell
Jill	mess	pass	miss

Lesson 29: The sound of *a* followed by double *l*. Explain that the vowel *a* stands for more than one sound. Take the words *Al* and *all* and see if the child can distinguish between the two *a* sounds. Review how *Al* rhymes with *Cal, gal, Hal, pal, Sal, Val.* Show how *all* rhymes with *ball, call, fall, gall, hall, mall, pall, tall, wall.*

Lesson 30: Final consonant blend *ng*.

bang	bing	bong	hung
dang	ding	dong	lung
gang	king	gong	rung
hang	ping	pong	sung
pang	ring	*song*	
rang	sing		
sang	wing		
	zing		

Irregular pronunciation: Note the variant pronunciation of the letter *o* in the word *song*.

Here is a mixed list of *ng* words for reading practice:

ring	hung	ping	bing	wing
bang	gong	gang	dang	sing
dong	king	zing	pong	hang
sung	hang	bong	rung	ding
ding	lung	sang	pang	rang

ding-dong	sing-song
Hong-Kong	ping-pong
bing-bang	ding-dang

Try the word *Washington* on the child, first dividing it into syllables, *Wash-ing-ton.*

Lesson 31: Explain how adding *ing* to many words gives us new words. Note how the single consonant following a short vowel is doubled when *ing* is added. The exception is *fix, fixing.*

fan	fanning	pack	packing
nap	napping	pick	picking
get	getting	yell	yelling
let	letting	sell	selling
kid	kidding	pass	passing
rob	robbing	sing	singing
run	running	ring	ringing
rub	rubbing	hang	hanging
dig	digging	fix	fixing
shop	shopping	wish	wishing
ship	shipping	rush	rushing

Suggested practice sentences:

Jan is singing a song.

Bill is ringing a bell.

Ken is getting all wet.

Rick is kicking a ball.

Dick is calling his dog.

Lesson 32: Final consonant blends *nd, nt.*

and	rant	Kent	land	tent	fond
bend	fund	rent	dent	wind	tint
went	hand	end	punt	gent	lent
sand	hint	send	bond	sent	band
bunt	hunt	mend	rend	fend	bunt

Lesson 33: Final consonant blends *ct, ft, pt.*

act	pact	lift
kept	apt	duct
fact	left	raft
aft	tact	gift

Lesson 34: Final consonant blend *nk.*

bank	mink	hunk	wink	link	Hank
honk	*monk*	ink	tank	duck	pink
rank	junk	bunk	lank	sink	rink

Note the irregular pronunciation of *monk* which rhymes with *junk.*

Lesson 35: Final consonant blends *sk, sp, st.*

ask	asp	last	must	vest
desk	lisp	best	fast	just
risk	gasp	fist	lest	zest
task		rest	list	vast
mask		bust	west	pest
dusk		cast	rust	mast
tusk		jest	gist	nest
		test	mist	

Lesson 36: Final consonant blends *xt, nch.*

next	ranch
text	bench
	inch
	pinch
	lunch

Lesson 37: Final consonant blends *lb, ld, lf, lk, lm, lp, lt.*

bulb	held	bulk	elf
	meld	sulk	self
	gild	milk	golf
	bald	silk	gulf
		talk	*calf*
		walk	*half*

elm	help	belt	quilt
helm	yelp	felt	tilt
film	gulp	melt	cult
	pulp	pelt	hilt
		jilt	

Note the irregular pronunciations of the *a* in *talk, walk,* and *bald.* The *a* is pronounced as the *a* in *all.* Also note that in the words *calf, half, walk* and *talk* the *l* is silent. Explain that the pronunciation of the words has changed over the centuries but that the spelling hasn't. Thus, although the words are still spelled with an *l,* the *l* is not pronounced.

Lesson 38: Final consonant blend *mp.*

camp	romp	hump	lump
hemp	limp	pomp	limp
bump	dump	jump	hemp
damp	lamp	ramp	pump

Lesson 39: Final consonant blend *tch.*

batch	itch	etch	botch
catch	pitch	hutch	fetch
witch	hatch	patch	hitch
dutch	match	latch	retch

Lesson 40: Final consonant blend *dge.* Explain that the final *e* is silent.

badge	Madge
edge	hedge
ridge	fudge
budge	ledge
lodge	wedge

hodge-podge

Lesson 41: Final consonant blends *nce, nse.* The final *e* is silent.

fence	mince	*once*
since	dance	
tense	hence	
dense	rinse	
sense	dunce	

Note the irregular pronunciation of *once,* which rhymes with *dunce.*

Lesson 42: General review of final consonant blends and digraphs:

batch	kept	desk	hunt	next	belt	act
left	duct	last	went	path	self	fetch
fund	link	pest	dance	itch	help	camp
ring	cash	lisp	much	film	milk	edge
jump	fudge	half	with	sing	fond	elf
bath	test	west	hint	rust	ink	dish
match	lung	tent	pitch	melt	bank	catch

Lesson 43: With some assistance, the pupil should be able to read these two-syllable words with regular short vowels and known consonant blends and digraphs:

disgust	dis-gust	rubbish	rub-bish
restless	rest-less	content	con-tent
enrich	en-rich	dancing	danc-ing
sandwich	sand-wich	enlist	en-list
enact	en-act	budget	bud-get
vanish	van-ish	polish	pol-ish
Kenneth	Ken-neth	Nashville	Nash-ville
consent	con-sent	compact	com-pact
within	with-in	contact	con-tact
selfish	sel-fish	engulf	en-gulf

suspect	sus-pect	shoplift	shop-lift
dentist	den-tist	conduct	con-duct
dishrag	dish-rag	exist	ex-ist
withheld	with-held	often	of-ten
absent	ab-sent	bathmat	bath-mat
fishnet	fish-net	bathtub	bath-tub
punish	pun-ish	dustpan	dust-pan
		offense	of-fense
		senseless	sense-less

The next series of lessons is devoted to teaching the child initial consonant blends in words with known short-vowel sounds and final consonant blends and digraphs. Work on those words first which are in the child's speaking vocabulary. Then let him try the others. At this point, we are still more concerned with his mastering the sound-symbol system than expanding his vocabulary. Until he can read every word in his own speaking vocabulary, he is not ready to concentrate on expanding his written vocabulary. However, if he shows an interest in the meaning of a new word, by all means take the time to define it.

Lesson 44: Initial consonant blend *bl.*

blab	bled	blink	block	blunt
black	blend	bliss	blond	blush
bland	bless		blop	
blank			blot	
blast				

Lesson 45: Initial consonant blend *br*.

bran	bred	brick	broth	brunt
brand		brig		brush
brash		bridge		
brass		brim		
brat		bring		
		brink		

Lesson 46: Initial consonant blend *cr*.

crab	crest	crib	crop	crud
crack		crisp		crum
cram				crush
crank				crutch
crass				crux

Lesson 47: Initial consonant blends *dr, dw*.

drab	dredge	drift	
draft	dress	drill	
drag		drink	
		drip	

drop	drug	dwell
	drudge	
	drum	

Lesson 48: Initial consonant blend *fl*.

flab	fled	flip	flock	flub
flack	flesh	flint	flog	flunk
flag		flit	flop	flush
flash				
flat				

Lesson 49: Initial consonant blend *fr*.

Fran	Fred	frill	frog
France	fret		frost
Frank	fresh		froth
	French		

Lesson 50: Initial consonant blend *gl*.

glad	glen	glib
gland		
glass		

glob	glum
glop	glut
gloss	

Lesson 51: Initial consonant blend *gr* and *gw*.

grab	Greg	grid	grub	Gwen
grad		grim	grudge	
gram		grin		
grand				
grant				
grass				

Lesson 52: Initial consonant blend *pl*.

plan	plop	plug
plank	plot	pluck
plant		plum
		plus

Lesson 53: Initial consonant blend *pr*.

prance	prep	prick	prod
		prig	prom
		prim	prompt
		prince	
		print	

Lesson 54: Initial consonant blend *shr.*

shrank   shred   shrimp   shrug

shrink   shrunk

Lesson 55: Initial consonant blend *sl.*

slab	sled	slid	slob	slum
slack		slick	slosh	slush
slam		slim	slot	slump
slant		slink		slung
slash		slit		slunk
slat		sling		

Lesson 56: Initial consonant blends *sm, sn.*

smack   smell   smog

smash

smut   snick   snob

snip

Lesson 57: Initial consonant blends *sp, spr*.

spam	speck	spick	spot	spun
span	sped	spill		spud
spank	spell	spin		
spat	spend	spit		
	spent			

sprang	spring	sprung

Lesson 58: Initial consonant blends *st, str*.

stab	stem	stick	stock	stub
stack	step	stiff	stomp	stuck
stag		sting	stop	stud
Stan		stink		stump
stank		stint		stunt
				stunk

strand	strep	string		strut
strap		strip		

Lesson 59: Initial consonant blend *sw*.

swam	swell	swim
swan		swish
		swift

Note the irregular pronunciation of the *a* in *swan*.

Lesson 60: Initial consonant blends *sc, scr, sk*.

scab	skid	scuff	scrub	scrod
scalp	skill	scum	scrunch	
scan	skim	skunk		
scant	skin			
scat	skip			
	skit			

Lesson 61: Initial consonant blends *thr, tr* and *tw*.

thrall	thresh	thrift	throb	thrum
thrash		thrill	throng	thrush
				thrust

track	trek	Trick	trod	truck
tram	trend	trim	trot	trudge
trance		trip		trunk
trap				trust
trash				
twang	twelve	twig		
		twill		
		twin		
		twist		
		twit		
		twitch		

Lesson 62: General review of single-syllable short-vowel words with initial and final consonant blends and digraphs. These words can be used in making up practice sentences with other known words, in spelling tests, in dictation.

truck	quick	blond	task	dwell	witch
skip	grudge	fudge	sash	slack	jump
swift	glass	dump	lisp	spring	bless

then	frill	edge	bank	trick	bring
spun	flag	golf	king	France	chance
slosh	cliff	elm	fond	hitch	flash
shrimp	crux	dutch	hint	next	plus
shack	draft	with	act	rich	grin
plum	chest	pest	lift	lunch	class
prom	bridge	dish	kept	patch	stink

Lesson 63: Show the pupil how by adding *s, es, ing,* or *ed* to many words, you can change the tenses:

hint	hints	hinting	hinted
lift	lifts	lifting	lifted
act	acts	acting	acted
miss	misses	missing	missed
pass	passes	passing	passed
jump	jumps	jumping	jumped
dump	dumps	dumping	dumped

vanish	vanishes	vanishing	vanished
visit	visits	visiting	visited
zigzag	zigzags	zigzagging	zigzagged

A great many practice sentences can be made up of the words the child already should know how to read. Here are a suggested few:

Dad lifted the dog.

The witch vanished off the cliff.

The king of France danced.

The cat jumped off the bridge.

Bill had fudge with his lunch.

Pam drank a glass of milk.

The skunk stank.

The bell kept ringing.

The wagon zigzagged up the hill.

Gwen put cash in the bank.

Jan scratched his skin.

Bill's wagon got stuck in the mud.

Pam slipped in the bathtub.

The next series of lessons is devoted to teaching the child how to read the remaining vowel sounds. The long-vowel sounds can be spelled in a variety of ways. However, the spelling patterns are quite distinctive and are easily learned. Despite the fact that there are also a large number of irregularly pronounced words among the long-vowel spelling families, there is still a very high degree of consistency among the words in any family. Thus, the pupil should have no problem mastering both the regular and irregular words of any one spelling pattern. Some of the irregular words are so common that they are learned through frequent usage. As we have pointed out previously, the exceptions and irregularities merely serve to confirm and reinforce the consistency of everything else.

The child has by now acquired the knowledge and, hopefully, the skill to be able to read such words as *goblin* and *vanishing*. However, he has still not been taught to read such simple words as *I, home, he, like, ate*, etc. This is because the child is still in the process of learning *how* to read. That process consists of learning to master the sound-symbol correspondences of our writing system. It is purely a technical skill that we are concerned with at this stage of the child's education. It is of course possible to revise the sequence of lessons so that the child learns more of the vowel sound-symbol correspondences before he learns the consonant blends. This might permit the child to start reading some outside material earlier. But until he completes his mastery of all the sound-symbol correspondences, there will be many words he will not be able to figure out easily. Fortunately, there are only a finite and not terribly large number of sound-symbol correspondences which the child must learn in order to become a proficient reader for his entire lifetime. It is the opinion of this writer that it is wiser to delay the child's reading of outside material until he has learned all the sound-symbol correspondences he needs to know.

There is much confusion among reading teachers today between the concept of learning *how* to read and reading. No such confusion exists, for example, among teachers of stenographic shorthand. The pupil has to learn the full range of sound-symbol correspondences before she can even begin to qualify as a stenographer. The same should be true of reading. It is too bad that the child should have to go through the process of learning *how* to read before he can actually read. The how-to process takes time, as does the acquisition of any skill, particularly a mental skill involving the use of a large number of abstract symbols. Present-day school instruction tends to minimize the difficulties involved in learning to use such a set of symbols. Most teachers expect the students to pick it up by osmosis, as if it could be learned "naturally" in the same way one learns to talk. Unfortunately, alphabetic writing consists of a highly sophisticated use of abstract symbols. It cannot be learned properly outside of a purely technical approach.

Anything of a technical nature, if it is to be learned well, must be learned systematically, in a logical, orderly way, beginning with the simplest skill and progressing to the more difficult. In learning the alphabetic system there is considerable room for varying the sequence of skill acquisition after the short vowels and consonant sounds are learned. Which means that if the tutor would like to teach the long-vowel sounds before teaching the consonant blends, so that the pupil can sooner acquire a reading knowledge of many common words, he can do so, provided he takes special care not to confuse the child. Part of what we are teaching the child while we are teaching him the sound-symbol system, is methodology. This should not be lost sight of in the impatience to get the child to read every word he speaks. Although the child by now may have acquired an ability to recognize some of the more common long-vowel words on the basis of their consonants alone, he should be taught their complete sound-symbol relationships. Every written word has its place in the sound-symbol scheme of things—either as a regular, irregular, or archaic construction. Although we do use monetary symbols and punctuation marks, there are no hieroglyphics in written English. Every word we utter can be written out alphabetically—spelling peculiarities notwithstanding. Tradition and convention compel us to put up with these peculiarities. After all, written English is the product of a people who still maintain a monarchy long after its use and logic has ceased to exist. It is also the product of a people who have produced some of the world's greatest writers. Their use of written English is a testament to its incredible versatility as an intellectual and esthetic tool.

Some nations are strongly bound to ancient traditions. These traditions are often reflected in their written language. Some of the irregularities in written English teach us a great deal about our language's history, which is what traditions are supposed to do. However, because these irregularities, regardless of their origins, are an integral part of our written language, they pose problems to the teacher of reading. We have taken these irregularities into great consideration in working out the sequence of lessons in this course of instruction. The result, we hope, will be more proficient readers—readers so much at home with their written language that reading will become for them an unlimited, lifelong source of enjoyment and learning.

Lesson 64: The long *a* sound. Tell the child that he has learned all of the short vowel sounds and how to read them, plus all of the consonants. Now he is going to learn the long vowel sounds. Explain that the long vowel sounds are pronounced the same as their letter names—*a, e, i, o, u.* Start with *a.* Ask the child if he can hear the difference between the words *at* and *ate.* Write them down to show him what they look like. Explain that the silent *e* changes the short *a* to a long *a.* Explain that both words have only two sounds each, but that the word *ate* has three letters, one of which is silent. Cover up the *e* in *ate* and show him how it becomes *at.* Remove the cover and he sees how *at* becomes *ate.* Now under the word *at* write the words *fat, hat, mat, rat.* Under the word *ate* write *fate, hate, mate, rate.* Ask the child to explain what happened when you added the silent *e* to the words under *at.* Next, write the words *Al* and *ale.* Ask the child if can read them. If the child has heard of ginger ale, he'll know the word *ale.* Show him what happens when you cover up the *e* in *ale.* It becomes *al,* which, because it is a proper name, must be spelled *Al.* Now, under *Al* write *pal.* Under *ale* write *pale.* Again you've demonstrated the power of the silent *e.* Now make a list with the following words: *cap, tap, mad, Sam, can, pan.* Then in a column to the right, write: *cape, tape, made, same, cane, pane.* Again, explain how the silent *e* changed the short *a* into a long *a.*

Now ask the child if he can think of any other words, like *ate* and *ale,* which begin with a long *a* sound. If he can't think of any, suggest *Abe, ace, age,* and *ape.* Expand the six words which begin with long *a* as follows:

Abe	ace	age	ale	ape	ate
babe	face	cage	bale	cape	date
	lace	page	dale	gape	fate
	pace	sage	hale	tape	gate
	race	wage	male	drape	hate
	brace	stage	pale	grape	Kate
	grace		sale	scrape	late
	place		tale		mate
	space		stale		rate
	trace				crate
					grate
					plate
					state

When the above words are learned, add the following:

fade	safe	bake	came	cane
jade		cake	dame	Dane
made		fake	fame	Jane
wade		Jake	game	lane
blade		lake	lame	mane
grade		make	name	pane
trade		quake	same	sane
		rake	tame	crane
		sake	blame	plane
		take	flame	
		wake	frame	
		brake		
		flake		
		shake		
		stake		
		ache		

bare	base	cave	daze
care	case	Dave	maze
dare		gave	craze
fare		*have*	graze
hare		pave	
mare		rave	
rare		save	
ware		wave	
share		brave	
stare		crave	
are		grave	
		slave	

Lesson 64a: Irregular pronunciations: *are, have.* Teach the child the correct pronunciations of these words.

Note that the *a* in the *bare, care* group is technically not quite a long *a*. The *r* following the long *a* modifies the sound of the *a*, but it is close enough to the long *a* and has the same consonant-silent *e* spelling pattern to justify its inclusion in this section. Note the spelling of *ache.*

Lesson 65: The long *a* as spelled *ai*. Explain to the child that the long *a* with the silent *e* is not the only way to spell the long *a* sound. It is also spelled *ai* as in the words *aid, aim,* and *air*. Expand these three words as follows:

aid	aim	air
laid	maim	fair
maid	claim	hair
paid		pair
raid		chair
said		Clair

Have the child compare the words *made* and *maid*. They are pronounced exactly the same. Explain the meaning of each. The reason why we spell the long *a* in more than one way is so that we can write different words which sound alike in different ways. Next, have the child learn the following words:

bail	bait	Cain	*again*
fail	wait	gain	*against*
Gail	trait	lain	
hail		main	
jail		pain	
mail		rain	
nail		vain	
pail		brain	
sail		chain	
wail		drain	
frail		plain	
trail		slain	
		Spain	
		stain	
		train	
		strain	
		twain	

Lesson 65a: Irregular pronunciations. Explain that *said* rhymes with *red*. Also explain that the *ai* in the words *again* and *against* is pronounced like short *e*.

Lesson 66: The next most common spelling of the long *a* sound is *ay* found in the following words:

bay	may	clay	*hey*
day	nay	gray	*grey*
Fay	pay	play	*they*
gay	ray	slay	*obey*
hay	say	stay	
jay	way	tray	
Kay		stray	
lay		sway	

Note the variant, irregular spelling of *hey*, *grey*, *they*, and *obey*. *Gray* and *grey* are two different spellings for the same word.

Lesson 67: Another, less common, way the long *a* is written is *ei,* as in these words:

rein	veil	heir	weigh	eight	reign
vein		their	sleigh	weight	

Explain that sometimes when three different words like *vein, vain,* and *vane* sound alike but mean totally different things, they are spelled differently so that the reader can tell which meaning is intended by the writer. The same is true of *rain, rein,* and *reign; veil* and *vale; heir* and *air; eight* and *ate.* Point out that the *h* in *heir* is silent. Also point out that the *g* in *reign* and the *gh* in *weigh, sleigh, eight,* and *weight* are silent. Take up the spellings and meanings of *their* and *there.*

It is not necessary for the pupil to remember everything you tell him about every irregular word. Most of them are our most common words and he will get to know their spelling and pronunciation peculiarities through repeated use of them in reading and writing. However, it is important for him to know that there *are* many exceptions to the rules. In this way he learns both the rules and the exceptions. Otherwise he might simply be confused by the inconsistencies and learn nothing. We often remember the rules by knowing the exceptions.

Lesson 68: General review of long *a* words. All of these words are in the child's speaking vocabulary and he should have no trouble reading them:

face	space	tail	vein	main	weigh
pain	scrape	dare	fake	flame	play
way	paid	brave	stain	grade	they
plate	chair	brain	care	cake	say
cage	their	gate	brake	day	ache

Lesson 69: Two- and three-syllable words composed of known short- and long-vowel pronunciation units. See how many the child can read on his own. Help him with the others. The purpose of the lesson is to teach the child how to look at multisyllabic words in terms of their separate syllables:

payday	pay-day	explain	ex-plain
railway	rail-way	complain	com-plain
airplane	air-plane	mailman	mail-man
careful	care-ful	inkstain	ink-stain
spaceship	space-ship	painful	pain-ful
away	a-way	tailgate	tail-gate
engage	en-gage	maintain	main-tain
waitress	wait-ress	embrace	em-brace
raining	rain-ing	graceful	grace-ful
enslave	en-slave	obtain	ob-tain
grateful	grate-ful		

engagement	en-gage-ment
lemonade	lem-on-ade
engraving	en-grav-ing
complaining	com-plain-ing
navigate	nav-i-gate
agitate	ag-i-tate

Lesson 70: Suggested sentences for practicing the long *a* in its various spelling forms:

The train is late but on the way.

Dave is complaining that it's raining.

Ray drank lemonade in the spaceship.

Clair and Ray went away on the same airplane.

The mailman came late again.

Jane said, "If it rains let's take the train."

Their train was late. But the train will take them there.

"Let's play a game," said Jane.

Lesson 70a: Quotation marks. Explain the use of quotation marks when the speech of a person is directly quoted. Make up more sentences for additional practice.

Lesson 71: Introduce the *a* sound as in *all, Paul, jaw.* Teach the following words:

all	halt	balk	haul	gaunt
ball	malt	calk	maul	haunt
call	salt	*talk*	Paul	jaunt
fall		*walk*	Saul	
gall		*chalk*	fault	
hall			vault	launch
mall				staunch
pall			Maud	
tall			fraud	
wall				
stall				

cause	awe	hawk	bawl	dawn
pause	jaw		brawl	fawn
	law		crawl	lawn
taut	paw		drawl	pawn
	raw			yawn
	saw			brawn
	claw			drawn
	draw			
	flaw			
	thaw			
	straw			

Irregular pronunciation: Note that in *talk, walk, chalk* the *l* is silent. (See also Lesson 34 concerning the silent *l*, and Lesson 26 concerning the *a* sound with the double *l*.)

Lesson 72: Irregular spellings. Take up the following group of irregularly spelled words all of which rhyme with *taut*. Note the silent *gh* and the mixed pattern of *au, ou* spellings. Most of the spellings are derived from ancient pronunciations and therefore reveal something of the linguistic origin of the words. How much of this you can make the child aware of depends on the curiosity, interest, and intelligence of the child. Most of our highly irregular words are frequently used and therefore learned with little or no trouble. In teaching correct spelling, it is a good idea to put special emphasis on these words and others like them:

ought	fraught
bought	nought
brought	sought
caught	taught
fought	thought

Lesson 72a: One of the most highly irregular words in our language is *drought,* meaning a long spell of dry weather. In pronunciation it rhymes with *out,* although it has the same spelling pattern as *brought* with the silent *gh.* Actually, it should be classified among those words in which the *ow* sound is spelled *ou.* (See Lesson 96 for the *ow* sound as spelled *ou.*) *Drought* is often confused with *draught,* which is pronounced *draft.*

Lesson 72b: There is another group of highly irregular one-syllable words with *au, ou* spellings, in which the *gh* stands for the *f* sound. They are common words and the child should pronounce them as he has heard them spoken:

cough - pronounced *cawf*

rough - pronounced *ruff*

tough - pronounced *tuff*

draught - pronounced *draft*

laugh - pronounced *laff*

laughter - pronounced *lafter*

Draught and *draft* are two accepted spellings of the same word.

In learning all of these irregular words, it is obvious that the child will have to devote some practice to reading them and writing them. The important thing is not to make any great fuss over them, except to point out that they are unusual spellings and represent something of a challenge in mastering them. Again, these irregularities merely confirm the consistency of most everything else. Our method makes it possible for the pupil to see the written language's eccentricities and irregularities in the context of a highly consistent and predictable system. In addition, the irregularities are in themselves consistent in that once they are learned, they do not change.

Lesson 73: Suggested practice sentences:

```
Tall Paul caught the ball.

Small Paul hit his jaw.

Saul walked and talked with Paul.

Paul taught Saul a lesson.

It was Saul's fault.
```

Lesson 74: Introduce the *a* sound as in *arm, art, ah, ma, pa*. Words with this *a* sound include the following:

bar	bard	scarf	ark	arm
car	card	*dwarf*	bark	farm
far	hard	*wharf*	hark	harm
jar	lard		lark	*warm*
par	yard		mark	
tar	*ward*		park	
war			Clark	
			spark	

barn	carp	art	farce	ah
darn	harp	cart		ma
yarn	tarp	dart	carve	pa
warn	*warp*	*heart*	starve	mama
		mart		papa
		part		
		tart		
		wart		
		quart		
		quartz		

Irregular spelling: *heart*

Irregular pronunciation: Notice the similar pronunciation of the *a* in *war, ward, wharf, dwarf, warm, warn, warp, quart, quartz*. Apparently when a *w* sound precedes *ar* it forces the mouth to pronounce the *a* in a narrower channel, thus making *ar* sound more like *or*. You needn't trouble the child with this explanation, unless you think he will be helped by it. Most of these words are in the child's speaking vocabulary and he knows how to pronounce them. His task is to simply recognize in written form what he says in spoken form.

Lesson 75: Introduce the long *e* sound by comparing such words as *bet* and *beet, fed* and *feed.* Show the child the *ee* as the most common written form of the long *e* sound. Show how *ee* can be expanded into *bee, fee, see,* etc. Then introduce the word *eel.* Expand *ee* and *eel* as shown:

bee	eel
fee	feel
gee	heel
Lee	peel
see	reel
free	steel
tree	wheel
knee	

Then create these additional words with the long *e* sound as spelled *ee:*

heed	beef	Greece	leek	deem
deed	reef	fleece	meek	seem
feed			reek	teem
need			seek	
reed			week	
seed				
weed				
breed				
creed				
greed				

been	beep	beer	beet	breeze	sleeve
seen	deep	deer	feet	freeze	
teen	keep	jeer	meet		
queen	jeep	peer	greet	geese	
green	peep	cheer	sweet	cheese	
screen	seep	queer	tweet		
	weep	steer			
	creep				
	sleep				
	steep				
	sweep				

Irregular pronunciation: The word *been* is pronounced in the United States as if it were spelled *bin*.

Special spelling: Acquaint the child with the *kn* construction in *knee*.

Lesson 76: There is a family of short common words in which the long *e* is spelled with a single *e,* as follows:

be
he
me
we
she

Lesson 77: Another way in which the long *e* sound is written is *ea.* Introduce the words *eat, ear, each.* Expand them as follows:

eat	ear	each
beat	*bear*	beach
feat	dear	peach
heat	fear	preach
meat	gear	reach
neat	hear	teach
peat	near	
seat	*pear*	
cheat	rear	
sweat	sear	
treat	tear	
threat	*tear*	
wheat	*wear*	
	year	
	swear	

Irregular pronunciations: The words *sweat* and *threat* rhyme with *wet*. The following words rhyme with *care: bear, pear, tear, wear,* and *swear.* Point out that regular *tear,* as in *teardrop,* is an entirely different word from irregular *tear,* which means to rip apart. Note, also, the two meanings of *bear.* The child can determine which meaning the author intends by the context in which the word is used.

Additional words with the long *e* sound as written *ea:*

pea	bead	*deaf*	beak	deal	beam
sea	*dead*	leaf	leak	heal	ream
tea	*head*		peak	meal	seam
	lead		teak	peal	steam
	lead		bleak	real	team
	read			seal	cream
	read			steal	dream
	bread			veal	stream
				weal	
				zeal	

bean	heap	east	ease	eave
dean	leap	beast	cease	leave
Jean	reap	feast	lease	heave
lean		yeast	tease	weave
mean			crease	
clean			please	

peace

Irregular pronunciations: The following words rhyme with *red: dead, head, lead, read, bread.* Explain that *lead* and *read,* both of which rhyme with *need,* have different meanings from the *lead* and *read* which rhyme with *red.* The reader can only determine the meaning of the word by the context in which the author uses it. The word *deaf* rhymes with *Jeff.*

Lesson 77a: Here are some suggested sentences to illustrate how the context will determine how to pronounce words with more than one pronunciation:

A neat cap is on his head.

Jean ate lean meat and bread.

Jean is deaf. Can she lead the way? She led the way.

She picked up a green leaf.

The ball is made of lead.

Did he read the ad? He read the ad last week.

Please bring peace, she pleaded with a tear.

"Tear it up," he said.

Lesson 78: Sometimes the long *e* sound is spelled *ie*, as in the following words:

niece	thief	pier	field
piece	chief	tier	yield
	grief	pierce	shield
		fierce	

siege	*sieve*	believe	fiend
		receive	*friend*

Irregular pronunciations: *sieve* is pronounced *siv; friend* rhymes with *trend.*

Irregular spelling: *receive, i* before *e* except after *c.*

Lesson 79: The long *e* is also commonly written as *y* at the end of a two-syllable word or name, as follows:

Abby	daddy	taffy	saggy
baby	caddy	daffy	baggy
Tabby	paddy	jiffy	Maggy
Libby	Teddy	puffy	foggy
lobby	giddy	stuffy	Peggy
	muddy		muggy
	study		Twiggy

Billy	mammy	Danny	happy	Harry
silly	mommy	Fanny	pappy	carry
Sally	mummy	Benny	peppy	Perry
rally	tummy	Jenny	poppy	Terry
hilly	Tommy	Lenny	puppy	merry
Molly	Timmy	Kenny		hurry
Polly		penny		sorry
bully		bunny		
chilly		funny		
frilly		sunny		
daily		*money*		
		any		
		many		

messy	batty	hazy
sissy	fatty	lazy
fussy	ratty	crazy
pussy	catty	dizzy
easy	city	fuzzy
busy	pity	
	pretty	
	nutty	

Irregular pronunciations: *pretty* rhymes with *city; busy* rhymes with *dizzy; money* rhymes with *sunny.* The *u* in *pussy* is pronounced the same as the *u* in *put.* This *u* sound, incidentally, is identical to the *oo* sound in words like *book, cook, took.* (See Lesson 95 for the *oo* sounds.) *Any* and *many* rhyme with *penny.*

Lesson 79a: The long *e* written as *y* is also found in such words as:

key   creamy   salty   buttery   bakery   monkey

Lesson 79b: Sometimes the long *e* is written as *ie* at the ends of words, as in:

Jackie   hippie   junkie   Minnie

In the plural, the final *y* becomes *ie*. However, this is more of a spelling problem than a reading problem, since the child should have no trouble identifying the *ie* as a long *e* symbol, as in these words:

baby	babies	bakery	bakeries
lobby	lobbies	bunny	bunnies
daddy	daddies	puppy	puppies
city	cities	caddy	caddies

However, if the *y* is preceded by *e* as in *key* and *monkey*, the plural is made by adding *s*, as in *keys* and *monkeys*. In the case of *money*, the plural is either *moneys* or *monies*. In other words, the rules of usage are not difficult to figure out, but there is some variation, and the dictionary should be consulted in case of doubt. As for the child who is learning how to read, do not complicate his problems by going into these fine details at this time. Let him simply learn that the long *e* is written as *ee, ea, ie, e, y,* or with a consonant and silent *e*, and let him become familiar with the families of words in which these long *e* spellings are present. Most of the one-syllable words in these spelling families are already in his speaking vocabulary, and he will learn to read them easily.

Lesson 79c: The long *e* sound written as *y* in the *ly* ending. Introduce the child to the familiar *ly* ending with the following combinations:

bad	badly	happy	happily	day	daily
sad	sadly			gay	gaily

Lesson 80: There are also a few words in which the long *e* is followed by a consonant and a silent *e*, as in *gene, scene, scheme, here, mere, these*. However, there are exceptions: *there* and *where* rhyme with *care; were* rhymes with *fur;* and *eye* is pronounced as the name of the letter *i*. Note that these are all very frequently used words and are learned through constant usage. Have the child read these words:

gene	here	these	eve	Pete
scene	mere		Steve	

Lesson 81: Review of words with the long *e* sound represented by *e, ee, ea, ie, y,* or with a consonant and silent *e*:

tea	please	stea¹	meet	treat	eve
week	queen	feet	tease	cheer	weep
fear	reach	eel	here	peace	feast
niece	sweet	ease	near	greet	breeze
beet	sea	clear	chief	mean	Steve
see	field	city	Pete	need	Jean
easy	she	beach	feel	bean	believe
Jeep	steer	read	she	seat	jeer
tree	greasy	dear	thief	these	leave
he	hear	gear	feat	we	leaf
key	meat	study	funny	baby	dizzy

Lesson 82: Suggested practice sentences with long *e* syllables:

Pete and Steve are sleeping on the beach.

Peggy ate a pretty peach. She picked it from a peachtree.

The busy airfield is near the big city.

It was peaceful. A green leaf fell from the tree.

We sent Merry Christmas greetings.

We ate meat, beets, beans and drank a cup of tea.

The paleface brought the Indian chief a gift.

The Indian chief was pleased.

Note that the *ch* in *Christmas* has the *k* sound.

Lesson 83: Many common English words have an *er* ending. Introduce the child to these words, all of which have known vowel sounds:

better	number	rather	bigger	sitter
sweeter	ginger	dealer	winter	fever
sweater	finger	maker	lumber	heater
teacher	sister	butter	baker	chatter
hunger	later	upper	bumper	bother
summer	slipper	pitcher	blister	letter

understand	letterbox	feverish
lumberjack	slippery	gingerbread

Lesson 84: Introduce the long *i* sound. Tell the child that the long *i* sounds the same as the name of the letter *i*. First teach the word *I*. *I am.*

I am
I take
I make
I have
I had
I met
I ran
I played

Next, show how the most common way to write the long *i* is with a consonant followed by a silent *e*. Illustrate with the word *ice* and the name *Ike*. Expand *ice* and *Ike* as follows:

ice	Ike
dice	bike
lice	dike
mice	hike
nice	like
rice	Mike
vice	pike
price	spike
slice	strike
spice	
twice	

Teach these additional words in these spelling families:

bribe	bide	life	bile	dime	dine
tribe	hide	rife	file	lime	fine
	ride	wife	mile	mime	line
	side	*knife*	Nile	rime	mine
	tide	strife	pile	time	pine
	wide		tile	chime	vine
	bride		vile	crime	wine
	chide		smile	grime	brine
	pride		while	prime	shine
	slide			slime	spine
			isle	clime	swine
			aisle	*climb*	thine
					twine

pipe	dire	rise	bite	dive	size
ripe	fire	wise	kite	five	prize
wipe	hire		site	*give*	
gripe	mire		quite	hive	
swipe	sire		trite	jive	
stripe	tire			live	
	wire			*live*	
	spire			chive	
				drive	
				strive	
				thrive	

Irregular spellings and pronunciations: The *kn* in *knife* stands for *n*. Both *isle* and *aisle* are pronounced the same as *ile*. The *s* in *isle* is silent. The *s* in *aisle* is silent, the *ai* is pronounced *i*. Explain the difference in meaning between the two words. *Give* and *live* are pronounced as if they were spelled *giv* and *liv*, with short *i* sounds. Note the difference in meaning between *live* (short *i*) and *live* (long *i*). Note the silent *b* in *climb*. (Additional silent *b* words are taken up in Lesson 112.)

Lesson 85: The long *i* sound is also sometimes written as *ie*, *y*, and *uy*, as in the following common words:

die	by	buy
lie	my	guy
pie	ply	
tie	sly	
vie	spy	
	cry	
	dry	
	fry	
	pry	
	try	

In the past tense, the *y* is changed to *ied:*

die	died
lie	lied
tie	tied
cry	cried
dry	dried
try	tried

Lesson 86: In some words the long *i* is also found in combination with a silent *g* or *gh* as in:

sign	high	fight
	sigh	light
	thigh	might
		night
		right
		sight
		tight
		bright
		fright
		slight

height

Irregular spelling: The word *height* rhymes with *light*, not *eight* or *weight*.

Lesson 87: Note the long *i* in the following spelling families:

bind	binder	child
blind	blindness	wild
find	finder	
hind	behind	
kind	unkind	
mind	kindness	
rind	kindly	
wind	remind	
wind	unwind	

Exceptions: Note the pronunciation of *wind* (short *i*) as opposed to *wind* (long *i*). Explain the meanings of the two words. The *i* is also short in *window* and *cinder*. Note also: *child, children; wild, wilderness*. In all of these cases, the spoken word is the guide to the word's correct pronunciation, not its spelling.

110

Lesson 88: Review of long *i* pronunciation units in two and three-syllable words:

alive	reply	delight
decide	define	beside
refine	apply	advise
desire	alike	retire
assign	design	tighten
admire	advice	behind
devine	arise	remind
inspire	aside	kindness
reptile	entwine	brighten
highest	rightful	driver

retirement	re-tire-ment
rightfully	right-ful-ly
delightful	de-light-ful
assignment	as-sign-ment
reminder	re-mind-er
designer	de-sign-er

Lesson 89: Suggested practice sentences with long *i* words:

The child cried.

The night was mild and dry.

I sat beside the driver. The driver was nice.

I tightened my seatbelt.

The light was in my eyes.

Mike and I are alike.

"Can I ride my bike?" Mike asked with a smile.

"I can ride five miles," Mike said.

I asked myself, "Did Mike lie?"

Lesson 90: Introduce the long *o* sound. Say the words *oak, old, oat* to make sure the child identifies the long *o* sound. Then tell him that the long *o* sound can be written in a number of ways and that it is easy to learn them all.

The most common way of spelling the long *o* is with a consonant and a silent *e*, in the same way that the long *a* and long *i* are commonly written. Show him how *rob* is changed to *robe* by adding the silent *e*, *cod* to *code*, *rod* to *rode*. Then take the word *dive* and show how inserting an *o* in place of the *i* makes it *dove*, the past tense of *dive*. Present him the following words:

robe	ode	coke	spoke	hole	dome	*one*	*done*
	code	joke	stoke	mole	home	bone	*none*
	mode	poke	stroke	pole	Rome	cone	*gone*
	rode	woke		role	*come*	lone	
		broke		sole	*some*	tone	
		choke		whole		zone	*once*
		smoke				phone	

cope	ore	dose	note	cove	doze
dope	bore	hose	vote	dove	froze
hope	core	nose	quote	*dove*	
pope	fore	pose		*love*	
rope	more	rose		*move*	
slope	tore	chose		rove	
	sore	close		wove	
	yore	close		clove	
	chore			drove	
	store			grove	
	swore			stove	
				glove	
				shove	

Irregular pronunciations:

come, some rhyme with *hum.*

one, done, none rhyme with *fun.*

once rhymes with *dunce.*

gone rhymes with *dawn.*

dove, love, glove, shove are pronounced as if they were spelled *duv, luv, gluv, shuv.*

move rhymes with *groove.*

Note *close,* meaning *shut,* rhymes with *rose,* while *close,* meaning *near,* rhymes with *dose.*

Lesson 91: A second common way in which the long *o* is spelled is *oa* as in the following words:

load	loaf	oak	coal	foam
road		soak	goal	roam
toad		cloak		

soap	oar	boast	oat
	roar	coast	boat
	soar	roast	coat
	board	toast	goat
	hoard		moat
			float
			gloat

Lesson 92: A third way in which the long *o* is spelled is *ow* as in the following words:

bow	blow	own
low	crow	blown
row	flow	grown
mow	grow	shown
sow	show	known
tow	slow	
know	snow	

Lesson 93: A fourth way in which the long *o* is written is in combination with a consonant blend or followed by *r*. When followed by *r* the long *o* undergoes a modification in sound simply because it is physically impossible to pronounce a full long *o* sound immediately before an *r*. However, for all practical purposes of vowel-sound classification, the *o* in *or* is a long *o*. Teach the child to identify the following words with their spoken counterparts:

old	host	cord	cork	dorm	born
bold	most	ford	fork	form	corn
cold	*cost*	lord	pork	norm	horn
fold	*lost*	chord	York	*worm*	morn
gold	post	*word*	stork		torn
hold					worn
mold					adorn
sold					
told					

fort	horse	boss	or
Mort	Morse	loss	for
port	Norse	moss	nor
sort		toss	
short			

Irregular pronunciations: Note that *cost* and *lost* have the same *o* sound as in *boss, loss, moss, toss*. This *o* sound is similar to the *aw* sound in *jaw*.

As spelled, *worm* should sound like *warm*, but it rhymes with *germ*.

Word rhymes with *herd*.

Lesson 94: In a few simple words, the long *o* is simply spelled with an *o*, as in the following:

oh
go
no
so
quo
yo-yo

The pronunciation of these words will be obvious to the child when he encounters them in reading. He should become aware of the exceptions in this group, namely:

do
to
two
who
you

Lesson 95: Introduce the *oo* sound as in *good* and *food*. There is a slight difference between the two sounds, but the *oo* stands for both of them. Remember that the spoken language is always the ultimate guide to a written word's pronunciation.

coo	boob	brood	goof	book
boo		food	hoof	cook
moo		good	roof	hook
too		hood	proof	look
woo		mood		nook
zoo		wood		took
		stood		brook
				crook
				shook
				spook

cool	boom	boon	coop	boor
fool	doom	moon	loop	*door*
pool	broom	noon	hoop	moor
tool	*tomb*	soon	poop	poor
wool		spoon	stoop	
drool			sloop	
school				

loose	boot	booth	ooze
moose	coot	tooth	booze
noose	foot	smooth	snooze
choose	hoot		
	loot		
	soot		
	root		
	toot		
	zoot		

Irregular pronunciation: *door* rhymes with *more*.
Irregular spelling: *tomb* rhymes with *doom*. (See Lesson 113 for silent *b*.)

Lesson 95a: Special spelling group. The following group of irregularly spelled words also rhyme with *good: could, would,
should.* After you discuss their meanings, explain also that these
words are often joined with *not* to make the following contractions:

could	could not	couldn't
would	would not	wouldn't
should	should not	shouldn't

Lesson 95b: The problem of vowel variants. One of the best
ways to illustrate the nature of most of the irregularities in
written English is by showing the variety of pronunciations which
can be found in one spelling family. For example:

both	bother	brother	broth
		other	
		mother	
		smother	

The *o* in *both* is long. The *o* in *bother* is short. The *o* in *brother* is
pronounced as short *u*. The *o* in *broth* is pronounced as *aw* in *raw.*
Despite these variations, the child should have no trouble utter-
ing the appropriate vowel sound for each word. Why? Because,
first, he has been taught to associate the written word with the
spoken word. Second, he has been taught that such irregularities
are common and of no great importance except in learning to spell
correctly. Third, the consonants are quite consistent, and it is only
the vowel sound which varies. The inconsistency of the vowel
sounds may give the child some trouble at the beginning stages of
reading when encountering unknown words. But as he reads more
and more, he develops the ability to identify familiar words and to
hear them in the context of what he is reading. The problem of
vowel-sound variation, if it ever existed for the child, simply dis-
appears. Experience, moreover, seems to indicate that children are
not bothered by such variations at all and that they accept them
as they accept everything else around them. To a child, incon-

sistency is quite a natural part of life. It is expected, lived with, and learned.

To have the child practice reading the vowel variants illustrated in this lesson, make up sentences like the following:

>Both mother and brother told father not to bother sister.
>
>Both brothers had broth for breakfast.
>
>One brother tried to bother the other.
>
>Mother saw the Smothers Brothers on TV.

Lesson 96: Suggested practice sentences for the *o* and *oo* sounds.

Mort sold the pork for gold and went home.

His brother Joe took some money and told his mother that he was **going** to the store to buy something.

He opened the door of the store.

The storekeeper was old, toothless, and spooky.

"What should I buy?" Joe thought. "I'll buy a broom, some tools, a wool hat, good food, some pieces of wood, a pair of boots, and a hoola-hoop."

"Could I have these things?" he asked.

"If you have gold," said the old man who walked with a stoop.

Lesson 97: Introduce the *ow, ou* sound as in *cow* and *ouch.* There are many common words in this vowel group, as shown below:

bow	owl	*own*	browse	ouch
cow	*bowl*	down		couch
how	cowl	gown		pouch
now	fowl	town		*touch*
pow	howl	brown		vouch
sow	jowl	clown		
vow	growl	crown		
wow		drown		
		frown		

loud	gouge	ounce	noun
proud		bounce	
cloud		pounce	
		flounce	
		trounce	

bound	count	our	douse	out
found	fount	*four*	house	bout
hound	mount	hour	louse	lout
pound		sour	mouse	pout
round		*tour*	rouse	rout
sound		*your*	souse	clout
wound		flour		*doubt*
wound				trout
ground				

mouth	bower	bough	*rough*
youth	cower	plough	*tough*
	flower	drought	*enough*
	power		
	tower		

Irregular pronunciations and spellings:

bowl rhymes with *role.*

own rhymes with *tone.*

touch rhymes with *much.*

four and *your* rhyme with *or*.

tour rhymes with *poor*.

youth rhymes with *tooth*, as *you* rhymes with *too*.

The *ou* in *wound* sounds like *oo* in *moon*.

Note the silent *b* in *doubt*.

rough, *tough*, *enough* rhyme with *stuff*.

The word *own* is actually in the spelling family of *low, know, known*. It rhymes with *bone*. Note that *one* is pronounced *wun* and is the written word for the numeral 1. Note the three spellings of *four, for,* and *fore*. Obviously, the three different spellings provide immediate visual cues to the meaning of each word.

Lesson 98: Here are some well-known two-syllable practice words with *ow, ou* sounds which the pupil should be able to read quite easily:

downtown	lousy	vowel	doubtful
towel	county	Mounty	countless
bow-wow	about	fountain	arouse
counter	mountain	sauerkraut	bouncing

Suggested practice sentences:

Mr. and Mrs. Powell went downtown to see clowns at the circus.

Later they sat down at the counter of a soda fountain.

They had hotdogs with sauerkraut and ice cream sodas.

It all cost about four dollars.

Explain the meaning of the abbreviations *Mr.* and *Mrs.*

Lesson 99: Introduce the *oy, oi* sound as in *boy* and *oil.* Here are some common words in that sound group:

boy	void	oil	coin	joint
coy		boil	join	point
joy		coil	loin	
Roy		foil		
soy		soil		
toy		toil		
		broil		
		spoil		

noise	hoist	Joyce	choice
poise	foist	Royce	
	moist		

Lesson 99a: Here are some simple two-syllable words with *oy, oi* syllables.

poison	toilsome	joyful
avoid	decoy	boyish
oily	spoiler	broiling
appoint	annoy	rejoice

Lesson 100: Introduce the long *u* sound. Give examples by pronouncing such words as *use, June, cube, mule.* These words are spelled with the *u* followed by a consonant and silent *e* as follows:

cube	dude	huge	cuke	mule	fume
lube	Jude		duke	rule	plume
Rube	nude		juke	Yule	
tube	rude		Luke		
	crude		puke		
	prude				

dune	dupe	cure	use	cute
June		pure	muse	jute
tune		*sure*	ruse	lute
prune				mute
				brute
				chute
				flute

Irregular pronunciation: The *s* in *sure* is pronounced *sh*.

Lesson 101: Here are some two- and three-syllable words with long *u* syllables which your pupil should be able to read easily:

cupid	assure	ice-cube	refusal
Yuletide	refuse	duty	cucumber
jukebox	prudent	parachute	musical
dilute	Neptune	tuneful	amusing
amuse	pupil	jury	insurance
tubeless	ruler	student	fumigate
rudeness	music	excuse	assurance

Lesson 102: The long *u* is also spelled *ue* and *ui* as in the following words:

cue	blue	duel	juice
due	clue	fuel	fruit
hue	flue	cruel	bruise
rue	glue		cruise
Sue	queue		
	true		

Lesson 103: The long *u* is also spelled *ew* and *eu* as in these words:

dew	blew	flew	lewd	feud
few	brew	grew		deuce
Jew	chew	stew		
Lew	clew	view		
mew	crew	screw		
new	drew			
news				
pew				
sew				

Irregular pronunciation: The word *sew* rhymes with *no*.

Lesson 104: The *er, ir, ur* sounds. Note the general inter-changeability of these sound symbols. A few *or* and *ear* words can be included in this group.

her	terse	earn	fir	shirt
jerk	verse	search	sir	squirt
clerk	berth	heard	bird	birth
germ	Perth	learn	gird	girth
term	nerve	yearn	firm	mirth
fern	serve	earth	girl	thirst
herd	verve	dearth	whirl	dirge
Bert	swerve		dirt	smirk
pert	Merv		flirt	quirk

fur	curl	urn	Curt	word
cur	hurl	burn	hurt	work
purr	furl	turn	curse	worm
curd	lurk	churn	nurse	worst
urge	murk	spurn	purse	worth
purge	Turk		burst	
splurge			curve	

Lesson 105: Here are some two- and three-syllable words with *er, ir, ur, ear,* and *or* units joined with other known sounds:

perfect	herself	terminal
birthday	Mervin	searchlight
nervous	return	thirsty
service	occur	further
dirty	workingman	learning

expert	wormy
urgent	intern
murky	worthless
worthwhile	hurtful
girlish	Turkish

Lesson 106: Many common English words have an *le* ending in which the *l* sound terminates the word with only the slightest hint of a vowel sound preceding it. This vowel sound is often called "the muttering vowel." These words will familiarize your pupil with this common spelling form:

able	apple	battle
cable	grapple	cattle
fable	paddle	rattle
gable	faddle	little
table	fiddle	brittle
sable	saddle	settle
stable	coddle	kettle
maple	riddle	tattle
idle	pebble	tittle
stifle	babble	turtle
bridle	bubble	
eagle		
rifle		
beagle		
trifle		

ample	jungle	dazzle	hustle
sample	juggle	razzle	bustle
simple	struggle	fizzle	rustle
dimple	ogle		wrestle
pimple	bungle	raffle	pestle
temple	wiggle	ruffle	
fumble	wriggle	piffle	
bumble	wrinkle		
humble	crinkle		
nimble	jingle		
rumble	jangle		
grumble	strangle		
stumble	bangle		
tumble	dangle		
jumble	single		
thimble			
gentle			
handle			

Note the silent *t* in *hustle, bustle,* etc. (See Lesson 112 for more on the silent *t*.)

Lesson 107: Show how these multisyllabic words are derived from the words learned in the previous lesson:

juggler	settler	unstable	cobbler
simply	rustler	gently	babbling
rattler	wrestler	handling	grumbling
tumbler	fizzled	fumbling	rifleman
littlest	gentleman	pimply	unsettled

Lesson 108: There are many words of Latin origin in English in which the *ce, sc, ci, ti, xi, su,* and *tu* are pronounced *sh, ch,* or *zh.* Here are some of them the pupil can become familiar with:

ocean	ancient	national
nation	fission	confusion
special	racial	facial
station	ration	fraction
fissure	rapture	patient
initial	fusion	capture
sure	crucial	insure
treasure	leisure	fracture

mission	nauseous
measure	issue
conscious	atrocious
patience	question
pleasure	tissue
motion	physician
picture	musician
obnoxious	transportation

Lesson 109: The pupil has already been introduced to several words beginning with the silent *k*, such as *knee* and *know*. Here are others he should become familiar with:

knack	knap	knave	knee
knight	knit	knob	knock
known	knowing	knuckle	kneeling

kneel   knelt   knickers

knot   know   knowledge

knitted   knocked   knotted

Lesson 110: Introduce the initial silent *g* in these words beginning with *gn:*

gnarl   gnarled   gnat   gnaw

gnawing   gnome   gnu

Lesson 111: Introduce the pupil to the silent *w* in words beginning with *wr:*

write	wrack	wrench	wrapping
wrap	wreath	wrist	writing
wrong	wring	wrath	wrought
wreck	wrote	writer	wry

wretch	wrestle
wretched	wrestling
wriggle	wrestled
written	wrestler

Lesson 112: Introduce the silent *t* with these words:

castle	hustle	nestle	often	listen
whistle	hustling	hastening	soften	listener
wrestle	bristles	thistle	rustling	moisten
hasten	christen	rustle	wrestling	whistling

Lesson 113: Introduce the silent *b* as in the following words:

dumb   thumb   plumber   limb   climb

lamb   comb   crumb   tomb   bomb

numb   debt

bombing   climbing

Note the interesting variant sounds of *o* in *comb*, *tomb*, and *bomb*.

Lesson 114: The *h* is silent in some words. For example:

honor   hour   ghost   honest

ghastly   ghetto   ghoul

Lesson 115: In some words *ch* stands for the *k* sound, as in the following:

Christ	chord	chorus
Christian	chrome	Christmas
cholera	psyche	psychic
character	scheme	chemist
chemical	chronic	chlorine
chlorophyll	chronicle	chemistry

Lesson 116: The pupil has already been introduced to the silent *g* and *gh* as found in such long *i* words as *sign* and *sight*. The silent *gh* is found in other common words as well. Here are some of them:

naughty	daughter	height
straight	weight	fought
weigh	slaughter	fight
lightning	caught	thoughful

thought	frightened
eighty	brighten
neighbor	eighteen
slaughtered	thoughtfully

Lesson 117: Review of *ph* and *gh* as the *f* sound:

phantom	Ralph	rough	cough
graph	pharmacy	physical	Phoenix
tough	phony	photo	graphic
emphasis	telephone	phase	photograph

laugh	laughter
physics	Philadelphia
telegraph	philosophy
phrase	philosopher

With the completion of the final lesson, the child has learned the English sound-symbol system thoroughly enough to permit him to read virtually anything he will encounter in print. He will have no problem understanding all of the written material which is within his present intellectual scope, and he will have an entry into everything beyond it. His knowledge of the written language is now equal to his knowledge of the spoken language, and he can express his own thoughts on paper. Now he can use his entry into the world of written language to expand both his knowledge of the spoken word and the written word.

Reading a book is, from a technical point of view, much like playing a roller-playback piano. Once the paper roll with punched holes starts turning, the piano plays a piece of music complete with harmonies and chords, as if played by a professional. Similarly, when a reader starts reading a book, he channels someone else's words and thoughts through his own brain and his own mouth. The words and thoughts flow rapidly through the reader's mind because all the work of thinking has already been done by the writer. But here the analogy between the playback piano and the reader ends. The piano is a mechanical instrument. The reader is a living being with a living mind. Thus, the author's thinking will, if it is interesting or challenging, in turn stimulate the reader's thinking. The result is mental exercise, the kind of exercise the intellect needs in order to grow. This is how mind expansion really takes place.

We have tried to teach the child a number of important things in this course of instruction. First, we have provided him with a fundamental knowledge of our language's sound-symbol system which will enable him to read the written word accurately and proficiently. He has learned how forty-four distinct language sounds can be combined in endless variation to produce thousands of easily understood spoken words. And he has seen how twenty-six letter symbols can be combined in an equally endless variation to write those thousands and thousands of spoken words.

He has discovered that most spellings (about eighty percent) are quite accurate in their sound-symbol representations. Some words—like *how* and *low*, for example—can be read in more than one way, either of which may be correct from a sound-symbol point of view, but only one of which will be correct from the written-word-spoken-word point of view. Some words like *worm, want, young, said, friend, pretty* are spelling peculiarities. But even with these words, it is only the vowel sound which is inaccurately represented. The consonants are all accurate. Ninety percent of our irregular words are of this kind. Even the most irregularly spelled words—like *eye, one, two, tomb*—have sufficient sound-symbol elements to keep them within a limited range of possibilities. But because most of these words are alternate spellings of words with the same sound but different meaning, their distinct spellings, associated with specific meanings, make them easy to learn.

One should also be reminded that in regional accents, it is the vowel sounds which vary rather than the consonants. These regional accents are easily accomodated by our flexible vowel-symbol system. In a language spoken from Glasgow to London, Sydney to Cape Town, Boston to Atlanta, there are bound to be significant differences in accent. Yet the same written words must be read by all of these people in their respective regional accents. Which bring us to our remarkable vocal system.

We use five vowel letters and occasionally the consonant *y* to stand for over three times as many speech sounds. In addition, because of our double *e*'s, double *o*'s, *ea, ie, ai*, etc., our vowel symbols have tremendous visual impact. We hear them loudly when we see them, not only because we often use two vowel letters to represent one vowel sound in a word, but because in our speech we emphasize our vowels much more than we do our consonants. English, unlike German, is not a guttural language with its stress on consonants. Its unique quality, which suits it so well for poetry and drama, is its range of vowel sounds. *Webster's New World Dictionary of the American Language* lists twenty-one vowel sounds in English. The phonetic Initial Teaching Alphabet has sixteen vowel symbols for sixteen sounds. In our traditional spelling we use thirty-one ways of writing our full range of vowel sounds. To achieve this with only five vowel letters, we use single letters, double letters, combined vowel letters, and vowel letters combined with consonants like *w* and *y*. The result is that 15 vowel symbols represent only one sound each; 9 represent 2 sounds each; 2 represent 3 sounds each; 3 represent 4 sounds each; 1 represents 5 sounds; and 1 represents 6 sounds. It is not surprising that this should be the case with so few letters required to do so much work. There is in English a great interchangeability of vowel sounds and symbols, and therein lies our teaching problem. But it is not as difficult a problem as it would seem once the teaching approach is logical and systematic.

This brings us to the method used in this course of instruction. We have used our method not only to make learning how to read easier, faster, and more efficient, but to also teach the child something about method itself; something about the problem of taking a highly complicated system of abstractions and making it manageable for a child's mind. We consider that lesson as important for the intellectual growth of the child as his learning how to read. And this is why we have insisted that the child should not be diverted by distracting pictures, irrelevant excursions, story interpretations, and vocabulary building at a time when he is mastering this complex system of symbols. Mastery of this system should form the heart of his elementary education. It will provide a foundation for literacy so solid, so indestructible, so thorough, that all his future work will be able to draw important intellectual sustenance from it.

Language is the basis of all intellectual work, and the system of abstractions which forms the basis of our writing should be mastered during the first years of schooling. Such mastery is the first real step toward literacy. It is also the first real step toward the understanding of logic. A sound-symbol system which enables us to use twenty-six letters to write thousands of words is an intellectual marvel of tremendous magnitude, a marvel that every child should be made aware of. And only a systematic, organized, and logical approach will make him aware of it.

Thus, we have stressed the basic consistency of the system and introduced the irregularities as they occur within each of the spelling groups. Even in the irregularities there is an important lesson to be learned. The number of irregularities in written English helps to develop mental flexibility—a tolerance and appreciation for variation, an ability to see that there is more than one way to write a sound or express a thought, and that the written language is a living instrument of thought. If the written language were one hundred percent consistent it would appear rigid, inflexible, and stultifying. Its inconsistencies breathe with life. They reflect the ever-changing, growing people who make them and use them. The only languages which do not grow and change are dead languages. And even if we devised a perfectly phonetic alphabet, with one symbol per sound, how would we deal with regional accents and changing pronunciations? And who would suppose that, in time, this writing system would not develop its own inconsistencies and irregularities? The simple fact is that inconsistency, the exception to the rule, the unique, is an important part of life, and it is only natural that the vehicle of man's thinking should reflect this.

The truth is that our writing system is a rich, ingenious system, capable of accomodating our most complicated feelings, emotions, and thoughts. Its peculiarities make it interesting, vital, and very human. Like each of us, it has its faults. But better than most of us, it functions superlatively well despite them. The English writing system is the most useful intellectual instrument ever devised by man. It has been used by philosophers, scientists, novelists, dramatists, and poets to create a legacy of unparalleled wealth for anyone who wants to draw from it. The skill required to make use of that legacy is easily the most precious skill a human being can acquire. It is our hope that this book will have made the acquisition of that skill as pleasant and interesting as possible.

133

Index of Lessons

Part Three

Writing

Of the three R's, writing has been the most neglected in the elementary school curriculum for the last thirty years. The reason for this (which is scarcely known by most educators and totally unknown by the lay public) is that ever since the introduction of print-script writing in our schools in the 1930s, American children have been required to learn *two* systems of writing. And of the two, cursive writing has gotten less and less attention in the changing primary school curriculum. Prior to the introduction of print-script, or "manuscript" as it is officially called, American children were taught only one way to write: cursive, which means "running," and describes the traditional flowing form of adult handwriting in which all the letters of a word are joined. In those days, children were taught "penmanship" and by the third grade had learned to write reasonably well by third-grade standards.

However, because cursive writing is a rather difficult skill for some first-graders to learn, it was thought desirable to introduce children to the art of writing via the simplified print-script invented by an Englishman and imported into this country in the 1920s. "Manuscript," as this print-script was later called, is a misnomer if there ever was one. "Manuscript" is simply a form of hand printing or lettering, very much like the kind that architects use on their drawings. But it has been considered and taught as a form of handwriting, which it really is not.

In today's curriculum, when a child reaches the third grade, he is generally considered ready to learn cursive: "real writing" or "grown-up writing" as some children call it. Unfortunately, most teachers expect the children to pick up cursive writing on their own without much practice or supervision. In addition, children are required to use their cursive handwriting extensively in their schoolwork before they have been fully trained in it. The result is poor, illegible scrawls and lots of bad handwriting habits. Some schools don't even bother to give formal instruction in cursive writing at all, expecting the students to pick it up completely on their own if they want to use it. The handwriting of these students generally reflects their lack of instruction.

This dual writing program, in which cursive writing gets the short end of the stick, has been criticized by some thoughtful educators. For example, one concerned educator,* writing in *Elementary English* of October 1960, commented:

> Such a duality of learning and performance is almost unknown in the areas of reading and arithmetic where the first learnings are simply reinforced and broadened through subsequent training rather than altered and changed as in the area of handwriting.

> However, this dual program in handwriting instruction seems to have been accepted by educators almost without question, for no more than one or two research studies dealing with the transitional aspect of handwriting instruction have been reported within the past two decades. However, a study recently completed by this investigator provides data which support the premise *that it is more difficult for a person to master two sets of handwriting symbols than it is for him to perfect one set*—whether that set be manuscript or cursive in style.

> For many children who apparently encounter little or no difficulty at the time of transition this duality of learning and performance in handwriting appears to create few problems. However, those of us who have been primary teachers for any length of time are aware that children vary considerably in their

---

*Elaine Templin, "Handwriting—the Neglected R."

ability to make the transition from one handwriting style to another and that some children experience considerable loss in handwriting facility during the transitional period.

Personal observation has led this author to conclude that it is the boys who are more likely to experience difficulty in developing a legible and fluent cursive style of handwriting. Indeed, a few boys known to the author have persisted in clinging to the manuscript style of writing long after their classmates have succeeded in completing the transition. . . .

However, if tradition demands a continuance of the dual program of handwriting instruction, it would seem advisable for educators to urge that more careful guidance and more thorough instruction be provided during the period of change-over, *for it is at this level where our youth are most likely to become handwriting cripples.*

Yet it is here that the greater laxity in handwriting instruction seems to occur, for many teachers and pupils appear to view the transition as a nuisance as well as a necessity. In addition, many of them seem to believe that the cursive style of handwriting can be acquired quickly and easily since the pupils already know how to write.

Nothing could be farther from the truth. A child's ability to reproduce the manuscript symbols does not preclude his need to practice and to master the cursive symbols when they are introduced to him.

That sums up quite well why the handwriting of so many students is so poor. They must master two sets of symbols, two styles of writing, and the transition from one to the other is, in most cases, very carelessly and thoughtlessly made. Because of this, some educators have advocated teaching one writing style only. One veteran teacher of handwriting, Luella Cole, addressed herself to that problem in the *Elementary School Journal* of November 1956. She wrote:

Perhaps the commonest "fault" in these lowest grades is an over-emphasis upon printing of the letters, that is, upon manuscript writing. If this type of writing could be continued indefinitely, its introduction would be defensible. However, the permanent use of printing has at least three shortcomings. First, it is, in general, somewhat slower than cursive writing. Second, it tends, from imitation of book printing, to be written vertically—a characteristic which is not in itself objectionable but which contributes to the slowness of its production for most right-handed people. Third, its use leads to the introduction of misleading spaces within words, because pupils have joined together their letters in groups of two or three but have not joined together all the letters within an entire word. Thus, such a sentence as "The earth began to tremble," emerges as "T he ear th be g an to trem ble." Even if every letter is perfectly formed, the result is still illegible because of the spacing. Since, therefore, on the judgment of the present writer, manuscript writing cannot be continued with an expectation of satisfactory permanent results, it is best never to let it become established. Whatever form a first-grade child voluntarily uses for first writing his name (block capitals, printed letters, or cursive) is acceptable for the moment, but the actual teaching should certainly introduce cursive handwriting, since these letter forms will be used throughout life.

There are other educators, however, who feel that the dual writing program, so deeply entrenched, is with us to stay, and they advocate strengthening the writing program all the way down the line, going from print-script, to slant print-script, to cursive—a three-stage program. This, however, would require a much greater emphasis on handwriting than many schools or teachers want to confer on the subject. There are also those who want to eliminate cursive writing altogether. Their views* were expressed in *Elementary English* of December 1971 as follows:

It is the position here that instruction in handwriting should consist of the development and maintenance of one writing style throughout the child's educational career; that the advantages which manuscript holds for children as a communication tool clearly point to this as the style to be utilized, and that instruction in cursive writing should be eliminated from the basic curriculum of the elementary school. . . .

The evidence of a growing body of comparative data would seem to support the instruction of manuscript as the writing style in the primary grades and its maintenance throughout children's educational careers. A transition to cursive writing is complicated by factors which may create unnecessary problems

---

*Emma E. Platter, of the University of Calgary Faculty of Education, and Ellsworth S. Woestehoff, of the University of Rochester College of Education, "Toward a Singular Style of Instruction in Handwriting."

for many children and therefore militate against a dual program of handwriting instruction.

Cursive writing style should be considered for what it really is: a complex, complicated skill that is difficult to acquire. The time allotted to introduction and maintenance of the cursive writing style might well be directed to more significant language experience.

Thus, there is considerable disagreement among educators not only on which of the two writing styles to teach but how to teach them. The ones to suffer in all this pedagogical confusion and debate are the students. For our purposes, however, let us be clear on several points. First, manuscript writing is not handwriting. It is a form of hand printing. Our language has only one universally acceptable handwriting system, and that is cursive. Second, since it is cursive writing instruction which suffers in the schools, it is cursive writing which the tutor must specialize in. Third, we share Luella Cole's view that since cursive writing is the one which will be used throughout life, it is the one to teach the child. If the time the child spends in formal instruction is to be used to the child's maximum future benefit, it should be spent learning a skill which he will be able to employ in every area of educational, personal, professional, and business life. In addition, unless you can write cursive yourself, it is not likely that you'll be able to read the handwriting of others very well. In short, cursive writing is one of the indispensable tools of literacy in our highly literate civilization, and it should be taught to every child thoroughly and systematically from grade one onward.

In teaching a child to write you must think of the task in the same way you would think of teaching the child a physical skill like playing tennis or ping-pong, or playing the violin, or crocheting, or touch typing. What is involved for optimum performance is good muscular control, relaxed nerves, good eyesight, and excellent coordination between hand and eye. To bring it down to an even simpler level, we might say that teaching a child to write is no more intellectual than teaching him how to eat with chopsticks. The task is one of physical dexterity and the earlier it is learned the better. Many a Chinese youngster of four or five can handle chopsticks quite adeptly while a Western adult might have to spend weeks practicing before he could do as well. But first the adult would have to be taught how to hold the chopsticks correctly before being able to use them proficiently, and it would take a great deal of practice before the adult could use them as easily and automatically as the Chinese child.

The same is true in teaching a child to write cursively. Holding a pencil is perhaps a lot less difficult than holding chopsticks. Learning to form each letter and numeral legibly takes time because there are sixty-two of them—twenty-six small letters, twenty-six capitals, and ten numerals. The child must be taught how to write each letter and numeral correctly. Since writing is a physical skill which must become automatic, the child must repeat writing the letters slowly, accurately, and legibly until he does it so well that speed picks up on its own.

Because learning to write is a purely physical and muscular task, all the procedures used in mastering a physical skill must be applied. Luella Cole, after a full career of teaching children how to write, summed up these procedures in six easy-to-understand precepts:

1. Base the teaching upon careful imitation of a good model, allowing only such minor variations as are necessary because of a pupil's age or size.

2. Continue the practice of simple skills under close supervision until the pupil can execute a series of movements perfectly.

3. Teach self-diagnosis and self-correction until you feel sure that the pupil has the habit of self-appraisal.

4. Then introduce intensive practice, but without competition.

5. Permit no strain or pressure. If the pupil voluntarily tries to hurry, stop him.

6. Wait for nature to take its course in the development of speed.

How do we write? It is obvious that we write with the hand and fingers, which hold the writing instrument; the wrist, which gives the hand flexibility; and the arm, which moves the hand across the page. There has always been much dispute over how much arm movement is involved in handwriting. It is of course possible to use the hand and fingers merely to hold the writing instrument and to have the arm perform most of the movements. This form of writing was called "muscular movement penmanship" and was more suited to writing the ornate script of the past than it is to our modern utilitarian sort of handwriting.

The most comfortable way to write is by having the forearm rest on the desk, with the elbow as the pivot from which the arm can move to the right or left, carrying the hand in the direction it has to go. But as far as shaping the letters is concerned, the fingers, hand, and wrist do most of the moving. True, we can feel the muscles in our arms contributing to the more obvious muscular activity of our hand and fingers, just as we feel the muscles in our back contributing to the more obvious muscular activity of our legs when we walk.

In fact, when we walk, we also find that swinging our arms helps us walk better, faster, and with a more even rhythm. This is exactly the extent to which the arm contributes to writing skill. We no more write with our arms than we walk with them. But they are important auxiliaries in promoting rhythm, speed, and good form. We use more arm or less arm depending on our writing position and the size of what we are writing. How much arm to use becomes a matter of personal adjustment over the years.

In walking, for example, the British army uses as much arm movement as leg movement to create the rhythmic, bold stride it is famous for. But it is hardly a natural way of walking. The same criterion must be applied to cursive handwriting skill. How much finger, hand, wrist, and arm movement is natural to the task? The child finds this out gradually by discovering what movements are needed to produce the script he wants. The script he wants should be one that is legible and as easy and comfortable as possible to write at a suitable speed.

Thus, in teaching a child to write, the first thing we do is introduce him to a comfortable and correct way of sitting and holding the writing instrument. The instrument is held about an inch above the writing tip by three fingers: the first joint of the middle finger supporting the instrument from the bottom, the thumb holding it from the left, the index finger holding it from the top right. If you turn your hand and look directly at the pencil point you will notice that it emerges from a triangular opening made by the three fingers. The pencil is supported in this triangular opening by the three fingers, which apply the necessary subtle pressure to move the pencil point in the direction the writer wants it to go. The upper part of the pencil rests in the arc made by the thumb and index finger. The fourth and fifth fingers, somewhat curled, support the writing fingers with the rest of the hand, which rests on the desk, and contribute to the hand's movement and position. This instrument-holding position is both comfortable and natural. It does not require a tight grip. In fact, the more relaxed it is, the better.

It should be pointed out that cursive writing evolved because it was natural for the human hand and arm (in the pursuit of speed, greater efficiency, fewer stops, and less fatigue) to write in a slant and to join the letters of a word. The result was the cursive alphabet. The cursive alphabet is not an arbitrary set of forms devised to make life difficult for first-graders. It is the ultimate refined product of hundreds of years of trial and error in which the need for both legibility and speed required such compromises and refinements as to maximize both. It was devised to make life easier, not more difficult, to provide man with one of his most useful tools of self-expression and communication.

Despite what some educators say about the difficulty of learning to write cursively, there is a basic simplicity at the heart of our cursive handwriting system. All cursive script can be reduced to three basic pen movements: the overcurve and undercurve, both of which originate in the oval, and the push-pull slant stroke. The entire cursive alphabet is made up of these three natural basic movements in a variety of combinations. The oval and push-pull, as writing expert E. A. Enstrom has pointed out, are nothing more than the graphic representations of the natural movements of the relaxed arm, wrist, hand, and fingers when the paper is placed at the proper angle to permit better arm leverage and vision. That is why the cursive letters took the shape they did. Cursive writing makes use of our most natural arm, wrist, hand and finger movements. There is nothing strained in these movements. The coordination that is required can be learned with practice, and learned so that in a relatively short time it becomes wholly automatic.

So first we make sure that the child is seated in the proper position, facing the desk or writing table squarely, his feet flat on the floor, his body in a natural erect position rather than humped or bent over. The paper is placed at the proper angle so that the writing arm is perpendicular to its bottom edge. The arm, when swung left or right from its elbow pivot permits the hand to form a rainbow arc from one side of the paper to the other. The illustration shows how the child is to hold the writing instrument and the angle in which the writing paper is placed.

What kind of writing instrument should the child begin with? A regular standard-size number-two pencil or a medium-point ball-point pen would be appropriate. The ball-point pen might be preferable. You might have the child test both to see which one he works better with. Children tend to grip a ball-point pen less tightly than they do a pencil. Also, the writing is a bit faster, and more thought is given before writing because of the inability to erase. Whether you use pencil or ball-point pen or both, use standard-size instruments. Children use them as easily as they do the so-called beginners' instruments.

What kind of paper to use? We suggest using regular 8½ by 11 sheets of white paper with one-half-inch rules. The texture should be good for the ball-point pen or number-two pencil. The size of the small letters at the outset can be written a half inch high, that is, the full width of the rules, so that the child learns to form them correctly. They will become smaller as writing skill increases. Any capitals written at the outset should be one-inch high, or the width of two rules. Have the child skip two lines when going to another line of writing, so that tall letters and letters that loop below the line will not interfere with the next line of writing.

We have correlated our writing instruction with our reading instruction, so that the one will reinforce the other. Thus, in learning the alphabet (the letter names and shapes) we recommended having the child draw the alphabet letters, perhaps on large sheets of paper with pencils, crayons, or felt-tipped pens. Please note that we specified *draw* and not write. The purpose of that exercise was to help familiarize the child with the shapes of the printed letters so that he could recognize them and name them. This drawing exercise is an aid to reading and not to be considered an introduction to writing. It can be limited to only the capital letters or can be extended to include some or all of the lower case letters. However, such drawing is not to be confused with writing and it should cease as part of the instruction after the alphabet has been learned and cursive writing instruction has begun.

We start our instruction in cursive writing at the same point that we complete Lesson One in our reading instruction, in which the child begins learning the sounds the letters stand for. We have stressed repeatedly that literacy is a two-way process. The child is being taught to write as well as read. He is to become a sender of messages as well as a receiver, a talker as well as listener. For that reason we believe that the means for sending messages should be taught at the same time that the means for receiving them are taught. In fact, the physical exercise of writing is an excellent relief from the mental exercise of reading. Therefore, we suggest that the reading lesson come first, with the last ten or fifteen minutes of the session being devoted to writing. In this way, what has been learned in the reading lesson will tend to be reinforced by the purely physical writing lesson.

There are other advantages obtained in correlating the reading instruction with the writing course. The child learns to spell as he learns to write. In addition, since the letter sounds are learned in family spelling groups, the child has a chance to write the same letter forms over and over again, giving him the practice he needs to perfect the letter forms.

Teaching the Left-Handed Child to Write

About one in ten children is left-handed. Being left-handed does not affect a child's learning ability. Some left-handed children can be taught to write with their right hands. Others, however, find it much too awkward and exhibit general incoordination, including speech reactions. Therefore, the tutor should discuss the problem with the child's parents before deciding which course to take. It appears that hand preference is so innate that one should not interfere with the natural coordination and balance that come with the use of the preferred hand. It has been found that when the left-handed are taught the best approach to handwriting, they can often write with greater speed and higher quality than the norms established for all writers in general.

If the child is left-handed it is preferable that he be seated to your left during handwriting instruction. Since our handwriting system was devised for the convenience of the right-handed, everything has to be reversed to accommodate the left-handed, except, of course the direction of writing. Both right- and left-handed must write from left to right. However, instead of tilting the paper to the right, the left-handed child tilts it to an extreme clockwise position. He also holds the pencil about one and three-eighths inches from the point, with the eraser end directed toward the left shoulder and he keeps his hand below the writing line. This permits the left-handed child to see what he is writing and to maintain the proper leverage.

The left-handed should use the same forward slant in writing as do the right-handed. If taught correctly, the handwriting of the left-handed should look exactly the same as that of the right-handed. It is important to make sure that the left-handed child's paper is tilted extremely clockwise. Too little turning will encourage the "hook" position which creates smearing problems and is in general an inferior writing position.

The tutor will find that the left-handed child tends to reverse letters more frequently than does the right-handed child. In fact, there is a tendency to mirror-write at early stages of learning because of the natural movement of the left hand. The tutor, therefore, must supervise the left-handed child's initial handwriting instruction quite closely so that the child not only learns the correct left-to-right direction of writing but also recognizes his reversals when he makes them. It is important to provide enough practice at the early stages of instruction to establish correct writing habits.

If, however, a left-handed child comes to the tutor with the habit of hooking already firmly fixed, he should be taught to write by placing the paper in the same position as does the right-handed writer. He keeps his wrist somewhat on edge and flexes it while writing.

Materials Used in Handwriting Instruction

Before starting handwriting instruction, supply yourself with the proper sheets of ruled paper, pencils, and ball-point pens. You will also need to use the blackboard. In addition, prepare a set of sixty-two cards on which the twenty-six small cursive letters, the twenty-six capital cursive letters, and the ten cursive numerals have been accurately drawn. These are to be used by the child at his desk as models to copy from. A simple way to prepare such a set of cards would be to make a Xerox copy of the complete cursive alphabet, then cut out the letters and paste them on index cards, one to a card. You will also need model cards of the words the child is expected to write.

Lesson 1: Introduce the subject of handwriting by telling the child that learning to read is only half of learning to use the alphabet. The other half is writing. Reading permits us to read the messages of others. Writing permits us to send messages of our own. Just as you learn to communicate with others by both talking and listening, you must also learn to communicate by reading and writing. We also use writing to put down our own thoughts which we don't want to forget.

In writing, we use the same alphabet as we do in reading, except that the letters have been made a little differently so that they can be written quickly. This form of the alphabet is called the cursive alphabet and was invented long ago by men who wanted a fast way to write. They discovered that the fastest way to write was by joining all the letters in a word together instead of printing each letter separately.

The most important thing in writing is to make the letters correctly so that others can read them easily. To do this it is important to hold the pencil or pen in the correct way, to tilt the paper at the correct angle, and to sit in our seats so that we can write in as comfortable a position as possible.

Introduce the cursive alphabet and tell the child that he is going to learn to write all twenty-six small letters, all twenty-six capitals, and the ten numerals—one at a time.

Aa Bb Cc Dd

Ee Ff Gg Hh

Ii Jj Kk Ll

Mm Nn Oo Pp

Qq Rr Ss Tt

Uu Vv Ww

Xx Yy Zz . , ?

1 2 3 4 5 6 7 8 9 10

Since the child has completed Lesson One of the Reading Primer, tell him that he is going to learn to write the letters he has already learned to read.

Introduce the cursive letter *a*. Supply the child with a large, clear model of the letter on an index card.

Write the *a* on the blackboard. Then take your index finger and trace the letter *a* on the board, then in the air. Have the child also trace the *a* in the air, simply to get the feel of the movement. Have him then trace the *a* on the card with his index finger so that he learns where the writing point starts and where it ends. Note that the index finger is the one we write with in the sand or on vapor-covered glass. Note how much arm movement we use in writing with our index finger. Some of that arm movement is used when we write with an instrument. However, the fingers must also hold the instrument while writing. This requires a greater degree of muscular coordination than the child is accustomed to. Thus it will take him time to write the *a* on his sheet of paper. Although he has traced the letter with his finger, do not have him trace it with his pencil. You learn to write by writing, not tracing. Have him write the *a* several times, moving his pencil as directed by the arrow in the model diagram.

Make sure the child holds the writing instrument in the proper manner and is seated in a comfortable position. At the beginning, as the child is trying to master the letter form, he will apply much more energy and many more muscles than the task requires. This is because the child's muscular control and coordination is still largely undeveloped. He does not know how much energy to use and which muscles are required to make the letter correctly. So he uses much more than he needs.

Joseph S. Taylor, former District Superintendent of Schools in New York described this physiological process in his book *Supervision and Teaching of Handwriting:*

When a child first learns to write, he energizes a great many muscles not needed in the process. After writing has been made automatic, only the necessary muscles are used. While the child is self-consciously trying to get a group of muscles to act in harmony the resulting movement is always crude and inaccurate. This is one of the reasons why the early attempts at writing are so unsuccessful. Even if the pupil correctly sees the form he is trying to imitate, he is unable to make his muscles execute his intention. Only by long practice is he able to reduce the process to habit and to achieve complete success.

Diffuseness in movement is tiresome because of the needless expenditure of energy. The young writer grips his penholder and holds many of the larger muscles of the body taut that are not concerned in the movement at all. Hence he soon tires. Habit corrects this overuse of energy and thus reduces fatigue. Conscious control of muscles requires attention. Habit hands the movement over to the lower centers and takes it out of consciousness. Walking is a very serious business to a child who is just learning how to do it. To the adult it is so nearly automatic that he can dodge automobiles and carry on a conversation at the same time. . . .

Writing at first is a coordinated movement of the voluntary kind. This means that many different muscles must be energized at just the right moment and with an exact degree of strength if the movement is to be successful. This harmony of action can be achieved only by long and careful practice. The object of the learner has been accomplished only when what was at first voluntary coordination has become involuntary or automatic.

Diffusion of effort is one of the early difficulties of the learner. He energizes groups of muscles which are not needed in writing. Nature attacks her problems of development by producing more than she needs and then picking out the best. Development means the selection of the right movements out of a total mass of diffuse movements.

Thus, the important things to stress at the beginning stages of writing is correct hand- and instrument-holding positions, comfortable seating, and accurate copying of the letter forms. At the beginning stage, the child is so intent upon copying the letter forms correctly that little refinement can be taught or expected. However, he should be instructed to follow the correct sequence of curves and strokes in every letter he writes.

How much time should be spent on each letter? As much time as necessary to learn the letter accurately from the model and then from memory. Most schools teach all the small letters in the first year, devoting approximately two weeks of practice to each letter. The capitals are learned in the second year. Since cursive writing is not introduced in most schools until the third grade, the tutored child will have an excellent head start. Thus, this handwriting course of instruction should take two years to complete. It should keep pace, more or less, with the reading instruction, but with reading perhaps somewhat ahead.

In the beginning, while good writing habits are being formed, speed is of no importance. Correct letter formation is our primary goal, and enough time should be given so that each letter is learned thoroughly. When it is a matter of creating lifelong habits, what is taught at the beginning should be taught well.

Lesson 2: Introduce cursive letter *m*. Provide the child with a large, clear model of the letter.

Write the *m* on the blackboard. Point out its physical characteristics. Then take your index finger and trace the *m* first on the board, then in the air. Have the child also trace the *m* in the air, simply to get the feel of the movement. Have him then trace the *m* on the card with his index finger. Then have him write a line of *m*'s on his paper.

Lesson 3: The child has already learned to write *a* and *m*. Show him now how to write the word *am* by joining the two letters together.

Provide the child with a model *am* on a card to copy from. Then write the word on the blackboard to show how the letters are joined. Point out that you can write the entire word without lifting your pen or pencil from the paper. Have the child practice writing *am* several times. Always make sure that the child is maintaining the correct positions while writing.

Lesson 4: Introduce the cursive letter *n* in the same manner used to introduce cursive *m*. Compare the *n* to *m*.

n   *m*

Have the child write a line of *n*'s.

Lesson 5: The child has already learned to write *a* and *n*. Introduce him to the word *an* by showing him how the two letters are joined together.

an

Have the child write the word *an* several times.

Lesson 6: Review. Have the child write *am* and *an* several times, pointing out the difference between *m* and *n*. Check the child's writing position.

Lesson 7: Introduce the cursive letter *s*. Follow the same procedures used in the previous lessons.

s   *s*

Lesson 8: The child has already learned to write *a* and *s*. Show him how to write the word *as*.

as

Lesson 9: Introduce the cursive letter *t*. Follow same procedures used in previous lessons.

t   *t*

Have the child note the details of the letter, particularly that it is half as much taller than *a* and is crossed.

Lesson 10: The child has already learned to write *a* and *t*. Write *at* on the board and have the child note the height of the *t* in relation to the *a*. Provide a word card and have the child write *at* on his paper several times.

at

Lesson 11: Review. Have the child practice writing *as, at, am,* and *an*. Make sure the child leaves enough space between the words.

Lesson 12: Introduce the cursive letter *x*. Follow the same procedures used in earlier lessons.

x   *x*

Lesson 13: The child has already learned to write *a* and *x*. Now teach him to join these two letters to write the word *ax*.

ax

Lesson 14: See if the child can tackle such three-letter words as *tax, tan, mat, sat,* made up of letters he has already learned to write. Supply him with models to copy from. Do not be concerned if the child lifts his pencil off the paper in the middle of the words. A three-letter word may be too fatiguing for him to negotiate without a pause. While the tutor should be aware of the slant of the writing and the spacing between the letters, the most important thing at this time is still the correctness of writing position and letter forms.

tax tan mat sat

Lesson 15: Introduce the cursive letter *h*. This is the first loop letter the child has been introduced to. Have the child write a line of *h*'s.

h   *h*

Lesson 16: With his newly learned *h* have the child write the words *hat, ham, has*. Provide the child with model word cards from which to copy.

hat ham has

Lesson 17: Introduce the child to cursive capital letter *S*. While the rest of the capital letters will be taken up after completing the small letters, we are introducing the capital *S* at this point to teach the child additional concepts.

S   *S*

Explain that capital letters are used at the beginning of proper names and sentences. Write the name *Sam* to illustrate. Have the child practice writing the capital *S* from a card model.

Lesson 18: Have the child write his first sentence: *Sam sat.* Explain that a sentence is a group of words forming a complete thought. It begins with a capital letter and ends with an end mark, in this case a period. If the sentence is a question, we end it with a question mark.

Sam sat.

Sam sat?

Lesson 19: Introduce the cursive letter *d*.

d   *d*

Have the child write a line of *d*'s and the words *dad, add.*

dad add

Lesson 20: Have the child add *d* to *an* to produce the word *and.*
Show the child how to write the words *and, sand, hand.*

and sand hand

Lesson 21: Introduce the cursive letter *l.* This is another loop
letter.

l   *l*

Have the child write a line of *l*'s and the word *lad.*

lad

Lesson 22: Introduce the cursive letter *w.* Compare *w* to *m.*

w   *w*

Have the child write a line of *w*'s and the word *wax.*

wax

Lesson 23: Introduce the cursive letter *b.* Note the loop and
height of the letter.

b   *b*

Have the child write a line of *b*'s and the words *bad, bat, ban*.

bad   bat   ban

Lesson 24: Introduce the cursive letter *c*.

Have the child write a line of *c*'s and the words *cat, can, cab*.

cat   can   cab

Lesson 25: Introduce the cursive letter *f*. Point out the loops above and below the line.

Have the child write a line of *f*'s and the words *fat, fan, fad*.

fat   fan   fad

Lesson 26: Introduce the cursive letter *g*. This is another letter with a loop below the line. Show how it starts as an *a*, then goes below the line.

Have the child write a line of *g*'s and the words *gag, gab, gas*.

gag   gab   gas

Lesson 27: Introduce the cursive letter *j*. This is another letter with a loop below the line. Note the dot over the *j*.

$$j \quad j$$

Have the child write a line of *j*'s and the words *jab, jam*.

$$jab \qquad jam$$

Lesson 28: Introduce the cursive letter *r*.

$$r \quad r$$

Have the child write a line of *r*'s and the words *rag, ran, rat*.

$$rag \quad ran \quad rat$$

Lesson 29: Introduce the cursive letter *v*.

$$v \quad v$$

Have the child write a line of *v*'s and the words *van, vat*.

$$van \qquad vat$$

Lesson 30: Introduce the cursive letter *p*.

$$p \quad p$$

Have the child write a line of *p*'s and the words *pat, pan*.

$$pat \qquad pan$$

Lesson 31: Introduce the cursive letter *y*.

$$y \quad ny$$

Have the child write a line of *y*'s and the words *yam, yap.*

$$yam \quad yap$$

Lesson 32: Introduce the cursive letter *z*.

$$z \quad z$$

Have the child write a line of *z*'s and the word *zag.*

$$zag$$

Lesson 33: Introduce the cursive letter *e*.

$$e \quad e$$

Have the child write a line of *e*'s and the words *egg, bed, fed,*
leg.

$$egg \quad bed \quad fed \quad leg$$

Lesson 34: Introduce the cursive letter *i*. Note the dot over the *i*.

Have the child write a line of *i*'s and the words *in, is, it, if, ill.*

$$in \quad is \quad it \quad if \quad ill$$

Lesson 35: Introduce cursive letter *o*.

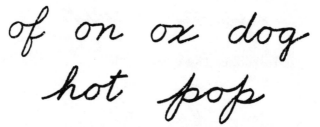

Have the child write a line of *o*'s and the words *of, on, ox, dog, hot, pop.*

of on ox dog
hot pop

Lesson 36: Introduce the cursive letter *u*.

Have the child write a line of *u*'s and the words *up, us, tub, rug.*

up us tub rug

Lesson 37: Introduce the cursive letter *q*. Compare it to *g*.

Explain that the *q* is always followed by *u* as in these words which the child should write after writing a line of *q*'s: *quit, quill.* Have the child note how the dot over the *i* helps us to visually separate the *i* from the *u*.

quit quill

Lesson 38: Introduce the cursive letter *k*.

Have the child write a line of *k*'s and the words *kick, kid, keg, kit*.

kick kid keg kit

The next series of lessons (39-63) teach the cursive capital letters. Start with the initial letter of the child's own name and have him learn to write his name. Then teach the other capitals in the proper sequence. If the child is about to begin arithmetic, however, teach him to write the cursive numerals first, before going on to the rest of the capitals. The cursive numerals are covered in lessons 64 through 71. The same procedures used in teaching the small cursive letters should be used in teaching the capitals and numerals. Always watch for correct writing position, good letter forms, and do not rush the student.

Lesson 39: Introduce cursive capital letter *A*.

Have the child write a line of *A*'s and the words *Ann, Anna, Al*.

Ann Anna Al

Lesson 40: Introduce cursive capital letter *B*.

Have the child write a line of *B*'s and the words *Ben, Bill, Bob*.

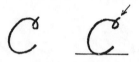

Lesson 41: Introduce cursive capital letter *C*.

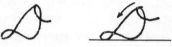

Have the child write a line of *C*'s and the words *Cal, Carl, Carol*.

Lesson 42: Introduce cursive capital letter *D*.

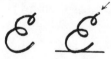

Have the child write a line of *D*'s and the words *Dan, Don, Dennis*.

Lesson 43: Introduce cursive capital letter *E*.

Have the child write a line of *E*'s and the words *Ed, Eli, Eliza*.

Lesson 44: Introduce cursive capital letter *F.*

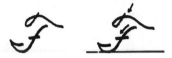

Have the child write a line of *F*'s and the words *Fred, Frank, France.*

Lesson 45: Introduce cursive capital letter *G.*

Have the child write a line of *G*'s and the words *Guy, Gail, God.*

Lesson 46: Introduce cursive capital letter *H.*

Have the child write a line of *H*'s and the words *Hal, Helen, Henry.*

Lesson 47: Introduce cursive capital letter *I.*

Have the child write a line of *I*'s and the words *I, Ida, Inez.*

I Ida Inez

Lesson 48: Introduce cursive capital letter *J*.

Have the child write a line of *J*'s and the words *Jean, John, Jim.*

Jean John Jim

Lesson 49: Introduce cursive capital letter *K*.

Have the child write a line of *K*'s and the words *Ken, Kathy, Kit.*

Ken Kathy Kit

Lesson 50: Introduce cursive capital letter *L*.

Have the child write a line of *L*'s and the words *Len, Lucy, Lil.*

Len Lucy Lil

Lesson 51: Introduce cursive capital *M.*

Have the child write a line of *M*'s and the words *Max, Mike, Millie.*

Max Mike Millie

Lesson 52: Introduce cursive capital letter *N.*

Have the child write a line of *N*'s and the words *Nat, Nick, Neil.*

Nat Nick Neil

Lesson 53: Introduce cursive capital letter *O.*

Have the child write a line of *O*'s and the words *Otto, Olga, Orson*.

Otto   Olga   Orson

Lesson 54: Introduce cursive capital letter *P*.

Have the child write a line of *P*'s and the words *Pete, Peg, Polly*.

Pete   Peg   Polly

Lesson 55: Introduce cursive capital letter *Q*.

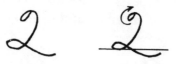

Have the child write a line of *Q*'s and the words *Quentin, Queenie, Quinn*.

Quentin   Queenie   Quinn

Lesson 56: Introduce cursive capital letter *R*.

Have the child write a line of *R*'s and the words *Ron, Rex, Ricky.*

Ron Rex Ricky

Lesson 57: Introduce cursive capital letter *T*.

Have the child write a line of *T*'s and the words *Tom, Tim, Tony.*

Tom Tim Tony

Lesson 58: Introduce cursive capital letter *U*.

Have the child write a line of *U*'s and the words *United States* and *U.S.A.* This will also give the child a chance to review cursive capital *S*, which was learned in Lesson 17.

United States
U.S.A.

Lesson 59: Introduce cursive capital letter *V*.

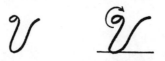

Have the child write a line of *V*'s and the words *Vince, Vicky, Vivian*.

Vince Vicky

Vivian

Lesson 60: Introduce cursive capital letter *W*.

Have the child write a line of *W*'s and the words *Wilma, Walter*.

Wilma Walter

Lesson 61: Introduce cursive capital letter *X*.

Have the child write a line of *X*'s and the words *X-ray, Xavier*.

X-ray Xavier

Lesson 62: Introduce cursive capital letter *Y*.

Have the child write a line of *Y*'s and the words *Yetta, York, Yuma*.

Lesson 63: Introduce cursive capital letter *Z*.

Have the child write a line of *Z*'s and the words *Zeke, Zoe, Zachary*.

The following lessons teach the cursive numerals. They should be taught when the child starts learning arithmetic. Use the same techniques in teaching the cursive numerals as were used in teaching the cursive letters, with the same attention to physical position and accurate forms.

Lesson 64: Introduce cursive numerals *1* and *2*.

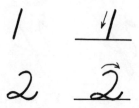

Have the child write alternating lines of *1*'s and *2*'s.

Lesson 65: Introduce cursive numeral *3*.

Have the child write a line of *3*'s. If he finishes this work quickly and is obviously ready to learn more, proceed to the next lesson.

Lesson 66: Introduce cursive numeral *4*.

4   4

Have the child write a line of *4*'s. Also review *1*, *2*, and *3*.

Lesson 67: Introduce cursive numeral *5*.

5   5

Have the child write a line of *5*'s.

Lesson 68: Introduce cursive numeral *6*.

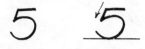

Have the child write a line of *6*'s. Review *1, 2, 3, 4,* and *5*.

Lesson 69: Introduce cursive numeral *7*.

Have the child write a line of *7*'s. If he finishes this work quickly and is obviously ready to learn more, proceed to the next lesson.

Lesson 70: Introduce cursive numeral *8*.

Have the child write a line of *8*'s.

Lesson 71: Introduce cursive numerals *9* and *0*.

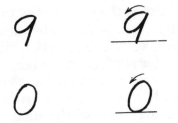

Have the child write alternating lines of *9*'s and *0*'s.

Lesson 72: General review of cursive numerals. Have the child write the entire numeral set in numerical order with attention to accurate form. Explain to him that these ten symbols are the basis for all arithmetic work. Have the child practice writing the numerals until he can write them correctly from dictation.

Lesson 73: Punctuation marks. Teach the question mark (?), comma (,), exclamation point (!), quotation marks ("/"), and apostrophe (') as they are required in the sentences to be written by the child.

After the child has learned all of the cursive letter and numeral forms and can write them reasonably well, the tutor should concentrate on improving legibility and making sure that the child's writing habits are good. Speed is developed when the writing of legible, well-formed letters is so automatic that the child no longer need think of that aspect of his writing. On the subject of speed, Luella Cole gave this excellent advice:

> The lesson from all sports is clear enough. There is only one road to speed in the use of any muscular skill: it lies through the development of perfect, undeviating form. Moreover, nothing kills good form so quickly and surely as hurrying. Far from being inversely related, speed and quality of performance are inseparable. As applied to handwriting this principle means that children should work only for correct form and should never be hurried. They should write at a deliberate rate enough words daily to be the equivalent of the swimmer's slow quarter-mile; it takes thousands of trials before even a simple motion is faultless. If this general policy was followed for the six years of elementary school, these pupils would be at the end not only good but rapid writers.

Thus, steady practice is the only means to develop and perfect a physical skill such as handwriting. Since legibility should be the primary aim of handwriting instruction, it is useful to know where most of our letter malformations occur. One research study showed that the letter *r* accounted for about 12 percent of all writing illegibilities. It was found that seven letters—*r, u, e, a, o, s, t*—accounted for over half of the illegibility problems. The most common letter malformations were: *n*'s like *u*'s, *r*'s like *i*'s, *e*'s closed, *d*'s like *cl*'s, and *c*'s like *a*'s. Sometimes illegible letters can be read because of the context in which the word is written. Context is an important aid in reading illegible handwriting. But the illegibilities invariably slow down reading and are not always helped by context.

Four types of difficulties in letters cause over one half of all illegibilities:

(a) failure to close letters like *a, g, d*

(b) closing looped letters like *e, l, f*

$$e\ l\ f$$

(c) looping non-looped strokes as in *t, i, d*

$$t\ i\ d$$

(d) straight up rather than rounded strokes of such letters as *r, l, i*

$$r\ l\ i$$

The curved letters with no distinguishing characteristic cause most of the illegibilities. The three biggest troublemakers among them are the letters *r, e,* and *a.*

$$r\ e\ a$$

This being the case, it is quite possible to devise drills and exercises which help the child overcome the tendency to make these malformations.

There is a basic simplicity at the heart of cursive handwriting which, if understood, can suggest the way to handwriting improvement. All cursive script is reducible to three basic pen movements: the overcurve and undercurve, both of which originate in the oval, and the push-pull slant stroke. The entire cursive alphabet is made up of these three natural basic movements in a variety of combinations. The oval and push-pull are nothing more than the graphic representation of the natural movements of the relaxed arm, wrist, hand and fingers when the paper is placed at the proper angle to permit better arm leverage and vision. That is why the cursive letters took on the shape they did. Cursive writing makes use of our most natural arm, wrist, hand and finger movements. There is nothing strained in these movements. The coordination that is required can be learned with practice, learned so that in a short time it becomes wholly automatic.

Since we know the causes of most illegibilities it would be helpful to devise exercises that can serve as preventive measures to their development. This can be done by grouping letters into the following three categories according to their initial strokes: (a) those with an initial downward overcurve, (b) those with an initial upward overcurve, and (c) those with an initial upward undercurve. Remember, the over- and undercurves originate in the oval, and they can be executed in a clockwise or counterclockwise direction, that is, upward or downward.

Letters with an initial downward overcurve are the ones that create the closing problem. They include *a, c, d, o, g, q.*

$$a\ c\ d\ o\ g\ q$$

Note that only the *c* does not close, which means that exercises with all of these letters can draw the child's attention to the need for closing the letters which require closing. Practice of the downward overcurve with counterclockwise ovals could be helpful to the youngster.

Letters with an initial upward undercurve are the ones which give rise to the closed looped-letter problem. These letters with an initial upward undercurve include *b, e, f, h, i, j, k, l, p, r, s, t, u, w.*

$$b\ e\ f\ h\ i\ j\ k\ l\ p\ r\ s$$
$$t\ u\ w$$

It is obvious that the mixture of looped and non-looped letters in this category cause the problem. The solution is to make the child aware of those with loops and those without.

The looped letters are *b, e, f, h, k, l.*

$$b\ e\ f\ h\ k\ l$$

The non-looped letters are *i, j, p, r, s, t, u, w.*

i j p r s t u w

The trick in looping the looped letters and not looping the non-looped letters is one of practiced muscular coordination, resulting from unhurried practice of letter forms.

Letters with an initial upward overcurve include *m, n, v, x, y, z.*

m n v x y z

Practice of these initial upward overcurves, the clockwise oval, can prevent *m*'s from looking like *w*'s, *n*'s from looking like *u*'s.

As for numerals, the *1* and *7* are often hard to distinguish in careless handwriting. Also, the careless writing of *3, 5,* and *8* has resulted in many calculating errors. It is estimated that these five numbers have caused business losses running into millions of dollars.

Maintain a benevolent supervision over the child's handwriting and try to diagnose his problems as they develop. To improve letter formation, have the child compare his product with the model. By comparing the two he can see how far off he is. Encourage the child to verbalize the discrepancies between his letter and the model. When a child can see and explain his error, he understands better what must be done to correct it.

After letter formation, the tutor must look for other things. Are the letters too crowded together? Is the spacing uneven? What about alignment? Do the words drift off the line? Perhaps the paper has not been placed at the proper angle. Observe the evenness of slant. Do the letters slant too much or too little, or haphazardly? Perhaps the child is not holding the pencil correctly. A poor, slow, crimped handwriting is usually the result of too much finger control at the exclusion of any other muscles. Try to get the child to relax his hand. Oval and push-pull exercises are useful in getting the child to relax his grip and to achieve more comfortable, more fluent coordinated movements of fingers, hand, wrist, and arm.

It is important to catch bad handwriting habits before they become fixed. This is why close supervision is needed during the early stages of writing instruction. Such careful initial teaching can prevent all but the rarest types of problems from developing.

While spelling and composition are beyond the scope of this primer, we suggest that handwriting practice follow essentially the same sequence as the reading instruction in this book. In this way the child will learn the most common spelling patterns in our language with their many irregularities. By learning the regular spelling patterns in the logical sound-symbol order presented in the reading primer, the child will be able to remember the spelling exceptions with little difficulty.

Index of Lessons

Part Four

Arithmetic

In reading, we teach the child the meaning and uses of the twenty-six alphabet symbols of which all our written language is composed. In writing, we teach him to write these symbols. In arithmetic we teach the child the meaning and uses of the ten numeral symbols—a set of symbols as important to the development of our civilization as the alphabet. All arithmetic calculation is performed with these ten remarkable symbols.

Like the alphabet, our decimal place-value arithmetic system is the product of a very long evolution in which man sought to find the best mental tools with which to express the tremendous intellectual potential he had within him. What man could do, provided he had the right tools and social conditions, can be measured by the incredible leap he made from the primitive agricultural civilization of the 1500s to the space-age civilization of the 1970s—a span of less than 500 years. Of that leap forward, the greatest progress was made in the last two hundred years. This is an unbelievably short time when measured against the total span of man's existence on earth. It indicates that for a long time man had the intellectual potential to make that leap, but for centuries he lacked the mental tools with which to realize it. The two necessary tools were the alphabet and the decimal place-value arithmetic system. Western man developed an alphabet about 1000 B.C. But he had to wait another two thousand years before he got the most effective mental tool for arithmetic calculation ever devised by the human race. Again, its hallmark, its genius, was simplicity—a simplicity which took centuries to develop.

The alphabet came to the West from the Phoenicians; the decimal place-value system came from the Hindus. Actually, man had started counting and using numbers very early in his upward climb toward civilization. As far back as 50,000 B.C. we find implements suggesting the existence of barter and the need for counting. By 17,000 B.C. man had advanced sufficiently to be able to recognize the common constellations and to create works of art, both of which required a rudimentary sense of calculation and geometric form. By 4241 B.C. we reach the earliest dated event in human history—the introduction of the Egyptian calendar of twelve months of thirty days each, plus five feast days. This achievement required a very high level of development in computation and astronomy. But like the hieroglyphic writing system, the Egyptian method of calculation was a complicated, unwieldy one which could never serve the needs of a society more advanced than its own.

In about 1000 B.C. came the first tool to provide the great intellectual leap forward—the alphabet. The Greeks adopted it from the Phoenicians and developed their highly literate civilization which marks the beginning of Western ascendancy. While the alphabet promoted the literary arts, philosophy, science, and mathematics, the Greek method of arithmetic was not much better than the Egyptian. It used no less than twenty-seven symbols—the twenty-four letters of the Greek alphabet plus three archaic symbols—and made no use of place value. It was a purely additive numeral notation. The first nine letters represented 1 through 9; the next nine represented the tens from 10 through 90; and the last nine represented the hundreds from 100 through 900. Thus the number 125 required a symbol for the hundred, a symbol for the twenty, and a symbol for the five. The symbols, regardless of their order, all added up to 125. Note that our number 125 adds up to 8. We understand its meaning because of place value or positional value.

While the Greek system was easy for addition and subtraction, it was difficult for multiplication, division, and fractions. To facilitate calculation, the Greeks, as well as everyone else in the ancient world, required the help of an abacus, a counting device derived from the primitive system of counting pebbles. In fact, the word calculate is derived from *calx*, the Latin word for pebble. Thus, in ancient Greece and in Europe right up to the 14th century, specialists had to be trained to do the kind of arithmetic calculation which today is performed by school children with little difficulty. Yet, the Greeks were able to develop Euclidean geometry and make other significant advances in mathematics. How was this possible? Here we must make the distinction between arithmetic, that is, the art of counting and calculation, and mathematics, the science or philosophy of relationships. In Greek times arithmetic was called *logistic* and was considered outside the domain of science and philosophy. Logistic was the tool of commerce. Mathematics, on the other hand, dealt with the abstractions of numbers and the relationships of geometric forms, most of which could be discussed rhetorically, without the use of arithmetic calculation. Euclid used no arithmetic or logistic at all and exercised a strict taboo against using it, while other mathematicians like Archimedes and Heron used it at will without philosophical prejudice. Mathematics was considered the purest form of philosophy, to be studied apart from any consideration for its practical use. Thus, while Greece made great advances in philosophical thought, its arithmetic was just as primitive as that of any other nation. On this subject, Tobias Dantzig*observed

> One who reflects upon the history of reckoning up to the invention of the principle of position is struck by the paucity of achievement. This long period of nearly five thousand years saw the fall and rise of many a civilization, each leaving behind it a heritage of literature, art, philosophy and religion. But what was the net achievement in the field of reckoning, the earliest art practiced by man? An inflexible numeration so crude as to make

---

Number, The Language of Science (New York: Macmillan, 1946).

progress well-nigh impossible, and a calculating device so limited in scope that even elementary calculations called for the services of an expert. And what is more, man used these devices for thousands of years without making a single worthwhile improvement in the instrument, without contributing a single important idea to the system! . . .

When viewed in this light, the achievement of the unknown Hindu who some time in the first centuries of our era discovered the principle of position assumes the proportions of a world event. Not only did this principle constitute a radical departure in method, but we know now that without it no progress in arithmetic was possible. And yet the principle is so simple that today the dullest school boy has no difficulty in grasping it.

The date of the first known appearance of a decimal place-value notation in India is 595 A.D. The oldest reference to the place-value system outside India is found in a work written by Severus Sebokht, a Syrian bishop, in 662. His comments about it are interesting:

I will omit all discussion of the science of the Hindus, a people not the same as the Syrians; their subtle discoveries in this science of astronomy, discoveries that are more ingenious than those of the Greeks and the Babylonians; their valuable methods of calculation; and their computing that surpasses description. I wish only to say that this computation is done by means of nine signs. If those who believe, because they speak Greek, that they have reached the limits of science should know these things they would be convinced that there are also others who know something.

The bishop referred to "nine signs" because the sign for zero had not yet been invented. The Hindus had derived the place value concept from their operation of the counting board in which each column stood consecutively for ones, tens, hundreds, thousands, etc. Somewhere along the line it became necessary to designate a symbol for an empty column so that the reader could tell the difference between 32, 302, 3002. "And so," writes Professor Dantzig, "from all appearances, the discovery of zero was an accident brought about by an attempt to make an unambiguous permanent record of a counting board operation."

We shall never know for certain whether the invention of zero was an accident or a stroke of genius, but it was, according to Dantzig,

. . . the turning-point in a development without which the progress of modern science, industry, or commerce is inconceivable. And the influence of this great discovery was by no means confined to arithmetic. By paving the way to a generalized number concept, it played as fundamental a role in practically every branch of mathematics. In the history of culture the discovery of zero will always stand out as one of the greatest single achievements of the human race.

How did the Hindu place-value system finally make its way into Western culture? It was carried there by the Arabs who had adopted the Hindu system for their own use and brought it to Europe in their invasion of Spain. It should be noted that all this took place after the rise of Christianity, the disintegration of the Roman Empire, and the subsequent sweep of Islam from Arabia to Gibraltar. The Moors established their rule in Spain in 747, but it took another 500 years before the place-value system finally swept the old Roman numerals and the abacus from Christendom.

Why did it take so long? In the wake of Rome's disintegration, Europe had entered the period known as the Dark Ages, during which all learning and intellectual progress seemed to come to a complete halt. The awakening finally came in the thirteenth century. The first book to systematically introduce the Arab-Hindu system in Europe was Leonardo of Pisa's *Liber Abaci*, published in 1202. But it wasn't until about 1500 that only Arabic numerals were used in commercial account books in Europe and the Roman numerals were discarded altogether. There were a number of reasons why the adoption of the Hindu-Arabic system took so long. The main reason, however, was the difficulty people had in adopting a new set of symbols for their numbers and *in using the symbols themselves in the calculating process*. It was quite difficult for many accountants to make the leap from abacus counting (that is, one-to-one concrete counting) to symbolic or abstract counting (that is, counting by the use of the abstract symbols alone). Symbolic counting won out, however, because it was so much faster and the place-value system permitted all calculation to be done with only ten symbols. It took time before people realized that the key to the most efficient use of this system was memory. Once you memorized the addition, subtraction, multiplication and division tables for the first ten numbers, you could perform any arithmetic calculation on paper with great speed. Once the key role of memory in this system was understood, the problem became one of developing the most efficient techniques of memorization—from which the notion of drills originated.

By the end of the fifteenth century, all the techniques (or algorithms, as mathematicians call them) which we now use to add, subtract, multiply and divide were fully developed. In other words, modern arithmetic is scarcely five hundred years old. Thus the gap between the abacus and the computer is less than five hundred years. It was the New Arithmetic which made our technology possible.

Pierre Laplace, the 18th-century French mathematician, eloquently summed up the importance of the place-value system when he wrote:

> It is India that gave us the ingenious method of expressing all numbers by means of ten symbols, each symbol receiving a value of position as well as an absolute value; a profound and important idea which appears so simple to us now that we ignore its true merit. But its very simplicity and the great ease which it has lent to all computations put our arithmetic in the first rank of useful inventions; and we shall appreciate the grandeur of this achievement the more when we remember that it escaped the genius of Archimedes and Apollonius, two of the greatest men produced by antiquity.

And thus it is probable that the space age would have never come into being had the place-value system and the symbol for zero not been invented.

In teaching the child arithmetic, it is important to convey to him the genius of the system itself. Next to the alphabet, it is the greatest mental tool ever devised by man. Therefore we should approach the subject with the excitement and interest it deserves. Any teacher who makes arithmetic dull does so because he or she does not understand its beautiful simplicity, its logic, and its facility which permit us to do so much with so little. The ten-symbol place-value system is perhaps the diamond of human intellect. It, and the alphabet are the child's greatest intellectual inheritance. Both sets of symbols represent the distilled genius of the human race. It is therefore obvious that such gifts must be presented in such a way as to make the child appreciate what these symbols can do for him in furthering his own potential and happiness.

At this point, it would be appropriate to discuss the matter of arithmetic and the New Math. Among educators today there is a tremendous confusion between what we mean by arithmetic and what we mean by mathematics. Arithmetic is no longer taught as arithmetic. It has been submerged, fragmentized, and scrambled in a much larger area of study called Elementary Mathematics—more popularly known as the New Math. Because of this, students scarcely become aware of the decimal place-value system as *a complete arithmetic system quite separate and distinct from the rest of the subject matter in elementary mathematics.* The result is that students learn arithmetic very poorly and very haphazardly.

With this tutoring book, the tutor can teach the basic arithmetic system without the distractions of the irrelevant mathematical theories and concepts taught in the New Math. Once the child has mastered the arithmetic system, he'll be in a much better position to deal with the often confusing theories and concepts of the New Math.

There has been some discussion among parents and teachers over the practical value of the New Math to the child. Most of us use a great deal of arithmetic throughout our lives—filling out income tax returns, balancing our checking accounts, buying on credit, figuring out mortgage payments, everyday purchasing at the supermarket, etc. But few of us ever use the algebra, geometry and trigonometry we were taught in school. This is not an argument against teaching algebra, geometry and trigonometry. But it is an argument *for* teaching arithmetic as thoroughly and systematically as possible in the primary grades.

Arithmetic, in the form of our decimal place-value system, is one of the most useful tools a child can learn to master. Since a knowledge of arithmetic is vital to an individual's economic survival and success, it should be given top priority in the curriculum of the elementary school. Unfortunately, arithmetic is considered a sort of stepchild in the house of mathematics and is given little attention by the curriculum developers. If it hadn't been for the ingenious invention of the Hindu place-value system, mathematicians wouldn't even bother to teach arithmetic at all. They would have left it to the counting specialist. As we mentioned earlier, the Greek mathematicians looked down on arithmetic as being unworthy of their attention. In today's primary school curriculum, arithmetic has been mathematized out of existence. Teachers no longer talk about arithmetic. They talk only of mathematics—the word arithmetic having been virtually stricken from the schoolroom vocabulary.

For most people, however, arithmetic, like the alphabet, is considered so simple a concept that we forget how complex it really is. Those of us who went to school in previous generations were taught arithmetic mainly by rote. We learned how to add, subtract, multiply, and divide without any trouble because we were taught to memorize our tables and drilled in them constantly. We knew that the multiplication and long-division methods worked, but we didn't know why they worked or who had invented these methods, or when they had come into use. For all we knew, man had been doing long division since the beginning of time. If something worked, we gave little thought as to why it worked or who first worked it out. Nor did it seem necessary for us to know why it worked or who invented it. The value of the methods we were using was so obvious that other considerations were of no importance. If a child discovers that a dollar bill is worth so much candy in a store, he is not interested in the history of money at that point or the theory of supply and demand. He is much more interested in learning how to get more dollars so that he can exchange them for more candy. If we stopped him in his tracks and told him that he ought to know the history of money before using it, he might find our history quite irrelevant to his immediate pursuit.

The same situation applies to the learning of arithmetic. When the child is being taught the rudiments of addition and subtraction, he is much more interested in the fact that the methods being taught work and permit him to master counting than in why the methods work. The *why* is quite irrelevant at this point in learning. That is why it was possible for children to become so proficient in arithmetic by rote learning. They saw, in the doing, that it *worked*—and they did it.

Today, all that rote learning has been thrown out of the school-room window and an attempt is being made to explain to the child how addition, subtraction, multiplication, and division work. Unfortunately, the explanations are not very good and often much too confusing and tiresome, with the result that children neither learn to perform arithmetic well nor understand it.

Therefore, in this book we shall teach the child both to perform his arithmetic well and to understand it, but with the strict proviso that in teaching a child to use a complex abstract system it is not always desirable to precede instruction with understanding. Sometimes such premature "understanding" can, in fact, retard performance. For example, if we taught a child the grammatic structure of our language before he began to speak, he might never speak for fear of being wrong. The child learns to speak completely on his own before he knows anything about grammar, correct pronunciation, parts of speech, or the origin of words. He speaks because he finds out by experience that speaking *works*. He finds himself understood, and he goes on to increase his speaking vocabulary and to improve his pronunciation so that he can make himself better understood. To explain to him at the earliest stages of his mastery *why* language works or *how* it works would be of little help, and in fact, might hinder and confuse him. So we leave the child alone and let him learn to speak on his own, making minor corrections here and there so that he can improve his pronunciation and be better understood.

Sometimes an understanding of a method comes automatically with the learning. Sometimes it has to be given quite separately and for reasons other than learning how to use the method. When we study the history of language or philology, we do so only peripherally to improve our working use of the language. Our main interest is in discovering how the human race developed linguistically. The same is true of arithmetic. When we study the history of arithmetic, it is not to help us use arithmetic better. That can only be done by drilling the tables until we know them cold. We study the history of arithmetic to give us insights into the development of civilization, the development of methods, etc., but only peripherally to improve our working mastery of arithmetic.

Therefore, in teaching the child arithmetic, we should not allow ourselves to confuse the idea of a *working knowledge* with that of *intellectual understanding*. In teaching an abstract system to a child, a working knowledge must precede intellectual understanding. It is on this principle that the child learns to speak. It is on this principle that civilization has advanced. Man progressed from the cave to complex civilization primarily because he imitated what *worked* for his predecessors. Children learn by imitating adults. When they become adults themselves and discover why something works, they make improvements. Their children imitate these improvements and thus a higher level of civilization is reached.

The interesting thing about arithmetic is that until the development of the Hindu decimal place-value system, very little improvement had been made in the art of calculation over a very long period of time. Nevertheless, advances were being made in every other field. However, the invention of the new decimal place-value system was so significant a breakthrough that it permitted us to make the leap from the primitive agricultural society of 1500 to our space-age technology of 1970 in less than five hundred years.

Until the 1950s, most of our children were taught the decimal place-value system of arithmetic by rote. The only people who were interested in the "how" and "why" of it were the theoretical mathematicians who were intrigued by this ingenious tool and began to take it apart to see what made it tick. Many who took it apart, however, couldn't quite put it together again. Others came up with some discoveries about the system which could later be applied in the building of computers. However, none of this information was of any use to a child learning to master our arithmetic system. The system, as a practical tool, had been perfected by its users over the centuries.

Since most people find that arithmetic is all the mathematics they will ever need in their lifetimes, it is important to distinguish between arithmetic and mathematics. Arithmetic is a tool of economic man. It helps him deal with quantity, money, and measurement, all of which relate to practical everyday living. It is the practical tool which enables man to conduct the economic business of his life with speed, accuracy, and efficiency. Arithmetic, in other words, is much more allied to the world of commerce and industry than it is to the world of mathematical speculation and theorization. Arithmetic goes with those areas of interest in which computation plays an important part:

economics, government, taxation, accounting, business management, etc. Mathematics, on the other hand, is more closely allied to physics, chemistry, engineering, astronomy, philosophy, metaphysics, etc. Thus, in developing a curriculum, it can be shown that arithmetic and mathematics lead toward two divergent paths of interest and activity. Of course, in our complex industrial civilization, all subject matter is interrelated. Reading, for example, is required in every field where the written word is used. But we teach reading as a separate and distinct skill. The same ought to be the case with arithmetic. Arithmetic is used in business as well as in mathematics and scientific calculation, and for this reason it should be taught as a separate and distinct discipline which the growing youngster can later adapt to his chosen field of interest.

What is arithmetic? Arithmetic is simply the art of counting. All arithmetic functions (addition, subtraction, multiplication, and division) are merely different ways of counting. In addition we count forward. In subtraction we count backward. In multiplication we count in multiples, which is merely a faster way of counting forward when dealing with great quantities. In division, the same principle is applied in the reverse direction. Until the invention of the Hindu place-value system all counting (or calculation and computing) was performed by way of abacuses and counting boards, in which quantitative units were represented by concrete objects such as pebbles or beads. Written numbers were used only to record totals.

The advent of the Hindu system marked a radical departure from this primitive concrete counting method. It permitted the accountant to do his calculating with the written symbols themselves. But to do this well, the accountant had to become proficient in the use of the abstract number symbols. The entire counting process had to be transferred from a pebble-manipulating process to a purely mental and written process—from the concrete to the abstract, and from the manipulation of things to the manipulation of symbols representing abstractions.

It is useful in dealing with the subject of abstraction (about which there is so much confusion in the minds of adults as well as children) to define our terms as accurately as possible. The words "abstract" and "abstraction" are used in so many different ways to mean so many different things, that people can easily be confused unless they understand the sense in which the term is used by a writer. One of the growing problems in communication today is the great proliferation of new words meaning new things, new words meaning old things, and old words being used in new ways. Dictionaries cannot keep up with the changes in spoken and written language, with the result that communication in complex areas of thought is on the verge of a breakdown. This is particularly true in modern pedagogy, where educators with different views and different axes to grind refuse to agree on definitions of terms. Sometimes the confusion is deliberately encouraged so that under the cover of verbal fog some educators can reap professional and financial benefits which clear verbal sunlight might make impossible.

In dealing with arithmetic in the context of the New Math it is very important to understand the terms being used, for the New Math has smothered arithmetic in a mass of so many new, complex, ill-defined words that both teacher and pupil can easily lose their way. Parents are so intimidated by the whole complicated approach, that they simply stay away from the New Math. Arithmetic wasn't always this coveted by the mathematician. In fact, arithmetic was of little interest to theoretical mathematicians while it was in its pebble-counting stage. The moment it began to use abstract symbols they took a closer look.

The verb *abstract* and the noun *abstraction* are derived from the Latin word *abstrahere*—to draw away from. This definition essentially describes how abstractions are created. The idea, or mental image, is drawn away from the concrete. It becomes an abstraction in our heads. How did this occur with numbers? The process probably started soon after man learned to use his vocal chords to create language. Undoubtedly man had mental images long before he began to speak. Those were his first abstractions. What he saw in outer reality could be seen in his head either in a dream or with his eyes closed. He also could hear the noises of outer reality in his dreams or by thinking of them. In other words, the ability to retain the impressions of the outer world which we receive through our senses is one of the properties of our nervous system. Those inner impressions, divorced from outer reality, were man's first experience with abstraction. It is probable that early man attributed to his dreams a reality they did not have, which is probably how much of our mythology originated.

Man's invention of spoken language was his first means of concretizing, by way of vocal sounds, elusive mental images and ideas, feelings and actions, so that he could get a firm grip on them. Spoken words became the first symbols to represent and thus communicate to others the abstractions in his head. By giving the ideas names he could anchor them down more securely, he could confirm their existence, and he could, in a sense, increase their reality. All of us know the power of words and man must have become aware of this phenomenon very early in his use of speech.

Also, spoken words enabled man to handle his abstractions with greater precision and thus to exert better mental control over them. The same was true of feelings and actions. By naming them he could better identify and understand them. To name something, it should be noted, is simply to designate it with a spoken expression. The common expression "What do you call it?" sums up the naming process.

Thus, our first spoken words were probably the names of persons and objects. These vocal expressions could only serve as a means of communication if more than one person agreed that the same sound meant the same thing. Language thus developed not only as a means of communication among people, but as a mental tool which individuals could use to develop their own powers of reasoning and understanding.

Did man start drawing before he started speaking? I doubt it. Drawing implies considerable cultural development. The most primitive aborigines speak but do not draw. In the evolution of abstractions, words like "mother" and "father" were probably first used as names, then generalized to mean all mothers and fathers. A word like "house" probably began as the name or designation of a specific living place and was later used to express the idea of a living place in general. The same can be said of "cat," "dog," "sister," "brother," and all the simple object names or nouns which infants learn when they start talking.

The important thing to understand here is the level of abstraction each word represents. The first level is a specific word applying to a specific object in reality. The relationship of the spoken symbol to the concrete is direct. The "drawing away" is only one step, or one level, away. On this level is also the generalized use of name words like "house," "cat," "dog" when referring to a specific entity. When we think of "feeding the cat" we are generally thinking of a specific cat. When the infant says "mama" and "dada" he is referring to specific people he knows, not to the concept of mother and father, or parenthood, or reproduction. When we use the word "sun" we are referring to that specific ball of yellow in the sky. Now, of course, we also speak of other suns in other solar systems.

Thus, in everyday speech we all use first-level abstractions in great abundance. The language of all children learning to speak is made up exclusively of first-level abstractions because they are the easiest to learn and have a direct connection to a concrete object. The child learns them by trial and error. He discovers which ones work and he is thrilled by the sense of discovery he experiences as he adds more and more words to his vocabulary. It should be noted that first-level abstractions include more than just names of objects. They include moral abstractions having to do with behavior as in such phrases as "good boy" and "bad boy," and action and feeling abstractions having to do with eating, drinking, walking, running, wanting, hurting, and the body functions.

The first arithmetic abstractions the child learns are those dealing with measurement: "big" and "little"; or quantity: "a little bit," "a lot," "more," "less," "one," "two," "three." Are these first-level abstractions? From what concrete objects are they drawn? "Big" and "little" are concepts having to do with comparisons. He learns the concepts of "big" and "little" because they are applied in concrete situations all around him: "big brother," "little baby," "small kitten," "big dog," "little puppy." "Big" and "little" become second-level abstractions because they are drawn away from first-level abstractions. Thus, the most elementary arithmetic concepts or ideas are second-level abstractions, twice removed from the concrete.

It is obvious that the transition to the use of second-level abstractions by a child represents a considerable intellectual development. He achieves this development all by himself through his own trial-and-error method of discovery. Obviously he is helped in this development by those around him whom he is trying to understand and imitate. It is also obvious that this transition to second-level abstractions is an uneven process. It takes time before one graduates from an understanding between "good boy," "bad boy," to "good behavior," "bad behavior," and the ethical concepts of good and evil.

The point we wish to make is that spoken language is a means of concretizing all abstraction and that there are different levels of abstraction, that is, ideas which may be once, twice, or three times removed from the original source in reality—including our own organic reality. It should be noted that no matter how complex our civilization becomes, we are always adding new first-level abstractions to our vocabulary: *rocket, missile, airplane, telephone, computer, light bulb, thermometer.* These are the easiest spoken abstractions to learn, no matter how complicated the origin of the words. They are simply names for concretes. While we are increasing the number of first-level abstractions in our vocabulary, we are also increasing the number of second- and third-level abstractions. Here is where we get into difficult problems of definition and here is the source of our present semantic confusion. The knowledge explosion has brought with it the abstraction explosion. In the field of mathematics the confusion is great. Much of it is due to the proliferation of undefined terms and the mixed use of alphabetic words with hieroglyphic symbols. The imposition of this mathematical confusion on arithmetic is causing many children great learning difficulties.

What is the origin of arithmetic abstraction? As primitive man's economic life grew, it became more and more necessary to keep track of larger quantities of goods and cattle. There is probably no concept more elusive than quantity. We can all conjure up mental images of two items, three items, four and five items. But very soon the mind simply cannot cope with larger quantities in this manner. The only way man could concretize and thus get a better grip on the idea of quantity was to give names to specific quantities. These names became known as numbers. Where did the names come from? Primitive man found that the easiest way to count (that is, to indicate exact quantity) was not by thinking about units in his head but by using his marvelous ten fingers. He gave each finger a name in a specific sequence: one through ten. Thus was born the first numbering system. Of course, we have no idea how many centuries it took primitive man to get this far. Obviously the idea of sequential position was closely related in his mind to that of total. He knew, for example, that he had five sons, and he knew the sequence of their birth. But for arithmetic it was easier to count fingers than children. In time, the names or numbers were "drawn away" from the actual fingers to become merely the names of quantities, each name easily remembered if recited in a specific sequence. *Sequential counting*, in other words, was the first aid to the memorization of number names.

Thus, language permitted man to concretize the elusive idea of quantity. By naming quantities man put a handle on something which does not exist in nature but exists in his head for his own use. As the quantities men dealt with increased, the number names over ten became compounds of the finger names, simplifying both the naming and the counting process. All this was done verbally, but because men were so used to calculating with the actual ten fingers, they easily learned to count in tens and to use a ten-base system. Permanent records were made with notches on wood, bundles of sticks, knots tied on a rope and other concrete devices.

In time man developed written symbols for the numbers, merely as a means of recording totals. All calculation, however, was performed by using such concretes as counting boards and abacuses.

With the advent of the alphabet, spoken numbers could also be written out phonetically. However, this was of no help from a computational point of view. Ideographic and hieroglyphic number symbols were still used for arithmetic notation and their use in computation was minimal. To clarify the distinction between ideographic and hieroglyphic numbers, we might say that line markings or a series of dots indicating units would be an ideographic way of writing numbers. They are the simplest graphic substitutes for concretes. The use of one symbol (a letter or a unique graphic design) to represent more than one unit would be a hieroglyphic number. All our Arabic numbers are hieroglyphics. The Greeks used alphabet letters as number hieroglyphics but failed to devise a place-value system whereby they could be used in computation. The Roman numbers were a mixture of ideographs and hieroglyphics, that is, a combination of unit marks and letters. This mixture of graphic concretes with symbols of abstractions proved to be quite unworkable for computation.

It is important to understand the complexity of the mental process involved in man's development of a counting system. When man first gave names to his fingers in order to count small quantities, he probably first conveyed the idea of a total by counting each unit until he reached the last one. Thus, to say "three" he had to say "one, two, three." Eventually he shortened the process so that whenever he said "three" everyone knew he meant the total, and not merely a position in sequence. What is significant is that each number came to represent not only a position in sequence and a specific quantity, but also the counting process itself which was implicit in the naming of a total. Thus, there was much more involved in the naming of quantities than one might suspect. By telescoping the counting process in each number over one, numbers took on an added abstract dimension. Thus, a number is a complex symbol with three important meanings: position in sequence (a first-level abstraction), quantity or total (a second-level abstraction), and the process whereby quantity is determined (another second-level abstraction). Remember, quantity or total does not exist in nature, and it is impossible for man to separate quantity from a counting process used to determine it. However, our minds, always eager to find shortcuts, combine the two concepts in one symbol with no difficulty whatever. It is the law of the conservation of energy which makes such efficient mental functioning possible.

All of this is true for the verbal numbers as well as our Arabic number symbols. All verbal numbers represent position in sequence, specific quantity, and the counting process. How do we know which meaning is intended? The context of our speech gives us clues. We say "He is third" or refer to "page 25" to indicate position. When we say "My house has ten windows" we indicate total as well as the fact that we counted the windows. When we say "I started with 100 dollars and have only 50 left" we are speaking about totals but the counting process is somewhat explicit. When we use our Arabic numbers, their meaning is further enhanced by the added dimension of place-value. For example, the number 123 represents the one-hundred-and-twenty-third position, the quantity of one-hundred-and-twenty-three units, and the counting process used to determine that total. But the position of the numerals in the number also determine their value in computation. It is quite possible to learn by sight-reading that the hieroglyphic 123 stands for one-hundred-and-twenty-three without knowing anything about place value. But if you want to compute with that number, you must know the meaning of place value.

Thus, our Arabic numbers have four meanings while our verbal numbers have only three. Is place value a first- or second-level abstraction? To answer that we must go back to the concrete from which place-value was drawn. That concrete was the counting board, in which each column represented ones, tens, hundreds, etc. We should imagine that this would make place value a first-level abstraction, except that in the counting board itself was incorporated the second-level abstraction of multiplication by tens in all the columns except the unit column. The zero was invented to indicate an empty column so that the accountant could indicate the different values of the digit 3 in 3, 30, 300. Thus, the zero was a first-level abstraction drawn from an empty column, but the digit 3 in 30 and 300 took on an additional second-level abstract meaning (i.e., multiplication by tens, hundreds, etc.). By transferring the second-level abstraction incorporated in the counting board directly to the numerals on paper, we can dispense with the counting board altogether, which is what happened when the Hindu system was adopted in Europe.

Thus, in place-value notation, each numeral assumes an additional second-level abstract meaning. This includes the zero. Although it started out as a first-level abstraction, it has taken on a second-level abstract dimension by becoming an integral part of a hieroglyphic number used in computation. Standing by itself, symbolizing the absence of quantity, the zero performs the unique function of concretizing the idea of nothing. In a way, it symbolizes man's awesome ability to deal with abstraction in daring, versatile, and ingenious ways.

What does all this mean? It means that behind the beautiful simplicity of our ten-symbol arithmetic system is a highly complex circuitry of abstraction. When we deal with numbers in arithmetic our minds are dealing simultaneously with four different meanings on two different levels of abstraction. This is no problem for an adult, but it is for a child of five or six. That is why arithmetic must be taught to children in a very orderly way—one thing at a time, to avoid the confusions that bad teaching can easily cause. Despite the complexity behind the system, once it is understood, the system easily suggests how it should be taught.

First, we must understand that arithmetic is nothing more than a tool for memory. Its prime function is to keep track of quantity and permit us to calculate quantity. The system's chief way of keeping track of quantity is by serial counting—that is, naming totals in sequence. Thus, the first step in teaching a child arithmetic is to teach him to count. As he is taught to count verbally, he is also taught to associate the number symbols with specific quantities. He does this by counting units. To do this he can use fingers or pennies. Since our ten-base system is derived from our fingers, our fingers are the most natural and convenient counting board the child can have. The use of these concrete units are only necessary up to ten, for beyond ten he is dealing with ten plus units of one, and all this can and should be done with the ten Arabic symbols he will be using for the rest of his life.

The instruction in this arithmetic primer has been arranged in "steps," rather than lessons, for the simple reason that the skills involved lend themselves more conveniently to this kind of an arrangement. A step may include concepts and skills which require a day to master, or a week, or a month before the child is ready to move on to the next step. It is important that the child master the material in one step before going on to the next. If the tutor finds the child becoming confused, one should then go back to the earliest point where the child was on solid ground and proceed again slowly in order to discover where the pupil missed the point. Do not proceed further until what was missed has been mastered.

It is suggested that the tutor read through the entire course of instruction before starting to teach. In that way the tutor will gain a better overall grasp of the methods and concepts used. It will be noted, for example, that once the child has learned the quantities the numbers 1 through 10 stand for, we use few problems with concretes for the child to solve. This is deliberate. Our arithmetic system is based on the manipulation of symbols—not apples, oranges, buttons, or other concrete units. These concretes hinder the development of automatic adding because they make the child think in terms of unit counting instead of adding, subtracting, multiplying or dividing with quantities or totals represented by number symbols.

Besides, most of these unit-counting problems are artifical, unreal, and boring. It isn't the numbers that bore children but the ridiculous items that textbooks attach to them. Children never have to perform arithmetic problems in real life with apples, balloons, cowboys, or peppermint sticks. They do count money, boxtops, trading stamps, and birthday candles. The child is not bored with arithmetic per se, which in itself is an interesting mental game. But he does get bored with meaningless "problems" which bind him to concrete unit counting and thereby retard his learning to add numbers automatically. The child wants to get on with the learning of arithmetic, not to determine how many monkeys you have left if you take two out of a cage holding five. No child will ever be confronted with the problem of counting monkeys and he doesn't know any adults who will have to count them either. It is such unreal problems which give children the feeling that arithmetic itself is unreal. Thus, avoid all counting problems which are clearly out of the realm of reality. Have the child count those things he would normally have to count or want to count, or those things which adults have to count but which lend themselves to instructional use by children. The child's weekly allowance or savings program might make an excellent basis for teaching elementary calculation.

Also, most of the arithmetic problems in today's primary textbooks are based on baby-think. It is assumed that a child must be surrounded by an array of baby chicks, circus clowns, and party hats in order to learn anything. We strongly disagree with this philosophy and suggest that the playful paraphernalia of babyhood not be permitted to smother the substance of learning. One should have respect for the child's intellectual capacity and curiosity, knowing how much he has learned by himself in his own way without the use of balloons and toy bugles. It should be noted that when children play games, they imitate adults not children. A little girl with a doll is trying to play the role of an adult mother to the best of her understanding. A little boy playing cowboys and Indians, or playing the role of a train motorman or jet pilot, is trying to act the part of a grown man.

Therefore, when we introduce the child to something as abstract as our arithmetic system, we must appeal to the budding adult in him, the part of him that has a curiosity about the outer world and wants to master basic skills. The way to instructional success is to teach one concept at a time, making that concept understandable and providing enough time and practice for the child to master what he is being taught.

All counting is a function of memory, and our arithmetic system depends on memorization for its most efficient use.

Children enjoy memorizing if it is taught well, with good humor and patience, and as a learning challenge. Any child can be taught to memorize. Because memorizing is based on imitation, it is the easiest form of learning. That is why our arithmetic system lends itself so readily to the primary school curriculum. Counting itself is simply the memorization of additions by one. If a child can learn to count from one to a hundred, he can be taught to memorize the multiplication tables as well.

Remember, we are preparing the child now for what he will be doing twenty years from now. It is important that we keep this long-range view in mind and not let the colorful but mentally empty paraphernalia of childhood obscure the fact that sooner than we think this child will be an adult using the skills we taught him each and every day of his life.

Step 1: Find out the extent of the child's understanding of arithmetic concepts. Children of six will vary greatly in the amount of arithmetic knowledge they have picked up through their informal way of learning. Discuss the meaning of such words and phrases as *more, less, a little bit, a lot, many, few.* Find out the extent of the child's verbal counting ability. Some children of six can count as high as thirty. Others may not be able to count to ten. The ability to count, however, does not necessarily mean that the child understands the meaning of the numbers he recites. Therefore, ask the child if he understands what the numbers mean and why we use them. If he cannot give adequate answers, explain to him that numbers are used so that we can know *exactly* how many of anything we have or may need. For example, if we know that a candy bar we want costs five cents, then we know exactly how many pennies to get from mother. If we know that our friend Tim will be six on his next birthday, then we'll know exactly how many candles to put on his cake.

Establish the idea of exactness with number. Number tells us exactly how many as opposed to "a few" or "a lot."

Step 2: Write the Arabic numbers 1 through 10 on the blackboard and have the child learn to read them in proper sequence. Our purpose is to teach the child to identify the spoken number with its hieroglyphic counterpart. Also teach the child to write the numbers in conjunction with his handwriting lessons. Since we only use the Arabic symbols in arithmetic, the phonetically written numbers should be taught as part of reading instruction and not arithmetic. To include the spelled-out numbers at this point would detract from the arithmetic purpose of his learning.

As the child learns to identify a spoken number with a number symbol, he is also learning to count. Counting consists of naming quantities in their proper sequence, the constantly repeated sequence being the best aid to memory of the quantity names. Remember, counting is a pure task of memorization, and it is as difficult for a child to learn to count by ones as it is for an older child or many an adult to count by sevens or nines. If the child is given many opportunities to use his counting he will learn it quickly. Counting is perfected when it becomes completely automatic, that is, the child can repeat the numbers in sequence without hesitation and without thinking about them. This is a goal which only repeated counting makes possible.

Learning to count *over* ten is a lot easier than learning to count *to* ten, for numbers over ten are compounds of ten or tens with units repeated in the same original sequence of one through ten.

If the child can already count to ten and beyond, review his counting ability and teach him to associate the verbal number with the number symbol as far as he can count verbally. Then use your discretion in expanding his verbal and symbolic counting ability at this time. If there is good indication that he can easily learn to count to fifty or one hundred at this time, let him do so. With today's inflation, children are exposed to much larger sums in their purchases than were the children of twenty and thirty years ago. However, do not assume that because a child of six verbalizes a large number, he knows what it means. In general, it is not very valuable to the child to learn counting in the higher decades if he does not know the meaning of the numbers one through ten.

Step 3: In teaching the numbers one through ten, make sure the child understands the meaning of each number. He learns sequential position (the ordinal sense of the number) through recitation, but he must be taught the quantities each number stands for (the cardinal sense of the number). This can be done by the use of concrete units, such as fingers or pennies.

An easy way to teach the child the meaning of each number is to have him show you how many fingers make 3, or 5, or 7, etc. Also, with the use of pennies you can ask the child to give you 3 cents, 5 cents, 4 cents, 8 cents, etc., until the quantity which each number stands for is firmly established in his mind.

Fingers make an excellent unit counting board since they are always available. Also, since our numbering system is based on finger counting, the correlation between number symbol and the concrete units is perfect. The ten fingers provide an excellent concrete reference for the ten-base system. They also provide an easy, visible proof of the fact that 5 and 5 are 10, and that 2 times 5 are 10. These number relationships are so solidly based on our own physical reality that they become the most useful reference points the child can have in the entire number system. Also, later, in unit counting over ten, the child will learn through the spoken number, number symbol, and his fingers that eleven is ten-plus-one, twelve is ten-plus-two, etc. The compound names suggest the addition process in terms of ten. Therefore, the use of the fingers makes an excellent introduction to the ten-base system.

It should be noted that elementary mathematics textbooks refer to the ordinal number and cardinal number when referring respectively to a number's sequential position or its quantity. We find the use of such rarefied technical terms more of a hindrance to the understanding of arithmetic than a help. Would it not be more appropriate to identify the intended meaning of a number by referring to its "positional sense" or "quantity sense"? This would make arithmetic more understandable for both teacher and pupil. Positional sense need not be confused with place value, which comes into the picture much later.

Step 4: After the child has learned to count to ten and knows the quantities each number stands for, you will want to teach him to count with the symbols rather than units. You can start doing this by demonstrating that each number symbol in sequence represents one unit more than the preceding number. Thus he learns the following additions by one, which you can write out on the blackboard, explaining the meaning of the plus and equal signs. You can do the first two alone, then enlist the child's assistance in figuring out the totals of the rest.

$$1 + 1 = 2$$

$$2 + 1 = 3$$

$$3 + 1 = 4$$

$$4 + 1 = 5$$

$$5 + 1 = 6$$

$$6 + 1 = 7$$

$$7 + 1 = 8$$

$$8 + 1 = 9$$

$$9 + 1 = 10$$

Go over these until the child knows them in any order. Ask him: "What is 5 plus 1, 8 plus 1, 2 plus 1?" etc. This will reinforce his understanding of the number quantities as well as the meaning of sequential counting.

Step 5: You can show the child the same arithmetic facts learned in Step 4 in another way so that he can appreciate the convenience of our number symbols:

$$1 + 1 = 2$$

$$1 + 1 + 1 = 3$$

$$1 + 1 + 1 + 1 = 4$$

$$1 + 1 + 1 + 1 + 1 = 5$$

$$1 + 1 + 1 + 1 + 1 + 1 = 6$$

$$1 + 1 + 1 + 1 + 1 + 1 + 1 = 7$$

$$1 + 1 + 1 + 1 + 1 + 1 + 1 + 1 = 8$$

$$1 + 1 + 1 + 1 + 1 + 1 + 1 + 1 + 1 = 9$$

$$1 + 1 + 1 + 1 + 1 + 1 + 1 + 1 + 1 + 1 = 10$$

Such a demonstration will convince the child how much time and energy he can save by using the quantity symbols. Children are always happy when they find shortcuts. Here you show him how to eliminate unit counting by the use of number symbols, symbols that stand for quantities.

Step 6: To further strengthen the child's ability to use the number symbols in calculation rather than to count units, teach the following additions by showing how units can be combined in number symbols more than one, or, to put it in the reverse, how numbers are used to represent more than one unit. You can demonstrate the process on the blackboard by encircling the units represented by the numbers in the additions. Take as much time as is needed to teach these additions. Explain each step as you go. Note that the child is to be taught that $1 + 2 = 3$ as well as $2 + 1 = 3$, etc. Children do not automatically assume that because $1 + 2 = 3$, that $2 + 1 = 3$. They have to be shown it.

$$1 + 1 = 2 \qquad \begin{array}{r} 1 \\ 1 \\ \hline 2 \end{array}$$

$$1 + 1 + 1 = 3$$
$$1 + 2 = 3 \qquad \begin{array}{r} 1 \\ 2 \\ \hline 3 \end{array} \quad \begin{array}{r} 2 \\ 1 \\ \hline 3 \end{array}$$
$$2 + 1 = 3$$

$$1 + 1 + 1 + 1 = 4$$
$$1 + 3 = 4$$
$$2 + 2 = 4 \qquad \begin{array}{r} 1 \\ 3 \\ \hline 4 \end{array} \quad \begin{array}{r} 2 \\ 2 \\ \hline 4 \end{array} \quad \begin{array}{r} 3 \\ 1 \\ \hline 4 \end{array}$$
$$3 + 1 = 4$$

1 + 1 + 1 + 1 + 1 = 5

1 + 4 = 5

2 + 3 = 5

3 + 2 = 5

4 + 1 = 5

$$\frac{1}{5} \quad \frac{2}{5} \quad \frac{3}{5} \quad \frac{4}{5}$$
$$\frac{4}{5} \quad \frac{3}{5} \quad \frac{2}{5} \quad \frac{1}{5}$$

1 + 1 + 1 + 1 + 1 + 1 = 6

1 + 5 = 6

2 + 4 = 6

3 + 3 = 6

4 + 2 + 6

5 + 1 = 6

$$\frac{1}{6} \quad \frac{2}{6} \quad \frac{3}{6} \quad \frac{4}{6} \quad \frac{5}{6}$$
$$\frac{5}{6} \quad \frac{4}{6} \quad \frac{3}{6} \quad \frac{2}{6} \quad \frac{1}{6}$$

1 + 1 + 1 + 1 + 1 + 1 + 1 = 7

1 + 6 = 7

2 + 5 = 7

3 + 4 = 7

4 + 3 = 7

5 + 2 = 7

6 + 1 = 7

$$\frac{1}{7} \quad \frac{2}{7} \quad \frac{3}{7} \quad \frac{4}{7} \quad \frac{5}{7} \quad \frac{6}{7}$$
$$\frac{6}{7} \quad \frac{5}{7} \quad \frac{4}{7} \quad \frac{3}{7} \quad \frac{2}{7} \quad \frac{1}{7}$$

$1 + 1 + 1 + 1 + 1 + 1 + 1 + 1 = 8$

$1 + 7 = 8$

$2 + 6 = 8$

$3 + 5 = 8$

$4 + 4 = 8$

$5 + 3 = 8$

$6 + 2 = 8$

$7 + 1 = 8$

1	2	3	4	5	6	7
7	6	5	4	3	2	1
8	8	8	8	8	8	8

$1 + 1 + 1 + 1 + 1 + 1 + 1 + 1 + 1 = 9$

$1 + 8 = 9$

$2 + 7 = 9$

$3 + 6 = 9$

$4 + 5 = 9$

$5 + 4 = 9$

$6 + 3 = 9$

$7 + 2 = 9$

$8 + 1 = 9$

1	2	3	4	5	6	7	8
8	7	6	5	4	3	2	1
9	9	9	9	9	9	9	9

$$1 + 1 + 1 + 1 + 1 + 1 + 1 + 1 + 1 + 1 = 10$$

$$1 + 9 = 10$$

$$2 + 8 = 10$$

$$3 + 7 = 10$$

$$4 + 6 = 10$$

$$5 + 5 = 10$$

$$6 + 4 = 10$$

$$7 + 3 = 10$$

$$8 + 2 = 10$$

$$9 + 1 = 10$$

1	2	3	4	5	6	7	8	9
9	8	7	6	5	4	3	2	1
10	10	10	10	10	10	10	10	10

Note how these unit-grouping exercises strengthen the child's understanding of the numbers and the quantity of units each number stands for. He learns the proofs of these additions by being shown how the units are combined into numbers. Now show the child how these addition facts can be arranged in a very useful addition table which the child can utilize in memorizing the addition facts. Memorization is the only way to automatic addition. If the child does not memorize the addition totals, he will be unit counting indefinitely, and this will hinder or retard his mastery of arithmetic.

	1	2	3	4	5	6	7	8	9	10
	1	2	3	4	5	6	7	8	9	10
1	2	3	4	5	6	7	8	9	10	
2	3	4	5	6	7	8	9	10		
3	4	5	6	7	8	9	10			
4	5	6	7	8	9	10				
5	6	7	8	9	10					
6	7	8	9	10						
7	8	9	10							
8	9	10								
9	10									
10										

Step 7: The additions in the table can also be put into column form. Write them out as follows so that the child can see the pattern:

$$\frac{1}{\frac{1}{2}} \quad \frac{2}{\frac{1}{3}} \quad \frac{3}{\frac{1}{4}} \quad \frac{4}{\frac{1}{5}} \quad \frac{5}{\frac{1}{6}} \quad \frac{6}{\frac{1}{7}} \quad \frac{7}{\frac{1}{8}} \quad \frac{8}{\frac{1}{9}} \quad \frac{9}{\frac{1}{10}}$$

$$\frac{1}{\frac{2}{3}} \quad \frac{2}{\frac{2}{4}} \quad \frac{3}{\frac{2}{5}} \quad \frac{4}{\frac{2}{6}} \quad \frac{5}{\frac{2}{7}} \quad \frac{6}{\frac{2}{8}} \quad \frac{7}{\frac{2}{9}} \quad \frac{8}{\frac{2}{10}}$$

$$\frac{1}{\frac{3}{4}} \quad \frac{2}{\frac{3}{5}} \quad \frac{3}{\frac{3}{6}} \quad \frac{4}{\frac{3}{7}} \quad \frac{5}{\frac{3}{8}} \quad \frac{6}{\frac{3}{9}} \quad \frac{7}{\frac{3}{10}}$$

$$
\begin{array}{cccccc}
1 & 2 & 3 & 4 & 5 & 6 \\
\underline{4} & \underline{4} & \underline{4} & \underline{4} & \underline{4} & \underline{4} \\
5 & 6 & 7 & 8 & 9 & 10
\end{array}
$$

$$
\begin{array}{ccccc}
1 & 2 & 3 & 4 & 5 \\
\underline{5} & \underline{5} & \underline{5} & \underline{5} & \underline{5} \\
6 & 7 & 8 & 9 & 10
\end{array}
$$

$$
\begin{array}{cccc}
1 & 2 & 3 & 4 \\
\underline{6} & \underline{6} & \underline{6} & \underline{6} \\
7 & 8 & 9 & 10
\end{array}
$$

$$
\begin{array}{ccc}
1 & 2 & 3 \\
\underline{7} & \underline{7} & \underline{7} \\
8 & 9 & 10
\end{array}
$$

$$
\begin{array}{cc}
1 & 2 \\
\underline{8} & \underline{8} \\
9 & 10
\end{array}
$$

$$
\begin{array}{c}
1 \\
\underline{9} \\
10
\end{array}
$$

Have the child read off these additions aloud repeating "one plus one is two, two plus one is three," etc., until he reaches "one plus nine is ten." Repeating the additions in sequential patterns helps memory. Just as it is easy to remember poems that rhyme, so it is easier to remember arithmetic facts when they are learned in progressive order. The child should articulate these additions so that the sounds of the combinations become familiar to him. You can also write out the same addition sequences on the blackboard without the sums and see how well he adds them up. You can later test him on how well he has learned these additions by giving him random addition combinations by flash card. Some he will know cold if they are easy, such as 5 plus 5 is ten. Others will be remembered by their position in sequence or relationship to other combinations, while yet others he will figure out by unit counting in his head or on his fingers. The optimum goal is to get him to know 4 plus 5 as automatically as he knows 1 plus 1, so that there is no need to unit count. Unit counting hinders speedy, effortless calculation, and some unit-counting habits picked up in early instruction can persist throughout one's life, constantly hindering easy calculation. If the child is permitted to rely on unit counting, he will not make the effort needed to memorize the addition facts.

Most modern textbooks give the child the kind of arithmetic problems that encourage unit counting in addition, negating the unique advantages that our arithmetic system has as a tool for memory. The instruction in this book excludes such teaching. Therefore, once the addition facts of numbers 1 through 10 are proven by demonstrations of unit counting, no further unit counting should be permitted in adding quantities over 1. The reason why we stress this is that the hardest habits to break are those learned by children in the early grades where they establish their ways of doing things. This goes for bad habits as well as good. It makes no sense to let a bad habit become established in the hope that it will eventually be replaced by a good one. Chances are that it won't. Thus, care should be taken to make sure that the child establishes good habits from the beginning. This can be done by being aware of the child's thinking methods and how he performs the additions we give him.

We have devised the instruction in this book to make it as easy as possible to establish good habits from the start and difficult to establish bad ones. However, no book of instruction is better than the teacher using it. Thus, it is up to the teacher to put the book's methodology into practice.

Step 8: By now the child will have spent about a year getting acquainted with numbers and learning his first forty-five addition facts. If he cannot as yet count to 100, teach him to do so. If he learns this much easily, proceed to teach him to count to 500 or 1000, depending on his ability. Since the hundreds repeat all the decade counting already learned, they will reinforce the child's counting ability from 1 through 100. In any case, he should have little trouble learning to count to 100 since he can easily discern the sequential pattern of 1 through 10 repeated in each line of tens. *At this point we are interested merely in getting the child to associate the verbal number with its hieroglyphic counterpart.*

Test his ability to name numbers from 1 to 100 by showing them to him at random on flash cards. Practice with higher numbers if you have taught him to count beyond 100.

1	2	3	4	5	6	7	8	9	10
11	12	13	14	15	16	17	18	19	20
21	22	23	24	25	26	27	28	29	30
31	32	33	34	35	36	37	38	39	40
41	42	43	44	45	46	47	48	49	50
51	52	53	54	55	56	57	58	59	60
61	62	63	64	65	66	67	68	69	70
71	72	73	74	75	76	77	78	79	80
81	82	83	84	85	86	87	88	89	90
91	92	93	94	95	96	97	98	99	100

Step 9: Teach the rest of the additions with numbers to ten. Use the addition groupings in Step 10 for drill purposes.

	1	2	3	4	5	6	7	8	9	10
1	2	3	4	5	6	7	8	9	10	11
2	3	4	5	6	7	8	9	10	11	12
3	4	5	6	7	8	9	10	11	12	13
4	5	6	7	8	9	10	11	12	13	14
5	6	7	8	9	10	11	12	13	14	15
6	7	8	9	10	11	12	13	14	15	16
7	8	9	10	11	12	13	14	15	16	17
8	9	10	11	12	13	14	15	16	17	18
9	10	11	12	13	14	15	16	17	18	19
10	11	12	13	14	15	16	17	18	19	20

Step 10: Drill the child on these additions in the same manner used in Step 7.

$$\frac{\begin{array}{r}10\\1\end{array}}{11} \quad \frac{\begin{array}{r}10\\2\end{array}}{12} \quad \frac{\begin{array}{r}10\\3\end{array}}{13} \quad \frac{\begin{array}{r}10\\4\end{array}}{14} \quad \frac{\begin{array}{r}10\\5\end{array}}{15} \quad \frac{\begin{array}{r}10\\6\end{array}}{16} \quad \frac{\begin{array}{r}10\\7\end{array}}{17} \quad \frac{\begin{array}{r}10\\8\end{array}}{18} \quad \frac{\begin{array}{r}10\\9\end{array}}{19} \quad \frac{\begin{array}{r}10\\10\end{array}}{20}$$

$$\frac{\begin{array}{r}9\\2\end{array}}{11} \quad \frac{\begin{array}{r}9\\3\end{array}}{12} \quad \frac{\begin{array}{r}9\\4\end{array}}{13} \quad \frac{\begin{array}{r}9\\5\end{array}}{14} \quad \frac{\begin{array}{r}9\\6\end{array}}{15} \quad \frac{\begin{array}{r}9\\7\end{array}}{16} \quad \frac{\begin{array}{r}9\\8\end{array}}{17} \quad \frac{\begin{array}{r}9\\9\end{array}}{18} \quad \frac{\begin{array}{r}9\\10\end{array}}{19}$$

$$\frac{\begin{array}{r}8\\3\end{array}}{11} \quad \frac{\begin{array}{r}8\\4\end{array}}{12} \quad \frac{\begin{array}{r}8\\5\end{array}}{13} \quad \frac{\begin{array}{r}8\\6\end{array}}{14} \quad \frac{\begin{array}{r}8\\7\end{array}}{15} \quad \frac{\begin{array}{r}8\\8\end{array}}{16} \quad \frac{\begin{array}{r}8\\9\end{array}}{17} \quad \frac{\begin{array}{r}8\\10\end{array}}{18}$$

$$\frac{\begin{array}{r}7\\4\end{array}}{11} \quad \frac{\begin{array}{r}7\\5\end{array}}{12} \quad \frac{\begin{array}{r}7\\6\end{array}}{13} \quad \frac{\begin{array}{r}7\\7\end{array}}{14} \quad \frac{\begin{array}{r}7\\8\end{array}}{15} \quad \frac{\begin{array}{r}7\\9\end{array}}{16} \quad \frac{\begin{array}{r}7\\10\end{array}}{17}$$

$$\begin{array}{cccccc}
6 & 6 & 6 & 6 & 6 & 6 \\
\underline{5} & \underline{6} & \underline{7} & \underline{8} & \underline{9} & \underline{10} \\
11 & 12 & 13 & 14 & 15 & 16
\end{array}$$

$$\begin{array}{ccccc}
5 & 5 & 5 & 5 & 5 \\
\underline{6} & \underline{7} & \underline{8} & \underline{9} & \underline{10} \\
11 & 12 & 13 & 14 & 15
\end{array}$$

$$\begin{array}{cccc}
4 & 4 & 4 & 4 \\
\underline{7} & \underline{8} & \underline{9} & \underline{10} \\
11 & 12 & 13 & 14
\end{array}$$

$$\begin{array}{ccc}
3 & 3 & 3 \\
\underline{8} & \underline{9} & \underline{10} \\
11 & 12 & 13
\end{array}$$

$$\begin{array}{cc}
2 & 2 \\
\underline{9} & \underline{10} \\
11 & 12
\end{array}$$

$$\begin{array}{c}
1 \\
\underline{10} \\
11
\end{array}$$

Here are the same additions arranged in another pattern to facilitate memorization:

$$\begin{array}{cccccccccc}
10 & 9 & 8 & 7 & 6 & 5 & 4 & 3 & 2 & 1 \\
\underline{1} & \underline{2} & \underline{3} & \underline{4} & \underline{5} & \underline{6} & \underline{7} & \underline{8} & \underline{9} & \underline{10} \\
11 & 11 & 11 & 11 & 11 & 11 & 11 & 11 & 11 & 11
\end{array}$$

$$\begin{array}{ccccccccc}
10 & 9 & 8 & 7 & 6 & 5 & 4 & 3 & 2 \\
\underline{2} & \underline{3} & \underline{4} & \underline{5} & \underline{6} & \underline{7} & \underline{8} & \underline{9} & \underline{10} \\
12 & 12 & 12 & 12 & 12 & 12 & 12 & 12 & 12
\end{array}$$

$$\begin{array}{cccccccc}
10 & 9 & 8 & 7 & 6 & 5 & 4 & 3 \\
\underline{3} & \underline{4} & \underline{5} & \underline{6} & \underline{7} & \underline{8} & \underline{9} & \underline{10} \\
13 & 13 & 13 & 13 & 13 & 13 & 13 & 13
\end{array}$$

$$\begin{array}{ccccccc}
10 & 9 & 8 & 7 & 6 & 5 & 4 \\
\underline{4} & \underline{5} & \underline{6} & \underline{7} & \underline{8} & \underline{9} & \underline{10} \\
14 & 14 & 14 & 14 & 14 & 14 & 14
\end{array}$$

10	9	8	7	6	5
5	6	7	8	9	10
15	15	15	15	15	15

10	9	8	7	6
6	7	8	9	10
16	16	16	16	16

10	9	8	7
7	8	9	10
17	17	17	17

10	9	8
8	9	10
18	18	18

10	9
9	10
19	19

10
10
20

To test the child's mastery of the addition facts, give the child random additions to perform. Note the ones that make him hesitate and note the ones he can add automatically. Make a list of the ones he is unsure of and drill him in them. Take plenty of time and be patient. Let him see and hear the more difficult combinations over and over again with the correct sums. In time they will become as easy to remember as 2 plus 2 is 4. Speed in response is important, because it permits us to detect unit counting. Make such speed drills as enjoyable and as pleasant as possible, telling the child that with sufficient practice he'll be able to perform perfectly. A good way to drill is to put addition combinations on flash cards. Such drills should be conducted in short spurts rather than in long tiresome sessions. But they should be repeated over a period of time until performance is perfect. We can all count from 1 to 100 at top speed without thinking because we have done it so often. Automatic knowledge is acquired by going over the same thing often enough so that a "path" in our minds is created. We acquire a great deal of automatic knowledge without being aware that we are doing so. However, with a system as complex yet compact and organized as arithmetic, such knowledge is best acquired through a systematic, deliberate approach. In the long run it prevents poor arithmetic habits from developing and saves the student time and effort all his life.

Step 11: Review counting and advance the child's counting capability to 1,000. Again, the purpose of the instruction is to teach the child to associate the verbal number with its proper hieroglyphic counterpart. This is done by teaching the child to see and hear the basic pattern of 1 through 10 in each decade of the hundreds. The child learns to count by remembering the recurring patterns in both verbal and symbolic numbers.

Step 12: Subtraction. Pose some simple subtraction problems to the child so that he can understand what subtraction is. Explain to him that while adding makes the quantity we started with more, subtraction makes that quantity less. As an example, ask the child if he had ten pennies and spent six, how many he would have left. He can use his fingers to see the subtraction process in concretes, or use pennies themselves. If he takes away three from five, how many does he have left? When the child firmly grasps the concept of subtraction in terms of units and in terms of a smaller quantity being taken away from a larger quantity, then give him the following simple subtractions in number symbols, explaining the meaning of the minus sign:

$$2 - 1 = ? \qquad 4 - 2 = ? \qquad 4 - 3 = ?$$
$$3 - 2 = ? \qquad 3 - 1 = ? \qquad 4 - 1 = ?$$

Explain that in addition we count forward. In subtraction, we really count backward.

Step 13: Teach the child to count backward from 20 to 1. Then demonstrate with the following how counting backward is really subtraction by ones, as counting forward is addition by ones:

9 + 1 = 10	10 - 1 = 9
8 + 1 = 9	9 - 1 = 8
7 + 1 = 8	8 - 1 = 7
6 + 1 = 7	7 - 1 = 6
5 + 1 = 6	6 - 1 = 5
4 + 1 = 5	5 - 1 = 4
3 + 1 = 4	4 - 1 = 3
2 + 1 = 3	3 - 1 = 2
1 + 1 = 2	2 - 1 = 1

Have the child learn the following subtractions with their addition counterparts. Show how subtraction can be checked by adding the difference (or remainder) to the subtractor (subtrahend):

8 + 2 = 10	10 - 2 = 8	7 + 3 = 10	10 - 3 = 7
7 + 2 = 9	9 - 2 = 7	6 + 3 = 9	9 - 3 = 6
6 + 2 = 8	8 - 2 = 6	5 + 3 = 8	8 - 3 = 5
5 + 2 = 7	7 - 2 = 5	4 + 3 = 7	7 - 3 = 4
4 + 2 = 6	6 - 2 = 4	3 + 3 = 6	6 - 3 = 3
3 + 2 = 5	5 - 2 = 3	2 + 3 = 5	5 - 3 = 2
2 + 2 = 4	4 - 2 = 2	1 + 3 = 4	4 - 3 = 1
1 + 2 = 3	3 - 2 = 1		

$6 + 4 = 10 \quad 10 - 4 = 6$ $\qquad$ $4 + 6 = 10 \quad 10 - 6 = 4$

$5 + 4 = 9 \quad 9 - 4 = 5$ $\qquad$ $3 + 6 = 9 \quad 9 - 6 = 3$

$4 + 4 = 8 \quad 8 - 4 = 4$ $\qquad$ $2 + 6 = 8 \quad 8 - 6 = 2$

$3 + 4 = 7 \quad 7 - 4 = 3$ $\qquad$ $1 + 6 = 7 \quad 7 - 6 = 1$

$2 + 4 = 6 \quad 6 - 4 = 2$

$1 + 4 = 5 \quad 5 - 4 = 1$ $\qquad$ $3 + 7 = 10 \quad 10 - 7 = 3$

$\qquad\qquad\qquad\qquad\qquad\quad\;\; 2 + 7 = 9 \quad 9 - 7 = 2$

$\qquad\qquad\qquad\qquad\qquad\quad\;\; 1 + 7 = 8 \quad 8 - 7 = 1$

$5 + 5 = 10 \quad 10 - 5 = 5$

$4 + 5 = 9 \quad 9 - 5 = 4$ $\qquad$ $2 + 8 = 10 \quad 10 - 8 = 2$

$3 + 5 = 8 \quad 8 - 5 = 3$ $\qquad$ $1 + 8 = 9 \quad 9 - 8 = 1$

$2 + 5 = 7 \quad 7 - 5 = 2$

$1 + 5 = 6 \quad 6 - 5 = 1$ $\qquad$ $1 + 9 = 10 \quad 10 - 9 = 1$

Through repeated recitations of these additions and sub-tractions, the child will not fail to detect the consistent counting patterns in our arithmetic system. In being exposed to it, his mind is bound to capture some of its logic. In our introduction we stated that our goal was to both teach arithmetic and have the child understand it. By detecting the consistency of the patterns, he will begin to understand the logic behind the system. The discovery of a logical consistency in a set of abstract symbols will be an exciting discovery for the child. It is more important for him to learn this than to solve unreal arithmetic problems which give him practice in unit counting, much to his own detriment.

Step 13a: The symbol for zero. Ask the child to give the answers to the following subtractions:

$$1 - 1 = ? \qquad 5 - 5 = ? \qquad 10 - 10 = ?$$

If he cannot give the correct answers, ask the child how much would be left if you took one away from one, or five from five, or ten from ten. If he answers "nothing is left," tell him that he is correct and that we use the zero, 0, to represent nothing. For example, when a baseball team scores nothing, we put down zero as the score. Give the child some additions and subtractions with zero, such as:

$$1 + 0 = 1 \qquad 5 + 0 = 5 \qquad 10 + 0 = 10$$

$$1 - 0 = 1 \qquad 5 - 0 = 5 \qquad 10 - 0 = 10$$

Tell the pupil that if he has any trouble adding or subtracting with zero to simply remember that zero stands for nothing, and that nothing added to something does not increase the something, and that nothing taken away or subtracted from something does not decrease the something. Thus, five plus nothing remains five, and five minus nothing remains five.

Step 14: Subtraction table. Show the child how to use the table in memorizing subtractions from 0 through 10.

	0	1	2	3	4	5	6	7	8	9	10
0		1	2	3	4	5	6	7	8	9	10
1		0	1	2	3	4	5	6	7	8	9
2			0	1	2	3	4	5	6	7	8
3				0	1	2	3	4	5	6	7
4					0	1	2	3	4	5	6
5						0	1	2	3	4	5
6							0	1	2	3	4
7								0	1	2	3
8									0	1	2
9										0	1
10											0

Step 15: The child may find it easier to memorize the following subtractions from sums up to 19 in this form. Show him how he can check his subtractions by adding the remainder and the subtractor, which should equal the sum subtracted from.

$$\frac{1}{-0}\ \frac{2}{-1}\ \frac{3}{-2}\ \frac{4}{-3}\ \frac{5}{-4}\ \frac{6}{-5}\ \frac{7}{-6}\ \frac{8}{-7}\ \frac{9}{-8}\ \frac{10}{-9}$$
$$\overline{1}\ \ \overline{1}\ \ \overline{1}\ \ \overline{1}\ \ \overline{1}\ \ \overline{1}\ \ \overline{1}\ \ \overline{1}\ \ \overline{1}\ \ \overline{1}$$

$$\frac{2}{-0}\ \frac{3}{-1}\ \frac{4}{-2}\ \frac{5}{-3}\ \frac{6}{-4}\ \frac{7}{-5}\ \frac{8}{-6}\ \frac{9}{-7}\ \frac{10}{-8}\ \frac{11}{-9}$$
$$\overline{2}\ \ \overline{2}\ \ \overline{2}\ \ \overline{2}\ \ \overline{2}\ \ \overline{2}\ \ \overline{2}\ \ \overline{2}\ \ \overline{2}\ \ \overline{2}$$

$$\frac{3}{-0}\ \frac{4}{-1}\ \frac{5}{-2}\ \frac{6}{-3}\ \frac{7}{-4}\ \frac{8}{-5}\ \frac{9}{-6}\ \frac{10}{-7}\ \frac{11}{-8}\ \frac{12}{-9}$$
$$\overline{3}\ \ \overline{3}\ \ \overline{3}\ \ \overline{3}\ \ \overline{3}\ \ \overline{3}\ \ \overline{3}\ \ \overline{3}\ \ \overline{3}\ \ \overline{3}$$

$$\frac{4}{-0}\ \frac{5}{-1}\ \frac{6}{-2}\ \frac{7}{-3}\ \frac{8}{-4}\ \frac{9}{-5}\ \frac{10}{-6}\ \frac{11}{-7}\ \frac{12}{-8}\ \frac{13}{-9}$$
$$\overline{4}\ \ \overline{4}\ \ \overline{4}\ \ \overline{4}\ \ \overline{4}\ \ \overline{4}\ \ \overline{4}\ \ \overline{4}\ \ \overline{4}\ \ \overline{4}$$

$$\frac{5}{-0}\ \frac{6}{-1}\ \frac{7}{-2}\ \frac{8}{-3}\ \frac{9}{-4}\ \frac{10}{-5}\ \frac{11}{-6}\ \frac{12}{-7}\ \frac{13}{-8}\ \frac{14}{-9}$$
$$\overline{5}\ \ \overline{5}\ \ \overline{5}\ \ \overline{5}\ \ \overline{5}\ \ \overline{5}\ \ \overline{5}\ \ \overline{5}\ \ \overline{5}\ \ \overline{5}$$

$$\frac{6}{-0}\ \frac{7}{-1}\ \frac{8}{-2}\ \frac{9}{-3}\ \frac{10}{-4}\ \frac{11}{-5}\ \frac{12}{-6}\ \frac{13}{-7}\ \frac{14}{-8}\ \frac{15}{-9}$$
$$\overline{6}\ \ \overline{6}\ \ \overline{6}\ \ \overline{6}\ \ \overline{6}\ \ \overline{6}\ \ \overline{6}\ \ \overline{6}\ \ \overline{6}\ \ \overline{6}$$

$$\frac{7}{-0}\ \frac{8}{-1}\ \frac{9}{-2}\ \frac{10}{-3}\ \frac{11}{-4}\ \frac{12}{-5}\ \frac{13}{-6}\ \frac{14}{-7}\ \frac{15}{-8}\ \frac{16}{-9}$$
$$\overline{7}\ \ \overline{7}\ \ \overline{7}\ \ \overline{7}\ \ \overline{7}\ \ \overline{7}\ \ \overline{7}\ \ \overline{7}\ \ \overline{7}\ \ \overline{7}$$

$$\frac{8}{-0}\ \frac{9}{-1}\ \frac{10}{-2}\ \frac{11}{-3}\ \frac{12}{-4}\ \frac{13}{-5}\ \frac{14}{-6}\ \frac{15}{-7}\ \frac{16}{-8}\ \frac{17}{-9}$$
$$\overline{8}\ \ \overline{8}\ \ \overline{8}\ \ \overline{8}\ \ \overline{8}\ \ \overline{8}\ \ \overline{8}\ \ \overline{8}\ \ \overline{8}\ \ \overline{8}$$

$$\frac{9}{-0}\ \frac{10}{-1}\ \frac{11}{-2}\ \frac{12}{-3}\ \frac{13}{-4}\ \frac{14}{-5}\ \frac{15}{-6}\ \frac{16}{-7}\ \frac{17}{-8}\ \frac{18}{-9}$$
$$\overline{9}\ \ \overline{9}\ \ \overline{9}\ \ \overline{9}\ \ \overline{9}\ \ \overline{9}\ \ \overline{9}\ \ \overline{9}\ \ \overline{9}\ \ \overline{9}$$

$$\frac{10}{-0}\ \frac{11}{-1}\ \frac{12}{-2}\ \frac{13}{-3}\ \frac{14}{-4}\ \frac{15}{-5}\ \frac{16}{-6}\ \frac{17}{-7}\ \frac{18}{-8}\ \frac{19}{-9}$$
$$\overline{10}\ \ \overline{10}\ \ \overline{10}\ \ \overline{10}\ \ \overline{10}\ \ \overline{10}\ \ \overline{10}\ \ \overline{10}\ \ \overline{10}\ \ \overline{10}$$

Step 16: Drill subtractions with random combinations taken from the subtraction tables.

Step 17: Drill the fundamental addition and subtraction facts by mixing random combinations from both the addition and subtraction tables.

Step 18: Elementary addition involves more than simply learning the fundamental addition facts. Further techniques are basic to development of addition skills. These include column addition, higher decade addition—which is needed in column addition—and carrying. In teaching column addition we start off with three single-digit numbers which add up to not over 10. For example, we give the child 2, 3, and 4 to add in a column. He first adds the 2 and 3, which gives him 5. Then he adds 5 and 4 to give him the final sum of 9. What is significant in this process is that in adding 2 and 3 the child sees both numbers. But in adding 5 and 4, the 5 is not seen on paper but is held as an idea or image in his head, to which he adds the 4. The process of adding a written number to an invisible or mental number is a more difficult computational task for the child to perform. So we start him off with very simple addition columns, all of which add up to not more than 10. Lots of practice in adding these columns will accustom the child to adding mental numbers to written numbers.

```
1   1   1   2   1   1   3   1   1   4   1   1   5   1   1
1   1   2   1   1   3   1   1   4   1   1   5   5   1   1
1   2   1   1   3   1   1   4   1   1   5   1   6   1   6
─   ─   ─   ─   ─   ─   ─   ─   ─   ─   ─   ─   ─   ─   ─
```

```
6   1   1   7   1   1   8   1   2   2   1   1   2   2   3
1   1   7   1   1   8   1   2   1   2   2   3   1   3   1
1   7   1   1   8   1   1   2   2   1   3   2   3   1   2
─   ─   ─   ─   ─   ─   ─   ─   ─   ─   ─   ─   ─   ─   ─
```

```
3   1   1   2   2   4   4   1   1   2   2   5   5   1   1
2   2   4   1   4   1   2   2   5   1   5   1   2   2   6
1   4   2   4   1   2   1   5   2   5   1   2   1   6   2
─   ─   ─   ─   ─   ─   ─   ─   ─   ─   ─   ─   ─   ─   ─
```

```
2   2   6   6   1   1   2   2   7   7   1   3   3   1   1
1   6   1   2   2   7   1   7   2   1   3   1   3   3   4
6   1   2   1   7   2   7   1   2   1   3   3   1   4   3
--  --  --  --  --  --  --  --  --  --  --  --  --  --  --

3   3   4   4   1   1   3   3   5   5   1   1   3   3   6
1   4   1   3   3   5   5   1   3   3   6   1   6   6   1
4   1   3   1   5   3   5   1   3   1   6   3   6   1   3
--  --  --  --  --  --  --  --  --  --  --  --  --  --  --

6   1   4   4   1   1   4   4   5   5   2   2   2   3   2
3   4   1   4   4   5   1   5   1   4   2   2   3   2   2
1   4   4   1   5   4   5   1   4   1   2   3   2   2   4
--  --  --  --  --  --  --  --  --  --  --  --  --  --  --

2   4   2   2   5   2   2   6   2   3   3   2   2   3   3
4   2   2   5   2   6   2   2   3   2   3   3   4   2   4
2   2   5   2   2   6   2   2   3   3   2   4   3   4   2
--  --  --  --  --  --  --  --  --  --  --  --  --  --  --

4   4   2   2   3   3   5   5   2   4   4   3   3   3   4
2   3   3   5   2   5   2   3   4   2   4   3   3   4   3
3   2   5   3   5   2   3   2   4   4   2   3   4   3   3
--  --  --  --  --  --  --  --  --  --  --  --  --  --  --
```

Step 19: The next series of column additions to be learned are those in which the three one-digit numbers add up to sums over 10. In the additions below, the sum of the first two numbers in the column do not exceed 9. In learning to do these additions, make sure that the child always adds from the top down. This is the direction in which the numbers are written. It is the direction in which he should add them. Later on when he is well habituated to downward adding and has learned to add one-digit numbers to two-digit numbers in what is known as higher decade addition, you might introduce him to upward adding merely as a check on the accuracy of his downward addition.

222

```
 1   1   1   1   1   1   1   1   1   1   1   1   1   1
 1   2   2   3   3   3   4   4   4   4   5   5   5   5
 9   8   9   7   8   9   6   7   8   9   5   6   7   8
___ ___ ___ ___ ___ ___ ___ ___ ___ ___ ___ ___ ___ ___

 1   1   1   1   1   1   1   1   1   1   2   2   2   2
 5   6   6   6   6   7   7   7   8   8   2   2   2   3
 9   6   7   8   9   7   8   9   8   9   7   8   9   6
___ ___ ___ ___ ___ ___ ___ ___ ___ ___ ___ ___ ___ ___

 2   2   2   2   2   2   2   2   2   2   2   2   2   2
 3   3   3   4   4   4   4   4   5   5   5   5   5   6
 7   8   9   5   6   7   8   9   5   6   7   8   9   6
___ ___ ___ ___ ___ ___ ___ ___ ___ ___ ___ ___ ___ ___

 2   2   2   2   2   2   3   3   3   3   3   3   3   3
 6   6   6   7   7   7   3   3   3   3   3   4   4   4
 7   8   9   7   8   9   5   6   7   8   9   4   5   6
___ ___ ___ ___ ___ ___ ___ ___ ___ ___ ___ ___ ___ ___

 3   3   3   3   3   3   3   3   3   3   3   3   4   4
 4   4   4   5   5   5   5   5   6   6   6   6   4   4
 7   8   9   5   6   7   8   9   6   7   8   9   4   5
___ ___ ___ ___ ___ ___ ___ ___ ___ ___ ___ ___ ___ ___

 4   4   4   4   4   4   4   4   4
 4   4   4   4   5   5   5   5   5
 6   7   8   9   5   6   7   8   9
___ ___ ___ ___ ___ ___ ___ ___ ___
```

Step 20: Higher decade addition. The purpose of this skill is to enable the child to add one-digit numbers to two-digit numbers mentally. It is a skill needed in order to become proficient in column addition. It is also useful in multiplication carrying. Basically it is a counting skill made automatic by much practice. Such exercises include the following kinds of additions in which we demonstrate how the fundamental addition facts relate to higher decade addition:

3	13	23	33		7	47	67	87
4	4	4	4		2	2	2	2
7	17	27	37		9	49	69	89

4	14	24	34		6	36	56	76
5	5	5	5		3	3	3	3
9	19	29	39		9	39	59	79

2	12	22	32		3	13	43	93
8	8	8	8		5	5	5	5
10	20	30	40		8	18	48	98

In all such higher decade additions, the reverses should also be practiced. That is, 87 plus 2 should also be practiced with 2 plus 87.

Step 21: Bridging in higher decade addition. What is important to note in higher decade addition is that the principle of learning them is the same applied to the basic addition facts. They are to be learned so that the pupil need not unit count in his head. Obviously, the key to proficient higher decade addition is a flawless, automatic knowledge of the basic addition facts. The skill of "bridging," that is adding mentally from one decade to the next as in 28 + 7 = 35, is more difficult for the child to master, but it can be done if taught systematically. Since higher decade addition should be learned as an automatic skill, an understanding of place value at this point is not necessary. The two-digit numbers are being used as single hieroglyphics designating specific quantities to which are added one-digit numbers designating specific quantities. In other words, the place value meaning of the two-digit number is irrelevant in this sort of adding. The verbal number and the recurring verbal and visual patterns in the higher decades are the keys to this kind of addition.

Place value only becomes a matter of importance when the child must start carrying when performing computation with two or more two-digit numbers. When we look at, say, the number 24 as a simple hieroglyphic, we see it as simply representing twenty-four single units. If we see it in terms of place value, we see it as 2 tens and 4 ones. It is easier to understand the process of carrying when we see the number in terms of place value. But in automatic counting, place value is only a help in that it provides certain visual and verbal number patterns which serve as effective aids to memory. But there is more to 24 than the fact that it is made up of 2 tens and 4 ones. It is also made up of two dozen, six fours, four sixes, three eights, eight threes. Thus, the place value meaning of 24 should be stressed when it is relevant to the arithmetic problem at hand.

Here are the addition exercises to teach bridging in higher decade addition:

9	19	29	39	49	59	69	79	89
2	2	2	2	2	2	2	2	2
11	21	31	41	51	61	71	81	91

8	18	28	38	48	58	68	78	88
3	3	3	3	3	3	3	3	3
11	21	31	41	51	61	71	81	91

7	17	27	37	47	57	67	77	87
4	4	4	4	4	4	4	4	4
11	21	31	41	51	61	71	81	91

6	16	26	36	46	56	66	76	86
5	5	5	5	5	5	5	5	5
11	21	31	41	51	61	71	81	91

5	15	25	35	45	55	65	75	85
6	6	6	6	6	6	6	6	6
11	21	31	41	51	61	71	81	91

4	14	24	34	44	54	64	74	84
7	7	7	7	7	7	7	7	7
11	21	31	41	51	61	71	81	91

| 3 | 13 | 23 | 33 | 43 | 53 | 63 | 73 | 83 |
8	8	8	8	8	8	8	8	8
11	21	31	41	51	61	71	81	91

| 2 | 12 | 22 | 32 | 42 | 52 | 62 | 72 | 82 |
9	9	9	9	9	9	9	9	9
11	21	31	41	51	61	71	81	91

| 9 | 19 | 29 | 39 | 49 | 59 | 69 | 79 | 89 |
3	3	3	3	3	3	3	3	3
12	22	32	42	52	62	72	82	92

| 8 | 18 | 28 | 38 | 48 | 58 | 68 | 78 | 88 |
4	4	4	4	4	4	4	4	4
12	22	32	42	52	62	72	82	92

| 7 | 17 | 27 | 37 | 47 | 57 | 67 | 77 | 87 |
5	5	5	5	5	5	5	5	5
12	22	32	42	52	62	72	82	92

| 6 | 16 | 26 | 36 | 46 | 56 | 66 | 76 | 86 |
6	6	6	6	6	6	6	6	6
12	22	32	42	52	62	72	82	92

| 5 | 15 | 25 | 35 | 45 | 55 | 65 | 75 | 85 |
7	7	7	7	7	7	7	7	7
12	22	32	42	52	62	72	82	92

| 4 | 14 | 24 | 34 | 44 | 54 | 64 | 74 | 84 |
8	8	8	8	8	8	8	8	8
12	22	32	42	52	62	72	82	92

3	13	23	33	43	53	63	73	83
9	9	9	9	9	9	9	9	9
12	22	32	42	52	62	72	82	92

9	19	29	39	49	59	69	79	89
4	4	4	4	4	4	4	4	4
13	23	33	43	53	63	73	83	93

8	18	28	38	48	58	68	78	88
5	5	5	5	5	5	5	5	5
13	23	33	43	53	63	73	83	93

7	17	27	37	47	57	67	77	87
6	6	6	6	6	6	6	6	6
13	23	33	43	53	63	73	83	93

6	16	26	36	46	56	66	76	86
7	7	7	7	7	7	7	7	7
13	23	33	43	53	63	73	83	93

5	15	25	35	45	55	65	75	85
8	8	8	8	8	8	8	8	8
13	23	33	43	53	63	73	83	93

4	14	24	34	44	54	64	74	84
9	9	9	9	9	9	9	9	9
13	23	33	43	53	63	73	83	93

9	19	29	39	49	59	69	79	89
5	5	5	5	5	5	5	5	5
14	24	34	44	54	64	74	84	94

$$
\begin{array}{ccccccccc}
8 & 18 & 28 & 38 & 48 & 58 & 68 & 78 & 88 \\
\underline{6} & \underline{6} & \underline{6} & \underline{6} & \underline{6} & \underline{6} & \underline{6} & \underline{6} & \underline{6} \\
14 & 24 & 34 & 44 & 54 & 64 & 74 & 84 & 94
\end{array}
$$

$$
\begin{array}{ccccccccc}
7 & 17 & 27 & 37 & 47 & 57 & 67 & 77 & 87 \\
\underline{7} & \underline{7} & \underline{7} & \underline{7} & \underline{7} & \underline{7} & \underline{7} & \underline{7} & \underline{7} \\
14 & 24 & 34 & 44 & 54 & 64 & 74 & 84 & 94
\end{array}
$$

$$
\begin{array}{ccccccccc}
6 & 16 & 26 & 36 & 46 & 56 & 66 & 76 & 86 \\
\underline{8} & \underline{8} & \underline{8} & \underline{8} & \underline{8} & \underline{8} & \underline{8} & \underline{8} & \underline{8} \\
14 & 24 & 34 & 44 & 54 & 64 & 74 & 84 & 94
\end{array}
$$

$$
\begin{array}{ccccccccc}
5 & 15 & 25 & 35 & 45 & 55 & 65 & 75 & 85 \\
\underline{9} & \underline{9} & \underline{9} & \underline{9} & \underline{9} & \underline{9} & \underline{9} & \underline{9} & \underline{9} \\
14 & 24 & 34 & 44 & 54 & 64 & 74 & 84 & 94
\end{array}
$$

$$
\begin{array}{ccccccccc}
9 & 19 & 29 & 39 & 49 & 59 & 69 & 79 & 89 \\
\underline{6} & \underline{6} & \underline{6} & \underline{6} & \underline{6} & \underline{6} & \underline{6} & \underline{6} & \underline{6} \\
15 & 25 & 35 & 45 & 55 & 65 & 75 & 85 & 95
\end{array}
$$

$$
\begin{array}{ccccccccc}
8 & 18 & 28 & 38 & 48 & 58 & 68 & 78 & 88 \\
\underline{7} & \underline{7} & \underline{7} & \underline{7} & \underline{7} & \underline{7} & \underline{7} & \underline{7} & \underline{7} \\
15 & 25 & 35 & 45 & 55 & 65 & 75 & 85 & 95
\end{array}
$$

$$
\begin{array}{ccccccccc}
7 & 17 & 27 & 37 & 47 & 57 & 67 & 77 & 87 \\
\underline{8} & \underline{8} & \underline{8} & \underline{8} & \underline{8} & \underline{8} & \underline{8} & \underline{8} & \underline{8} \\
15 & 25 & 35 & 45 & 55 & 65 & 75 & 85 & 95
\end{array}
$$

$$
\begin{array}{ccccccccc}
6 & 16 & 26 & 36 & 46 & 56 & 66 & 76 & 86 \\
\underline{9} & \underline{9} & \underline{9} & \underline{9} & \underline{9} & \underline{9} & \underline{9} & \underline{9} & \underline{9} \\
15 & 25 & 35 & 45 & 55 & 65 & 75 & 85 & 95
\end{array}
$$

9	19	29	39	49	59	69	79	89
7	7	7	7	7	7	7	7	7
16	26	36	46	56	66	76	86	96

8	18	28	38	48	58	68	78	88
8	8	8	8	8	8	8	8	8
16	26	36	46	56	66	76	86	96

7	17	27	37	47	57	67	77	87
9	9	9	9	9	9	9	9	9
16	26	36	46	56	66	76	86	96

9	19	29	39	49	59	69	79	89
8	8	8	8	8	8	8	8	8
17	27	37	47	57	67	77	87	97

8	18	28	38	48	58	68	78	88
9	9	9	9	9	9	9	9	9
17	27	37	47	57	67	77	87	97

9	19	29	39	49	59	69	79	89
9	9	9	9	9	9	9	9	9
18	28	38	48	58	68	78	88	98

After the pupil becomes familiar with these bridging patterns and sees the relationship between 9 plus 8 and 79 plus 8, you can arrange these additions in another pattern to aid memorization as in the following sample:

9	9	9	9	9	9	9	9
2	3	4	5	6	7	8	9
11	12	13	14	15	16	17	18

19	19	19	19	19	19	19	19
2	3	4	5	6	7	8	9
21	22	23	24	25	26	27	28

```
29    29    29    29    29    29    29    29
 2     3     4     5     6     7     8     9
───   ───   ───   ───   ───   ───   ───   ───
31    32    33    34    35    36    37    38


39    39    39    39    39    39    39    39
 2     3     4     5     6     7     8     9
───   ───   ───   ───   ───   ───   ───   ───
41    42    43    44    45    46    47    48
```

All these bridging additions should be studied and practiced in the context of the patterns so that the child forms in his mind the necessary number pattern aids to memory. Then you can flash random bridging additions on cards to see how well the pupil can perform them mentally. If there is much hesitation or obvious unit counting, find out which combinations cause the most trouble and practice them until the pupil can add them without difficulty. Mastery will require much practice, but mastery has its rewards. The child gains confidence in himself and in his ability to learn and use arithmetic. Memorization is the easiest form of learning, and arithmetic is basically a memorization system. The key aids to the use of the fundamental addition facts in higher decade addition are the recurring verbal and visual patterns. If more time is given to the more difficult combinations, they will be learned as thoroughly as the easier ones.

After the pupil has had sufficient practice in higher decade addition and bridging, give him sufficient column addition to put his skill to work. The tutor can prepare column additions which start off easy and get progressively more difficult, as in the following examples:

Higher decade combinations in the teens:

```
2     3     2     2     2     6     5     3     3
3     3     4     1     2     1     2     5     6
5     5     5     8     7     3     6     7     4
5     8     5     2     1     6     4     3     4
─     ─     ─     ─     ─     ─     ─     ─     ─
```

```
2   2   2   1   8   5   6   4   2
6   8   1   3   1   4   3   4   3
3   1   8   6   2   8   6   8   7
5   8   4   3   7   1   3   1   2
```

```
3   3   1   7   5   4   1   5   4
1   3   4   2   1   5   6   2   3
7   8   5   4   5   7   3   9   7
2   1   4   5   4   2   9   2   2
```

Higher decade combinations in the twenties:

```
8   2   7   9   6   5   7   8   6
2   8   8   3   6   5   4   3   8
5   4   2   3   6   5   6   9   2
8   9   4   6   3   8   7   5   5
```

```
7   8   5   7   6   4   6   5   9
3   1   6   8   7   6   5   7   8
9   7   2   2   6   9   7   7   3
2   6   7   8   7   4   6   1   9
```

```
7   8   4   6   4   4   3   9   6
7   8   6   4   9   8   9   6   9
3   3   8   4   1   2   6   3   3
6   8   7   7   8   6   2   9   4
```

Higher decade combinations in the twenties with five numbers:

8	9	6	7	9	8	4	7	5
4	2	6	4	6	3	7	7	8
3	5	7	2	2	1	7	3	1
7	4	4	9	9	6	7	3	8
3	8	2	5	3	2	2	6	4

3	8	6	8	3	7	9	5	9
7	3	5	3	2	6	9	4	8
2	8	7	1	9	3	1	6	2
8	3	3	9	7	8	6	5	5
4	3	4	6	6	3	3	8	2

7	8	4	6	4	4	9	4	8
7	8	6	4	9	8	3	8	7
3	3	8	4	1	2	1	5	1
6	8	7	7	8	6	8	6	3
2	1	3	2	6	5	7	4	9

More addition columns can be prepared by the tutor for the practice of higher decade additions, including some into the thirties.

Step 22: Place value. With the child now ready to start adding more than one two-digit number, we can introduce him to place value in order to give him an understanding of how these additions are performed. First point out how the number 10 was created by the addition of ten ones. Demonstrate how the ones can be added in column form. Then show how 20, 30, 40, 50, 60, 70, 80, 90, and 100 are created by the additions of 10s in the same way:

```
1
1
1
1
1
1
1
1
1
1
‾‾
10   10   10   10   10   10   10   10   10   10
     10   10   10   10   10   10   10   10   10
     ‾‾   10   10   10   10   10   10   10   10
     20   10   10   10   10   10   10   10   10
          ‾‾   10   10   10   10   10   10   10
          30   10   10   10   10   10   10   10
               ‾‾   10   10   10   10   10   10
               40   10   10   10   10   10   10
                    ‾‾   10   10   10   10   10
                    50   10   10   10   10   10
                         ‾‾   10   10   10   10
                         60   10   10   10   10
                              ‾‾   10   10   10
                              70   10   10   10
                                   ‾‾   10   10
                                   80   10   10
                                        ‾‾   10
                                        90   10
                                             ‾‾
                                             100
```

Explain that in a two-digit number, the digit on the right represents the ones or units column, while the digit on the left represents the tens column. Thus, the number 10 indicates that there are no ones and one ten. The number 20 indicates no ones and two tens, and so on. The number 12 indicates two ones and one ten. Give the child random two-digit numbers and see if he can identify how many ones and how many tens each digit stands for. Thus, in our decimal place-value system, each number of two digits tells us how many tens and ones it is made up of. This information is a built-in feature of our numbering system.

Then explain how in a three-digit number like 100, the third digit to the left stands for hundreds. Have the pupil read the following three-digit numbers and explain how many ones, tens, and hundreds each number has:

125   206   333   490   521   685   709   820   999

To further demonstrate the place-value concept and how we add numbers in place-value columns, show how the above three-digit numbers can be written out in the form of column additions as follows:

5		3		1	5			9
20	6	30	90	_0	80	9	20	90
100	200	300	400	ͻ00	600	700	800	900
125	206	333	490	521	685	709	820	999

Explain that in our arithmetic system we add each column starting at the right and proceeding to the left.

Step 23: Give the pupil simple two- and three-digit combinations to add in which no column adds up to more than nine, as in the following sample:

13	21	74	52	60	25	44	53	40	27
12	18	23	25	28	24	11	26	22	61

49	120	302	625	550	921	256	137	471	765
50	142	140	321	42	33	103	601	404	233

Step 24: Carrying. If in adding combinations of two-digit numbers the sum of the tens column is over nine, we put down the ones digit of the sum in the ones column and "carry" to the tens column the tens digit. Then we add up the tens column to get its sum. For example:

		1	1
	12	12	12
	19	19	19
		1	31

		1	1
	11	11	11
	19	19	19
		0	30

Give the pupil carrying exercises with the additions below. You can devise as many as you need for practice purposes.

```
19    18    37    26    18    27    26    29    37
21    32    23    54    23    35    47    65    28
```

```
            38    49    19
            58    18    39
```

In this next group, the sums are over 100:

```
85    66    96    82    75    87    53    84    63
36    76    88    18    26    74    69    99    67
```

```
            99    57
            99    88
```

Step 25: Adding three-digit numbers with no carrying. The columns are added from right to left.

```
123   202   333   420   511   433   683   770   856   284
405   141   333   419   238   542   205   217   143   603
```

Step 26: Adding three-digit numbers with carrying in the tens column. Explain each step.

```
        1        1        1
119     119      119      119
 24      24       24       24
                   3       43      143
```

```
  1        1        1        1
119      119      119      119
124      124      124      124
                    3       43      243
```

Have the pupil practice with these additions and others you may devise:

238	427	209	109	336	288	175	637	288	347
142	534	609	208	424	607	315	236	409	235

Step 27: Adding three-digit numbers with carrying in the hundreds column. Explain each step:

```
                  1      1
191    191      191    191
191    191      191    191
       ___      ___    ___
         2       82    382
```

```
                  1      1
170    170      170    170
462    462      462    462
       ___      ___    ___
         2       32    632
```

Have the pupil practice with these additions below. Note that the sum of the tens column is less than ten.

284	373	365	457	571	563	222	775	286	620
194	184	362	352	336	282	192	164	182	294

Step 28: Adding three-digit numbers with carrying in the tens and hundreds columns. Explain each step:

```
                  1     11     11
199    199      199    199
123    123      123    123
       ___      ___    ___
         2       22    322
```

```
            1        11       11
185        185      185      185
115        115      115      115
          ─────    ─────    ─────
            0        00      300
```

Have the pupil practice with the following additions, to which can be added more. Make sure that the pupil places the carried digit on top of the proper column and writes it as legibly but not as large as the other digits in the numbers. The purpose of this is to distinguish the carried numbers from the addends, that is, the numbers being added.

```
166      167      158      383      298
266      177      468      417      289


256      375      296      488
465      457      147      152
```

Step 29: Adding three-digit numbers with carrying in the tens and hundreds columns adding up to sums over 999. Explain each step.

```
            1        11       11
899        899      899      899
101        101      101      101
          ─────    ─────    ──────
            0        00      1000
```

Explain that in a four-digit number, the fourth digit to the left is the thousands column. Have the pupil practice with these additions:

```
956   874   548   832   639   751   388   473   927   654
655   357   453   878   363   659   756   847   996   889
```

Step 30: Subtraction with two-digit numbers in which borrowing is not needed. Provide more practice with additional combinations if needed:

```
53    64    79    85    78    99
-21   -43   -45   -32   -50   -75
```

```
86    47    57    69    71
-61   -35   -43   -21   -40
```

Step 31: Subtraction terms.

```
 28    minuend (the sum subtracted from)
-13    subtractor (the amount subtracted)
 15    remainder (what's left)
```

In some textbooks the *subtractor* is called the *subtrahend* and the *remainder* is referred to as the *difference*.

Step 32: Borrowing in subtraction. The method used in this instruction is known by three different names: the take-away-carry method, the method of equal additions, or the borrow-and-pay-back method. It's most accurate description is as the method of equal additions. Thus, when the "ones" digit in the minuend is lower than the "ones" digit in the subtractor, we add ten to the "ones" digit in the minuend and one to the "tens" digit in the subtractor. Over the centuries this adding process has come to be known as "borrowing." The operation works as follows:

1. We start with this subtraction problem.

```
 72
-26
```

2. We "borrow" ten and add it to the 2 in the minuend. This makes it 12. We then subtract 6 from 12. We write the remainder of 6 under the "ones" column.

$$
\begin{array}{r}
7^12 \\
-2\ 6 \\
\hline
6
\end{array}
$$

3. But we must also add ten to the "tens" digit of the subtractor. We do this by adding 1, remembering that the digits in the "tens" column represent multiples of ten.

$$
\begin{array}{r}
7^12 \\
-^12\ 6 \\
\hline
6
\end{array}
$$

4. Now we subtract 3 from 7 leaving us 4. The answer to the subtraction problem is 46.

$$
\begin{array}{r}
7^12 \\
-^12\ 6 \\
\hline
4\ 6
\end{array}
$$

5. To check our subtraction, we add the subtractor and the remainder, which give us the minuend.

$$
\begin{array}{r}
26 \\
46 \\
\hline
72
\end{array}
$$

In expanded form, the equal adding or "borrowing" process can be demonstrated as follows:

1. $\begin{array}{r} 72 \\ -26 \\ \hline \end{array}$

2. $\begin{array}{cc} 70 & 2 \\ 20 & 6 \end{array}$

3. $\begin{array}{cc} 70 & 2 + 10 \\ \underline{10 + 20} & \underline{6} \end{array}$

4. $\begin{array}{cc} 70 & 12 \\ -30 & -\ 6 \\ \hline 40 & 6 \end{array}$

5. $40 + 6 = 46$

In teaching the technique of equal additions or "borrowing," it is important to use terms which the child can understand so that he can easily recall what must be done. For this reason many teachers have used the terms "borrow and pay back" to describe the procedure. Children seem to take to it (even though it is technically inaccurate) because it reminds children that the borrowing process requires two actions: adding to the "ones" digit in the minuend and to the "tens" digit in the subtrator. A common error in subtraction is forgetting to add one to the "tens" digit in the subtractor. Thus, when the teacher refers to the operation as "borrowing" and "paying back" the child remembers that it is a two-step operation.

In this regard it is wise to get the child in the habit of performing the "borrowing" and the "paying back" in automatic sequence so that the second addition is not forgotten. Showing the child how the process works in the expanded form will help him retain the equal adding principle in his mind. If the child can understand the idea of subtraction by equal adding as demonstrated in the expanded form, you can refer to the process as "equal adding" rather than "borrowing and paying back." In this instance, an intellectual understanding of the process may be a much better way of helping the child master subtraction than rote memory.

Step 33: Have the child practice the technique of equal adding in these subtractions.

$$
\begin{array}{cccccc}
92 & 64 & 60 & 75 & 88 & 96 \\
-34 & -27 & -35 & -59 & -59 & -48 \\
\end{array}
$$

$$
\begin{array}{ccccc}
73 & 52 & 80 & 66 & 77 \\
-46 & -18 & -67 & -37 & -38 \\
\end{array}
$$

Step 34: Equal adding in subtractions in which the minuend is a three-digit number and the subtractor a two-digit number. Explain to the pupil that the zero in the hundreds column of the subtractor is invisible.

$$
\begin{array}{cccccc}
194 & 262 & 460 & 375 & 688 & 496 \\
-67 & -56 & -49 & -38 & -69 & -38 \\
\end{array}
$$

$$
\begin{array}{ccccc}
873 & 152 & 380 & 266 & 477 \\
-47 & -35 & -42 & -59 & -68 \\
\end{array}
$$

Step 35: Subtractions with three-digit numbers without equal adding or "borrowing."

```
 684      795      982      588      827
-362     -674     -871     -425     -605


          757      926      498      629
         -423     -604     -320     -413
```

Step 36: Subtractions with three-digit numbers with equal adding or "borrowing" in the "ones," "tens," and "hundreds" columns. The subtraction is performed in the following steps:

1.
```
 621          6 2 1
-267         -2 6 7
```

2.
```
 621          6 2 1①      add 10 here
-267         -2 ⑥ 7      add 1 here
```

3.
```
 621          6 2¹1
-267         -2¹6 7       subtract 7 from 11
  4              4
```

4.
```
 621          6⑫2¹1      add 10 here
-267         ⑫¹6 7       add 1 here
  4              4
```

5.
```
 621          6¹2¹1
-267         ¹2¹6 7       subtract 7 from 12
 54            5 4
```

6.
```
 621          6¹2¹1
-267         -¹2¹6 7      subtract 3 from 6
354           3 5 4
```

7.   267
       354
      621   checking the subtraction

Step 37: Subtraction exercises with three-digit numbers requiring equal adding. Help the child where he may have difficulty subtracting with zeros.

523	604	830	946	712	657
-298	-387	-266	-377	-475	-289

750	822	905	574	631
-253	-366	-306	-196	-258

Step 38: Multiplication. Explain to the pupil that multiplication is a short way of adding a lot of the same numbers. For example, in addition we write:

$$2 + 2 + 2 + 2 + 2 = 10$$

In multiplication we write the same thing as:

$$5 \times 2 = 10$$

We use the X to signify multiplication. Here's another example. In addition we write:

$$4 + 4 + 4 + 4 = 16$$

In multiplication we write the same thing as:

$$4 \times 4 = 16$$

Explain that multiplication saves us a lot of time. It is a very useful way of solving many simple problems. Supposing you had six boxes of pencils in which there were six pencils to each box and you wanted to know how many pencils you had altogether. You could add up six sixes in this way:

$$
\begin{array}{r}
6 \\
6 \\
6 \\
6 \\
6 \\
\underline{6} \\
36
\end{array}
$$

Or you could multiply 6 x 6 to get the same answer. The multiplication table gives us the answers to all multiplications with two numbers up to 12. The reason why we go as high as 12 is because 12 is a very common number in our measurement systems. There are 12 months to a year, 12 in a dozen, 12 inches to a foot.

Step 39: The multiplication table. There are a number of ways of learning the multiplication facts. One way to do it is to learn to count by twos, threes, fours, etc. Twos, fives, and tens are the easiest. Once they are learned, start the child learning to count by threes, fours, sixes, sevens, eights, and nines in conjunction with the learning of the multiplication facts. Save elevens and twelves until the pupil has fully mastered the multiplications through nine. Elevens and twelves are not that often used. Thus the child can learn to count by elevens to the ninth place and twelves to the eighth place, which is more than he will ever need in daily use. The multiplication table is an excellent guide to counting by numbers 2 through 12:

1	2	3	4	5	6	7	8	9	10	11	12
2	4	6	8	10	12	14	16	18	20	22	24
3	6	9	12	15	18	21	24	27	30	33	36
4	8	12	16	20	24	28	32	36	40	44	48
5	10	15	20	25	30	35	40	45	50	55	60
6	12	18	24	30	36	42	48	54	60	66	72
7	14	21	28	35	42	49	56	63	70	77	84
8	16	24	32	40	48	56	64	72	80	88	96
9	18	27	36	45	54	63	72	81	90	99	108
10	20	30	40	50	60	70	80	90	100	110	120
11	22	33	44	55	66	77	88	99	110	121	132
12	24	36	48	60	72	84	96	108	120	132	144

Step 40: The multiplication facts. The multiplication facts can be taught in equation or column form. For the purpose of verbal memorization, the equation is the better form in that it is easier to "read" rhetorically. Therefore, in teaching the child to memorize the multiplication facts we suggest using such sentences as "two times two is four; two times three is six." Some teachers prefer to say "two twos are four" or "three sixes are eighteen." This is perfectly good form except that it gives a more additive connotation to the process. By using the word "times" the idea of multiplication as distinct from addition is conveyed. Actually, multiplication is merely the memorization of multiple arithmetic facts or counting by numbers over one. The tutor should bear this in mind when teaching a child who is having dif-

ficulty grasping the concept of multiplication—which is really the concept of multiples, or specific quantities counted forward in multiples. Division, on the other hand, deals with specific quantities counted backward in multiples.

The multiplication facts are memorized rhetorically in two ways, either in such sentences as "two times two is four" or in counting as "two, four, six, eight," etc. If both methods are used, the child will have his mastery doubly reinforced. The key to addition is counting by ones. The key to multiplication is counting by numbers over one. Here are the multiplication facts in equation form. Note that we place multiplication by one at the end because some children have trouble understanding what we mean by $1 \times 1 = 1$ before they've grasped the concept of multiplication.

$2 \times 1 = 2$	$3 \times 1 = 3$	$4 \times 1 = 4$
$2 \times 2 = 4$	$3 \times 2 = 6$	$4 \times 2 = 8$
$2 \times 3 = 6$	$3 \times 3 = 9$	$4 \times 3 = 12$
$2 \times 4 = 8$	$3 \times 4 = 12$	$4 \times 4 = 16$
$2 \times 5 = 10$	$3 \times 5 = 15$	$4 \times 5 = 20$
$2 \times 6 = 12$	$3 \times 6 = 18$	$4 \times 6 = 24$
$2 \times 7 = 14$	$3 \times 7 = 21$	$4 \times 7 = 28$
$2 \times 8 = 16$	$3 \times 8 = 24$	$4 \times 8 = 32$
$2 \times 9 = 18$	$3 \times 9 = 27$	$4 \times 9 = 36$

5 x 1 = 5	6 x 1 = 6	7 x 1 = 7
5 x 2 = 10	6 x 2 = 12	7 x 2 = 14
5 x 3 = 15	6 x 3 = 18	7 x 3 = 21
5 x 4 = 20	6 x 4 = 24	7 x 4 = 28
5 x 5 = 25	6 x 5 = 30	7 x 5 = 35
5 x 6 = 30	6 x 6 = 36	7 x 6 = 42
5 x 7 = 35	6 x 7 = 42	7 x 7 = 49
5 x 8 = 40	6 x 8 = 48	7 x 8 = 56
5 x 9 = 45	6 x 9 = 54	7 x 9 = 63

8 x 1 = 8	9 x 1 = 9	1 x 1 = 1
8 x 2 = 16	9 x 2 = 18	1 x 2 = 2
8 x 3 = 24	9 x 3 = 27	1 x 3 = 3
8 x 4 = 32	9 x 4 = 36	1 x 4 = 4
8 x 5 = 40	9 x 5 = 45	1 x 5 = 5
8 x 6 = 48	9 x 6 = 54	1 x 6 = 6
8 x 7 = 56	9 x 7 = 63	1 x 7 = 7
8 x 8 = 64	9 x 8 = 72	1 x 8 = 8
8 x 9 = 72	9 x 9 = 81	1 x 9 = 9

Note that multiplying by one is really another way of counting by ones. Thus, when we say 1 x 1 = 1, etc., we are simply saying that one one is one, one two is two, one three is three. However, the child must know these multiplication-by-one facts because he will require them in multiplying numbers with more than one digit. Note how the products of multiples of three or six or nine give us the patterns of counting in these multiples. The pupil should be encouraged to memorize these multiple counting patterns as they will be extremely useful in remembering multiplication facts. Also note that any multiplication fact can be demonstrated by writing it out in addition form—in a column or equation. Thus,

$$5 \times 9 = 45$$

or

$$9 + 9 + 9 + 9 + 9 = 45$$

or

$$
\begin{array}{r}
9 \\
9 \\
9 \\
9 \\
9 \\
\hline
45
\end{array}
$$

It can also be written out as a position in a counting sequence by nines:

$$9 \quad 18 \quad 27 \quad 36 \quad 45$$

Step 41: Multiplication by zero. Since zero appears in many numbers of two or more digits, the pupil will have to know how to multiply by zero as follows:

$$0 \times 0 = 0 \qquad 0 \times 0 = 0$$

$$0 \times 1 = 0 \qquad 1 \times 0 = 0$$

$$0 \times 2 = 0 \qquad 2 \times 0 = 0$$

$$0 \times 3 = 0 \qquad 3 \times 0 = 0$$

$$0 \times 4 = 0 \qquad 4 \times 0 = 0$$

$$0 \times 5 = 0 \qquad 5 \times 0 = 0$$

$$0 \times 6 = 0 \qquad 6 \times 0 = 0$$

$$0 \times 7 = 0 \qquad 7 \times 0 = 0$$

$$0 \times 8 = 0 \qquad 8 \times 0 = 0$$

$$0 \times 9 = 0 \qquad 9 \times 0 = 0$$

You can demonstrate these equations by translating them into addition. Since zero means the absence of quantity, that is, nothing, point out that one nothing equals nothing and nine nothings still equal nothing. You can demonstrate this by writing out an equation of five zeros:

$$0 + 0 + 0 + 0 + 0 = 0$$

Point out that there are five zeros, but they all add up to zero. Point out that 0×5 is another way of saying no five, or nothing. In other words when you multiply anything by zero or multiply zeros you still get zero.

Step 42: Familiarize the pupil with the multiplication facts in column form in anticipation of his performing written multiplication problems:

$$\frac{1}{2} \quad \frac{2}{4} \quad \frac{3}{6} \quad \frac{4}{8} \quad \frac{5}{10} \quad \frac{6}{12} \quad \frac{7}{14} \quad \frac{8}{16} \quad \frac{9}{18}$$

$$\frac{1}{3} \quad \frac{2}{6} \quad \frac{3}{9} \quad \frac{4}{12} \quad \frac{5}{15} \quad \frac{6}{18} \quad \frac{7}{21} \quad \frac{8}{24} \quad \frac{9}{27}$$

$$\frac{1}{4} \quad \frac{2}{8} \quad \frac{3}{12} \quad \frac{4}{16} \quad \frac{5}{20} \quad \frac{6}{24} \quad \frac{7}{28} \quad \frac{8}{32} \quad \frac{9}{36}$$

$$\frac{1}{5} \quad \frac{2}{10} \quad \frac{3}{15} \quad \frac{4}{20} \quad \frac{5}{25} \quad \frac{6}{30} \quad \frac{7}{35} \quad \frac{8}{40} \quad \frac{9}{45}$$

$$\frac{1}{6} \quad \frac{2}{12} \quad \frac{3}{18} \quad \frac{4}{24} \quad \frac{5}{30} \quad \frac{6}{36} \quad \frac{7}{42} \quad \frac{8}{48} \quad \frac{9}{54}$$

$$\frac{1}{7} \quad \frac{2}{14} \quad \frac{3}{21} \quad \frac{4}{28} \quad \frac{5}{35} \quad \frac{6}{42} \quad \frac{7}{49} \quad \frac{8}{56} \quad \frac{9}{63}$$

$$\frac{1}{8} \quad \frac{2}{16} \quad \frac{3}{24} \quad \frac{4}{32} \quad \frac{5}{40} \quad \frac{6}{48} \quad \frac{7}{56} \quad \frac{8}{64} \quad \frac{9}{72}$$

$$\frac{1}{9} \quad \frac{2}{18} \quad \frac{3}{27} \quad \frac{4}{36} \quad \frac{5}{45} \quad \frac{6}{54} \quad \frac{7}{63} \quad \frac{8}{72} \quad \frac{9}{81}$$

$$\begin{array}{ccccccccc}
1 & 2 & 3 & 4 & 5 & 6 & 7 & 8 & 9 \\
\underline{1} & \underline{1} & \underline{1} & \underline{1} & \underline{1} & \underline{1} & \underline{1} & \underline{1} & \underline{1} \\
1 & 2 & 3 & 4 & 5 & 6 & 7 & 8 & 9
\end{array}$$

Note how graphically we see that multiplication is really a form of counting in multiples. Each line of products gives us the counting sequence of the multiplier, starting with one, which is our basic counting sequence by one, the foundation on which the entire structure of arithmetic rests.

Step 43: Multiplication terms.

$$\begin{array}{ll}
5 & \text{multiplicand} \\
\underline{2} & \text{multiplier} \\
10 & \text{product}
\end{array}$$

Step 44: Multiplication without carrying. Teach the pupil to perform these multiplications which give him practice in the multiplication facts. Point out that the digits in the multiplicand are multiplied from right to left in the same sequence that additions and subtractions are performed. You can give the pupil these multiplications as soon as he has acquired a preliminary mastery of the multiplication facts by verbal drilling and flash cards.

$$\begin{array}{cccccccccc}
11 & 21 & 31 & 41 & 51 & 61 & 71 & 81 & 91 & 12 \\
\underline{2} & \underline{2} & \underline{2} & \underline{2} & \underline{2} & \underline{2} & \underline{2} & \underline{2} & \underline{2} & \underline{2}
\end{array}$$

$$\begin{array}{cccccccccc}
22 & 32 & 42 & 52 & 62 & 72 & 82 & 92 & 13 & 23 \\
\underline{2} & \underline{2} & \underline{2} & \underline{2} & \underline{2} & \underline{2} & \underline{2} & \underline{2} & \underline{2} & \underline{2}
\end{array}$$

$$\begin{array}{cccccccccc}
33 & 43 & 53 & 63 & 73 & 83 & 93 & 14 & 24 & 34 \\
\underline{2} & \underline{2} & \underline{2} & \underline{2} & \underline{2} & \underline{2} & \underline{2} & \underline{2} & \underline{2} & \underline{2}
\end{array}$$

$$\begin{array}{cccccccccc}
44 & 54 & 64 & 74 & 84 & 94 & 40 & 50 & 60 & 70 \\
\underline{2} & \underline{2} & \underline{2} & \underline{2} & \underline{2} & \underline{2} & \underline{2} & \underline{2} & \underline{2} & \underline{2}
\end{array}$$

80	90	21	81	42	91	41	81	63	61
2	2	5	7	4	8	6	9	3	7

51	72	51	72	61	81	51	62	41	83
5	4	8	3	9	6	7	4	5	2

71	61	71	41	81	41	92	71	61	71
8	6	9	7	8	9	2	4	8	7

30	52	60	80	40	52	90	90	30	20
9	4	2	5	8	2	7	3	7	8

82	30	90	90	42	50	51	90	30	70
3	6	5	9	3	9	6	4	5	6

31	32	91	21	20	21	52	61	71	82
8	4	6	9	7	6	3	5	5	4

Step 45: Multiplication with carrying. Since carrying in multiplication is similar to carrying in addition, the pupil should have little difficulty in understanding or catching on to the process. The same place-value principles apply. For example, in adding five fifteens, we do as follows:

1.	15	2.	$\overset{2}{15}$	3.	$\overset{2}{15}$

1.
```
   15
   15
   15
   15
   15
   ──
```

2.
```
    2
   15
   15
   15
   15
   15
   ──
    5
```

3.
```
    2
   15
   15
   15
   15
   15
   ──
   75
```

In multiplying 15 x 5, we do as follows:

1.	15	2.	$\overset{2}{15}$	3.	$\overset{2}{15}$
	5		5		5
	—		—		—
			5		75

Note that we add the carried 2 to the product of the 5 x 1 in the tens column. Thus, the carrying process actually combines multiplication with addition.

Step 46: Multiplication exercises with carrying. The more difficult multiplication facts are given greater emphasis toward the end.

65	46	57	79	63	32	84	45	35
2	3	5	2	4	6	2	4	3

43	32	22	26	27	25	22	43	26
5	2	8	3	5	7	9	6	4

28	46	47	53	52	96	74	28	53
3	4	2	5	4	2	3	5	8

45	35	49	28	54	35	37	23	96
6	3	5	2	7	9	4	7	3

67	42	89	24	37	29	28	19	62
5	9	4	8	4	7	5	3	8

46	35	27	62	38	62	46	17	37
2	9	3	4	2	9	6	8	5

35 × 8	18 × 4	49 × 5	68 × 7	59 × 6	84 × 3	74 × 9	57 × 2	87 × 6
16 × 5	84 × 8	49 × 4	91 × 9	35 × 3	19 × 2	37 × 7	57 × 7	59 × 4
98 × 9	72 × 6	69 × 3	95 × 5	79 × 8	84 × 8	68 × 6	48 × 3	97 × 9
79 × 7	74 × 4	86 × 7	79 × 6	48 × 9	69 × 8	93 × 3	98 × 4	34 × 7
73 × 8	36 × 9	43 × 6	63 × 4	76 × 3	43 × 3	39 × 8	93 × 7	67 × 6
74 × 7	97 × 3	98 × 6	73 × 4	43 × 6	48 × 8	73 × 9	48 × 9	76 × 8

It is important to become aware of the pupil's working habits as he performs these multiplications. See which ones he performs easily and those that give him trouble. At the heart of any difficulty will probably be a weakness in the more difficult multiplication or addition facts. The remedy is to go back to the facts and drill them more thoroughly. Children pick up poor arithmetic habits as a result of their trying to overcome weaknesses in their knowledge of the basic facts when trying to solve difficult problems. The problem of 44 x 2 is, in essence, actually no more difficult than 99 x 7. The difficulty of the latter lies in the fact that we don't bother to put the same effort in learning to count by nines that we do in learning to count by ones and twos. Thus, we may go through life having trouble multiplying with nines because we were not given enough drill with nines in the primary grades to give us the kind of automatic knowledge which makes arithmetic as effortless as possible. Therefore, we suggest that more time be spent on automatizing arithmetic knowledge than performing problems of no consequence. The problems should be given as tests of knowledge, not as means of reinforcing bad arithmetic habits. Therefore it is much more important to find out how a pupil performs his arithmetic problems than merely to check for correct answers. If a correct answer is arrived at by way of tortuous unit-counting, it should alert us to the remedial work which should be done at this stage of learning.

Step 47: Division. Just as multiplication is a form of counting forward in multiples, division is basically counting backward in multiples. We start with a maximum quantity which we reduce by a divisor to a single smaller multiple. For example, if you want to divide a box of 250 oranges among five people, you divide 250 by 5, giving each fifty. In other words, the 250 has been divided into multiples of fifty. We apply a reverse knowledge of the multiplication facts to achieve the answer. We know that $5 \times 5 = 25$. In reverse we know that $25 \div 5 = 5$. Therefore, since our basic division facts are reverses of the multiplication facts, they should be learned together. The pupil's knowledge of his multiplication facts will help him learn the division facts. To help the child understand the practical uses of division, describe problems in which, for various reasons, quantities are divided into multiples. For example, if three children were running a lemonade stand as equal partners and took in 90 cents that day, how would they determine how much each partner had earned? They would use division to find out. When the child has grasped the idea of division, have him learn the division facts.

$2 \times 1 = 2$	$2 \div 2 = 1$	$3 \times 1 = 3$	$3 \div 3 = 1$
$2 \times 2 = 4$	$4 \div 2 = 2$	$3 \times 2 = 6$	$6 \div 3 = 2$
$2 \times 3 = 6$	$6 \div 2 = 3$	$3 \times 3 = 9$	$9 \div 3 = 3$
$2 \times 4 = 8$	$8 \div 2 = 4$	$3 \times 4 = 12$	$12 \div 3 = 4$
$2 \times 5 = 10$	$10 \div 2 = 5$	$3 \times 5 = 15$	$15 \div 3 = 5$
$2 \times 6 = 12$	$12 \div 2 = 6$	$3 \times 6 = 18$	$18 \div 3 = 6$

$2 \times 7 = 14 \quad 14 : 2 = 7$ $\qquad 3 \times 7 = 21 \quad 21 \div 3 = 7$

$2 \times 8 = 16 \quad 16 \div 2 = 8$ $\qquad 3 \times 8 = 24 \quad 24 \div 3 = 8$

$2 \times 9 = 18 \quad 18 \div 2 = 9$ $\qquad 3 \times 9 = 27 \quad 27 \div 3 = 9$

$4 \times 1 = 4 \quad 4 \div 4 = 1$ $\qquad 5 \times 1 = 5 \quad 5 \div 5 = 1$

$4 \times 2 = 8 \quad 8 \div 4 = 2$ $\qquad 5 \times 2 = 10 \quad 10 \div 5 = 2$

$4 \times 3 = 12 \quad 12 \div 4 = 3$ $\qquad 5 \times 3 = 15 \quad 15 \div 5 = 3$

$4 \times 4 = 16 \quad 16 \div 4 = 4$ $\qquad 5 \times 4 = 20 \quad 20 \div 5 = 4$

$4 \times 5 = 20 \quad 20 \div 4 = 5$ $\qquad 5 \times 5 = 25 \quad 25 \div 5 = 5$

$4 \times 6 = 24 \quad 24 \div 4 = 6$ $\qquad 5 \times 6 = 30 \quad 30 \div 5 = 6$

$4 \times 7 = 28 \quad 28 \div 4 = 7$ $\qquad 5 \times 7 = 35 \quad 35 \div 5 = 7$

$4 \times 8 = 32 \quad 32 \div 4 = 8$ $\qquad 5 \times 8 = 40 \quad 40 \div 5 = 8$

$4 \times 9 = 36 \quad 36 \div 4 = 9$ $\qquad 5 \times 9 = 45 \quad 45 \div 5 = 9$

$6 \times 1 = 6 \quad 6 \div 6 = 1$ $\qquad 7 \times 1 = 7 \quad 7 \div 7 = 1$

$6 \times 2 = 12 \quad 12 \div 6 = 2$ $\qquad 7 \times 2 = 14 \quad 14 \div 7 = 2$

$6 \times 3 = 18 \quad 18 \div 6 = 3$ $\qquad 7 \times 3 = 21 \quad 21 \div 7 = 3$

$6 \times 4 = 24 \quad 24 \div 6 = 4$ $\qquad 7 \times 4 = 28 \quad 28 \div 7 = 4$

$6 \times 5 = 30 \quad 30 \div 6 = 5$ $\qquad 7 \times 5 = 35 \quad 35 \div 7 = 5$

$6 \times 6 = 36 \quad 36 \div 6 = 6$ $\qquad 7 \times 6 = 42 \quad 42 \div 7 = 6$

$6 \times 7 = 42 \quad 42 \div 6 = 7$ $\qquad 7 \times 7 = 49 \quad 49 \div 7 = 7$

6 x 8 = 48	48 ÷ 6 = 8	7 x 8 = 56	56 ÷ 7 = 8
6 x 9 = 54	54 ÷ 6 = 9	7 x 9 = 63	63 ÷ 7 = 9

8 x 1 = 8	8 ÷ 8 = 1	9 x 1 = 9	9 ÷ 9 = 1
8 x 2 = 16	16 ÷ 8 = 2	9 x 2 = 18	18 ÷ 9 = 2
8 x 3 = 24	24 ÷ 8 = 3	9 x 3 = 27	27 ÷ 9 = 3
8 x 4 = 32	32 ÷ 8 = 4	9 x 4 = 36	36 ÷ 9 = 4
8 x 5 = 40	40 ÷ 8 = 5	9 x 5 = 45	45 ÷ 9 = 5
8 x 6 = 48	48 ÷ 8 = 6	9 x 6 = 54	54 ÷ 9 = 6
8 x 7 = 56	56 ÷ 8 = 7	9 x 7 = 63	63 ÷ 9 = 7
8 x 8 = 64	64 ÷ 8 = 8	9 x 8 = 72	72 ÷ 9 = 8
8 x 9 = 72	72 ÷ 8 = 9	9 x 9 = 81	81 ÷ 9 = 9

Step 48: Division terms. The most important fact in any division problem is the quantity or number you start with—the *dividend,* or that which is to be divided. The Latin word *dividere,* from which we derive our term division, means to separate, divide, distribute. In arithmetic it means to separate into equal parts by a *divisor.* Thus, in division we start with a quantity which is to be divided or distributed into equal parts or multiples by a *divisor.* Since not all numbers or quantities can be divided into equal parts, we may have a few units left over. For example, 252 oranges divided among 5 people gives us 50 oranges each with 2 left over. In division we call the 50 the *quotient* and the 2 left over the *remainder.* This is not to be confused with the remainder in subtraction, which is also called the difference in order to avoid confusing it with the remainder in division.

Step 49: Division skills should be developed through sets of exercises which become progressively more complex. We start with a review of the primary division facts, proceeding into exercises with one-digit divisors but two- and three-digit quotients without carrying.

$4\overline{)32}$ $2\overline{)18}$ $3\overline{)27}$ $4\overline{)24}$ $5\overline{)35}$ $7\overline{)49}$ $8\overline{)56}$

$6\overline{)48}$ $9\overline{)72}$ $8\overline{)64}$ $9\overline{)63}$ $8\overline{)72}$ $4\overline{)88}$ $3\overline{)69}$

$7\overline{)357}$ $6\overline{)486}$ $9\overline{)549}$ $3\overline{)216}$ $8\overline{)408}$ $2\overline{)148}$ $4\overline{)248}$

$5\overline{)205}$ $7\overline{)427}$ $5\overline{)255}$ $3\overline{)189}$ $9\overline{)729}$ $6\overline{)246}$ $8\overline{)728}$

$4\overline{)168}$ $7\overline{)567}$ $5\overline{)105}$ $3\overline{)156}$ $5\overline{)305}$ $6\overline{)126}$ $7\overline{)147}$

$9\overline{)189}$ $6\overline{)546}$ $4\overline{)128}$ $8\overline{)248}$ $6\overline{)426}$ $5\overline{)155}$ $4\overline{)364}$

$6\overline{)306}$ $9\overline{)459}$ $3\overline{)126}$ $9\overline{)819}$ $5\overline{)455}$ $6\overline{)186}$ $3\overline{)246}$

$8\overline{)168}$ $7\overline{)217}$ $3\overline{)273}$ $7\overline{)637}$ $2\overline{)104}$ $8\overline{)328}$ $5\overline{)405}$

$2\overline{)122}$ $4\overline{)208}$ $9\overline{)279}$ $7\overline{)497}$ $8\overline{)488}$ $4\overline{)284}$ $2\overline{)184}$

$9\overline{)369}$ $8\overline{)648}$ $7\overline{)287}$ $9\overline{)639}$ $8\overline{)568}$ $4\overline{)328}$ $5\overline{)355}$

Step 50: Primary division facts with remainders. Explain to the pupil that it is not always possible to divide a number evenly. Go back to the lemonade stand example and ask how much would each partner have gotten if they had earned only 29 cents instead of 90. We divide 29 by 3 to find out:

1. $3\overline{)29}$

2. To divide 29 by 3 we look for the number closest to 29, but not higher than 29 that can be divided by 3—or that 3 "goes into." That number is 27. Thirty obviously is too high. So we write 9 as the quotient, multiply it by the divisor—3. This gives us the dividend closest to 29 which can be evenly divided into three multiples. We write that dividend under the original dividend of 29, thus:

$$\begin{array}{r} 9 \\ 3\overline{)29} \\ 27 \end{array}$$

3. Then we subtract 27 from 29, which gives us the remainder, or how much extra is left over:

$$\begin{array}{r} 9 \\ 3\overline{)29} \\ \underline{27} \\ 2 \end{array}$$

To check division we multiply the quotient by the divisor and add the remainder. This gives us the dividend.

What do the partners do with the extra 2 cents? Perhaps some candy shop might sell them something which they can then divide into three parts.

Here are a series of division exercises with remainders. Some children will have difficulty finding the right divisible number into which the divisor can go. Let the child refer to the division table for help if necessary. If he has learned to count by numbers over two, this knowledge will be useful in finding the closest divisible number. Have the pupil write out the full process and check each division answer.

2)5̄	2)7̄	2)9̄	2)1̄1̄	2)1̄5̄	2)1̄7̄	2)1̄9̄
3)7̄	3)1̄0̄	3)1̄3̄	3)1̄9̄	3)2̄2̄	3)2̄5̄	3)2̄9̄
4)6̄	4)9̄	4)1̄5̄	4)2̄1̄	4)2̄7̄	4)3̄0̄	4)3̄9̄
5)1̄3̄	5)2̄2̄	5)3̄1̄	5)3̄7̄	5)3̄9̄	5)4̄3̄	5)4̄8̄
6)1̄5̄	6)1̄9̄	6)2̄1̄	6)2̄8̄	6)3̄3̄	6)3̄7̄	6)4̄0̄
6)4̄5̄	6)5̄0̄	6)5̄5̄	6)5̄7̄	6)5̄9̄		
7)1̄3̄	7)1̄6̄	7)2̄0̄	7)2̄5̄	7)3̄0̄	7)3̄4̄	7)4̄0̄
7)4̄7̄	7)5̄1̄	7)5̄5̄	7)5̄8̄	7)6̄2̄	7)6̄5̄	7)6̄8̄
8)1̄8̄	8)2̄8̄	8)3̄1̄	8)4̄4̄	8)4̄7̄	8)5̄1̄	8)5̄5̄
8)5̄8̄	8)6̄0̄	8)6̄5̄	8)6̄8̄	8)7̄0̄	8)7̄3̄	8)7̄7̄
9)1̄2̄	9)1̄7̄	9)2̄1̄	9)2̄6̄	9)3̄2̄	9)3̄5̄	9)4̄0̄
9)4̄4̄	9)4̄8̄	9)5̄2̄	9)5̄5̄	9)6̄0̄	9)6̄2̄	9)6̄5̄
9)6̄9̄	9)7̄1̄	9)7̄5̄	9)7̄9̄	9)8̄3̄	9)8̄5̄	9)8̄7̄

Step 51: Division with carrying, with and without remainders. The carrying process is performed by the process of "bringing down" as demonstrated in the examples below. An X is placed under the number brought down to indicate the bringing down process.

1. Without a remainder	1. With a remainder
3)84̄	3)89̄

2. How many 3's go into 8? Two.

$$\begin{array}{r} 2 \\ 3\overline{)84} \\ \underline{6} \\ 2 \end{array}$$

2.

$$\begin{array}{r} 2 \\ 3\overline{)89} \\ \underline{6} \\ 2 \end{array}$$

3. Bring down 4

$$\begin{array}{r} 2 \\ 3\overline{)84} \\ 6^{\times} \\ \overline{24} \end{array}$$

3. Bring down 9

$$\begin{array}{r} 2 \\ 3\overline{)89} \\ 6^{\times} \\ \overline{29} \end{array}$$

4. How many 3's go into 24? Eight.

$$\begin{array}{r} 28 \\ 3\overline{)84} \\ 6^{\times} \\ \overline{24} \\ \underline{24} \end{array}$$

4. How many 3's go into 29? Nine, with a remainder of 2.

$$\begin{array}{r} 29 \\ 3\overline{)89} \\ 6^{\times} \\ \overline{29} \\ \underline{27} \\ 2 \end{array}$$

The following exercises give practice in division facts with carrying, but without remainders:

2)56 2)74 2)138 2)156 2)178 2)194

3)78 3)81 3)195 3)234 3)258 3)297

4)76 4)96 4)268 4)296 4)356 4)392

5)95 5)135 5)190 5)245 5)315 5)420

6)156 6)198 6)264 6)396 6)444 6)594

7)196 7)252 7)315 7)406 7)553 7)679

8)256 8)352 8)472 8)544 8)696 8)784

9)351 9)477 9)585 9)702 9)774 9)891

The following exercises give practice in division with carrying and remainders. Make sure that the pupil places each figure of the quotient directly over the last figure of the partial dividend being used. A way for the pupil to keep track of the dividend digits brought down is to place a small x mark under the dividend digit as it is brought down.

3)206 7)325 5)172 2)31 6)224 4)311

8)217 4)139 9)716 3)74 6)334 7)132

9)318 5)284 6)115 2)75 3)239 8)412

$7\overline{)197}$ $3\overline{)172}$ $9\overline{)832}$ $4\overline{)50}$ $5\overline{)391}$ $6\overline{)279}$

$4\overline{)387}$ $5\overline{)473}$ $8\overline{)306}$ $2\overline{)97}$ $7\overline{)389}$ $3\overline{)40}$

$7\overline{)261}$ $9\overline{)415}$ $8\overline{)395}$ $5\overline{)63}$ $6\overline{)169}$ $8\overline{)129}$

$2\overline{)119}$ $4\overline{)225}$ $9\overline{)732}$ $2\overline{)53}$ $8\overline{)765}$ $5\overline{)116}$

Step 52: Three-digit quotients. The following practice examples require two carrying operations. Some come out even, but most have remainders. Make sure the pupil places the quotient figures in their proper position over the dividend and places a small x mark under each digit in the dividend as it is brought down. This will help him keep track of each step of the operation.

$5\overline{)933}$ $3\overline{)2810}$ $2\overline{)972}$ $6\overline{)5591}$ $8\overline{)3087}$ $4\overline{)1077}$ $9\overline{)2550}$

$2\overline{)719}$ $7\overline{)4490}$ $3\overline{)741}$ $9\overline{)6831}$ $6\overline{)1724}$ $8\overline{)1395}$ $6\overline{)2740}$

$4\overline{)734}$ $4\overline{)2299}$ $3\overline{)556}$ $7\overline{)1986}$ $5\overline{)2862}$ $7\overline{)6705}$ $9\overline{)5776}$

$2\overline{)592}$ $5\overline{)1974}$ $4\overline{)931}$ $8\overline{)2156}$ $7\overline{)4545}$ $9\overline{)7097}$ $6\overline{)5921}$

Step 53: Zeros in the quotient. Some children find it difficult to deal with zeros in the quotient. The following exercises are designed to give the child practice with handling zeros in the quotient. The rule to remember is that every time a digit in the dividend is brought down, a figure must be written in the quotient.

$$2\overline{)40} \quad 2\overline{)204} \quad 2\overline{)2004} \quad 2\overline{)41} \quad 3\overline{)62} \quad 2\overline{)410}$$

$$3\overline{)621} \quad 3\overline{)322} \quad 3\overline{)622} \quad 4\overline{)819} \quad 4\overline{)962} \quad 5\overline{)654}$$

$$6\overline{)605} \quad 7\overline{)4214} \quad 8\overline{)7265} \quad 9\overline{)8156} \quad 7\overline{)3563} \quad 6\overline{)4838}$$

$$5\overline{)1043} \quad 8\overline{)5610} \quad 9\overline{)5436} \quad 3\overline{)3232} \quad 4\overline{)3625} \quad 6\overline{)4082}$$

$$7\overline{)286} \quad 8\overline{)3841} \quad 5\overline{)901} \quad 9\overline{)187} \quad 7\overline{)3546} \quad 9\overline{)6316}$$

Note this fundamental principle: zero divided by any number equals zero. Also, no number can be divided by zero for the simple reason that something cannot be divided by nothing.

Step 54: Fractions. Children start understanding concepts of fractions quite early, as words and expressions like "a half" and "a quarter" become part of their vocabulary. But they also speak in terms of the "bigger half" and the "smaller half," which means that their understanding of fractions as a precise arithmetic concept is still lacking. An arithmetic fraction, in symbolic terms, represents one or more of the equal parts of a whole. The tutor should find out how much the child does know about fractions and then help the child to understand them in specific arithmetic terms. Since operations with fractions are not taught until the fourth grade, this primer will merely suggest a sequence of instruction leading into operations with fractions. The purpose of the instruction here is to find out how much the child already knows about fractions and to expand on that.

Since decimals are merely another way of writing fractions in place-value notation, you might teach some elementary facts about decimals, particularly in relation to money. (See Step 61.) The pupil will no doubt know by now that there are 100 cents in a dollar and that fifty cents are a half dollar and twenty-five cents are a quarter.

First, it is necessary to make sure that the child grasps the concept of a fraction—that is, a part of a whole or an aggregate. One pie can be divided into two, three, four parts, etc. A dozen eggs can be divided into a half dozen. One dollar can be divided into two halves, four quarters, ten dimes, twenty nickels, one hundred cents. Since the use of money is already in the child's experience, you might teach the fractions 1/2, 1/4, and 1/10 in relation to money. Fractions such as 1/3, 1/8, 1/5, etc., can be taught in relation to dividing up a whole pie into a number of pieces.

Fractions should also be taught in relation to line measurement: 1/2 inch, 1/4 inch, etc.; and in relation to weight: 1/2 pound, 1/4 pound; in relation to liquid measurement: 1/2 gallon, 1/2 pint; and in relation to time: half-hour, quarter-hour.

The first step is to teach the child to read fractions. Start with:

$$1/2 \quad 1/3 \quad 1/4 \quad 1/5 \quad 1/6 \quad 1/7 \quad 1/8 \quad 1/9 \quad 1/10$$

Demonstrate these fractions on the blackboard by dividing a pie or a candy bar into fractional parts. A fraction is one or more of the equal parts of a whole. We call the number above or to the left of the stroke the numerator and the number below or to the right of the stroke the denominator. The denominator tells us how many parts the whole has been divided into. It also tells us the comparative size of the parts—if we are dealing with wholes of similar size. The numerator tells us how many parts have been taken. A unit fraction, such as those above, is a fraction whose numerator is 1. The child should note from the above fractions that the larger the demoninator, the smaller the fraction. The larger the numerator, the larger the fraction. You can use blackboard drawings to demonstrate this.

It is important for the child to understand the difference between the numerator and the denominator and their relation to each other. This can be done by demonstrating that the numerator and the denominator of a fraction can be multiplied or divided by the same number without changing the value of the fraction. For example, demonstrate how 1/2 is the same as 2/4 or 5/10. But explain that we use fractions in their lowest terms by reducing 2/4 and 5/10 to 1/2. You can demonstrate this on the blackboard by dividing up a rectangle into two halves, four fourths, ten tenths, and showing how one half is the equivalent of two fourths or five tenths.

Step 55: Adding unit fractions. By teaching the child to add unit fractions we can acquaint him with other common fractions. We add fractions with the same denominators by adding the numerators only. For example:

$$1/3 + 1/3 = 2/3$$

$$1/4 + 1/4 = 2/4 = 1/2$$

Notice how in adding $1/4 + 1/4$ we reduced the $2/4$ to its lowest terms, $1/2$.

$$1/4 + 1/4 + 1/4 = 3/4$$

$$1/8 + 1/8 + 1/8 = 3/8$$

$$1/5 + 1/5 = 2/5$$

$$1/5 + 1/5 + 1/5 = 3/5$$

$$1/5 + 1/5 + 1/5 + 1/5 = 4/5$$

$$1/8 + 1/8 + 1/8 + 1/8 + 1/8 = 5/8$$

$$1/8 + 1/8 + 1/8 + 1/8 + 1/8 + 1/8 + 1/8 = 7/8$$

Adding common fractions. Show how some of the above fractions can be obtained as follows:

$$2/5 + 1/5 = 3/5$$

$$3/5 + 1/5 = 4/5$$

$$2/5 + 2/5 = 4/5$$

$$3/8 + 3/8 + 1/8 = 7/8$$

Also demonstrate the following deduced from the above, and see if the pupil can figure out what must be done to add fractions with different denominators:

$$1/2 + 1/4 = 3/4$$

$$1/4 + 1/8 = 3/8$$

$$3/8 + 1/4 = 5/8$$

$$1/2 + 3/8 = 7/8$$

Comparing fractions. Have the child compare the size of unit fractions by drawing circles on the blackboard divided into smaller and smaller unit fractions. Then have the child compare the size of 1/2 to 2/3 to 3/4, etc. These exercises will help the child learn that the larger the denominator the smaller the fraction and the larger the numerator the larger the fraction if the denominator remains the same. These exercises also teach the child to understand that when the numerator and the denominator are equal, the fraction always equals 1. For example:

$$1/2 + 1/2 = 2/2 = 1$$

$$1/3 + 1/3 + 1/3 = 3/3 = 1$$

$$1/4 + 1/4 + 1/4 + 1/4 = 4/4 = 1$$

$$1/5 + 1/5 + 1/5 + 1/5 + 1/5 = 5/5 = 1$$

Note that fractions in which the numerator exceeds the denominator equal more than one. For example: 5/4 = 1 1/4; 8/7 = 1 1/7; 9/5 = 1 4/5. A whole number (or integer) with a fraction is called a *mixed number*. A fraction in which the numerator is less than the denominator is called a *proper fraction*. A fraction in which the numerator is equal to or greater than the denominator is called an *improper fraction*.

Changing the denominator of a fraction. Comparing fractions also enables the child to discover the equivalence of fractions which have different numerators and different denominators. The child learns how common denominators are found for adding fractions with different denominators, and also how fractions are reduced to their lowest terms. For example, you can show how 6 sixths can be written with different fractions as follows:

$$1/6 + 1/6 + 1/6 + 1/6 + 1/6 + 1/6 = 6/6 = 1$$

$$2/6 \quad + \quad 1/6 \quad + \quad 3/6$$

$$1/3 \quad + \quad 1/6 \quad + \quad 1/2 \quad = \quad 6/6 = 1$$

Reducing fractions to their lowest terms. The important principle for the pupil to learn is that the numerator and the denominator of a fraction can be divided by the same number without changing the value of the fraction. In preparing exercises, use those fractions which are obtained as the result of adding or subtracting fractions. Fourths, sixths, eighths, tenths, twelfths, sixteenths, twentieths, and twenty-fourths will occur fairly often. Here are some practice examples to be reduced to their lowest terms:

4/10	5/20	8/12	14/24	4/24	12/16
4/6	2/24	10/20	6/8	8/24	4/12
4/16	3/6	8/16	10/24	2/12	4/8
14/16	18/24	16/24	9/24	6/20	4/20
12/24	16/20	6/24	2/16	8/20	14/20
10/12	15/20	4/16	10/16	6/10	5/10

Here are additional practice examples of fractions to be reduced to their lowest terms. These fractions are not as frequently encountered as those in the first group. In reducing these fractions to lowest terms the pupil can divide the numerator and denominator by two or more numbers. However, to save time the pupil should learn to divide by the largest number that he can see that will divide both the numerator and denominator:

6/15	15/48	30/48	12/15	12/30	9/48	8/64
6/48	24/32	3/18	14/64	5/30	10/25	3/9
4/18	20/32	16/48	15/18	6/9	42/48	4/14
12/18	21/30	24/64	9/15	20/25	10/18	10/15
36/64	2/14	5/25	48/64	16/32	12/32	12/14
26/30	30/32	56/64	15/25	24/30	28/32	10/14
6/18	24/48	20/64	5/15	6/14	10/30	6/32

With the completion of the above instruction the pupil should be ready to start learning to add, subtract, multiply and divide with fractions and mixed numbers. However, since these operations are beyond the scope of the primary grades, the instruction on the pages which follow has been added basically for reference purposes.

Step 56: Adding fractions with different denominators. In order to add fractions with different denominators, we must first make them have the same denominator—or a common denominator. To find the common denominator, we multiply the two denominators with each other, and to get the correct new numerators, we cross multiply the denominators with the numerators. For example:

$$\frac{1}{4} + \frac{1}{3} = \frac{3}{12} + \frac{4}{12} = \frac{7}{12}$$

First we cross multiply 3 x 1 and 4 x 1 in order to get the correct numerators. Then we multiply the two denominators 4 x 3 to get the common denominator. Here are more examples:

$$\frac{1}{2} + \frac{1}{3} = \frac{3}{6} + \frac{2}{6} = \frac{5}{6}$$

$$\frac{2}{3} + \frac{4}{5} = \frac{10}{15} + \frac{12}{15} = \frac{22}{15} = 1\frac{7}{15}$$

$$\frac{2}{7} + \frac{3}{8} = \frac{16}{56} + \frac{21}{56} = \frac{37}{56}$$

Step 57: Subtracting fractions. In subtracting fractions we go through the same process of finding the common denominator and the new numerators, and then we merely subtract numerators instead of adding them:

$$\frac{1}{3} - \frac{1}{4} = \frac{4}{12} - \frac{3}{12} = \frac{1}{12}$$

$$\frac{3}{4} - \frac{2}{5} = \frac{15}{20} - \frac{8}{20} = \frac{7}{20}$$

The following fraction table reveals how the pattern of numerators and denominators is directly related to our multiplication facts. Since the greatest aids to memory in arithmetic are the number patterns, the table is worth studying. It will reinforce the pupil's understanding of the advantages of memorizing counting by numbers over one and knowing the basic multiplication facts cold.

$$\frac{1}{2} = \frac{2}{4} = \frac{3}{6} = \frac{4}{8} = \frac{5}{10} = \frac{6}{12} = \frac{7}{14} = \frac{8}{16} = \frac{9}{18} = \frac{10}{20}$$

$$\frac{2}{3} = \frac{4}{6} = \frac{6}{9} = \frac{8}{12} = \frac{10}{15} = \frac{12}{18} = \frac{14}{21} = \frac{16}{24} = \frac{18}{27} = \frac{20}{30}$$

$$\frac{3}{4} = \frac{6}{8} = \frac{9}{12} = \frac{12}{16} = \frac{15}{20} = \frac{18}{24} = \frac{21}{28} = \frac{24}{32} = \frac{27}{36} = \frac{30}{40}$$

$$\frac{4}{5} = \frac{8}{10} = \frac{12}{15} = \frac{16}{20} = \frac{20}{25} = \frac{24}{30} = \frac{28}{35} = \frac{32}{40} = \frac{36}{45} = \frac{40}{50}$$

$$\frac{5}{6} = \frac{10}{12} = \frac{15}{18} = \frac{20}{24} = \frac{25}{30} = \frac{30}{36} = \frac{35}{42} = \frac{40}{48} = \frac{45}{54} = \frac{50}{60}$$

$$\frac{6}{7} = \frac{12}{14} = \frac{18}{21} = \frac{24}{28} = \frac{30}{35} = \frac{36}{42} = \frac{42}{49} = \frac{48}{56} = \frac{54}{63} = \frac{60}{70}$$

$$\frac{7}{8} = \frac{14}{16} = \frac{21}{24} = \frac{28}{32} = \frac{35}{40} = \frac{42}{48} = \frac{49}{56} = \frac{56}{64} = \frac{63}{72} = \frac{70}{80}$$

$$\frac{8}{9} = \frac{16}{18} = \frac{24}{27} = \frac{32}{36} = \frac{40}{45} = \frac{48}{54} = \frac{56}{63} = \frac{64}{72} = \frac{72}{81} = \frac{80}{90}$$

$$\frac{9}{10} = \frac{18}{20} = \frac{27}{30} = \frac{36}{40} = \frac{45}{50} = \frac{54}{60} = \frac{63}{70} = \frac{72}{80} = \frac{81}{90} = \frac{90}{100}$$

Step 58: Adding more than two fractions with different denominators.

1. $\quad \frac{3}{4} + \frac{2}{3} + \frac{5}{6} =$

2. Add the first two fractions:

$$\frac{3}{4} + \frac{2}{3} = \frac{9}{12} + \frac{8}{12} = \frac{17}{12}$$

3. $\quad \frac{17}{12} + \frac{5}{6} = \frac{17}{12} + \frac{10}{12} = \frac{27}{12} = 2\frac{3}{12} = 2\frac{1}{4}$

4. $\quad \frac{3}{4} + \frac{2}{3} + \frac{5}{6} = 2\frac{1}{4}$

Another example:

1. $$\frac{6}{7} + \frac{2}{3} + \frac{4}{5} =$$

2. $$\frac{6}{7} + \frac{2}{3} = \frac{18}{21} + \frac{14}{21} = \frac{32}{21}$$

3. $$\frac{32}{21} + \frac{4}{5} = \frac{160}{105} + \frac{84}{105} = \frac{244}{105} = 2\frac{34}{105} = 2\frac{1}{3}$$

Note that 34/105 is close enough to be considered 1/3.

4. $$\frac{6}{7} + \frac{2}{3} + \frac{4}{5} = 2\frac{1}{3}$$

Step 59: Multiplying with fractions. In multiplying fractions, the numerators are multiplied with one another and the denominators are multiplied with one another. Note that we convert whole numbers into fractions to simplify the process:

$$\frac{1}{2} \times 4 = \frac{1}{2} \times \frac{4}{1} = \frac{4}{2} = 2$$

$$\frac{1}{2} \times \frac{1}{4} = \frac{1}{8}$$

$$\frac{3}{4} \times \frac{7}{8} = \frac{21}{32}$$

$$\frac{5}{6} \times 6 = \frac{5}{6} \times \frac{6}{1} = \frac{30}{6} = 5$$

$$\frac{1}{22} \times 11 = \frac{1}{22} \times \frac{11}{1} = \frac{11}{22} = \frac{1}{2}$$

$$\frac{1}{2} \times 1\frac{1}{2} = \frac{1}{2} \times \left[\frac{2}{2} + \frac{1}{2}\right] = \frac{1}{2} \times \frac{3}{2} = \frac{3}{4}$$

$$2\frac{1}{4} \times 1\frac{5}{8} = \left[\frac{8}{4} + \frac{1}{4}\right] \times \left[\frac{8}{8} + \frac{5}{8}\right] =$$

$$\frac{9}{4} \times \frac{13}{8} = \frac{117}{32} = 3\frac{21}{32}$$

Step 60: Dividing by fractions. Dividing by a fraction is the same as multiplying by the same fraction turned upside down. The upside down fraction is known as the reciprocal. Study the following examples.

$$\frac{1}{2} \div 2 = \frac{1}{2} \div \frac{2}{1} = \frac{1}{2} \times \frac{1}{2} = \frac{1}{4}$$

$$\frac{1}{2} \div \frac{1}{2} = \frac{1}{2} \times \frac{2}{1} = \frac{2}{2} = 1$$

$$\frac{3}{4} \div 3 = \frac{3}{4} \times \frac{1}{3} = \frac{3}{12} = \frac{1}{4}$$

$$\frac{3}{4} \div \frac{1}{8} = \frac{3}{4} \times \frac{8}{1} = \frac{24}{4} = 6$$

$$1\frac{1}{2} \div 3\frac{1}{4} = \frac{3}{2} \div \frac{13}{4} = \frac{3}{2} \times \frac{4}{13} = \frac{12}{26} = \frac{6}{13}$$

Checking above division:

$$\frac{6}{13} \times 3\frac{1}{4} = \frac{6}{13} \times \frac{13}{4} = \frac{78}{52} = 1\frac{26}{52} = 1\frac{1}{2}$$

Step 61: Decimals. The simplest way to introduce the pupil to the concept of decimals (that is, fractions expressed in place-value notation) is through an understanding of how we deal with money in decimals. A decimal is a numerator of one or more digits with an unwritten denominator of ten or some power of ten depending on the position of the digit or digits in relation to the decimal point. For example:

.5	=	5/10	.85	=	85/100
.05	=	5/100	.805	=	805/1000
.005	=	5/1000			

In other words, the digit columns to the right of the decimal point represent 10ths, 100ths, 1000ths, etc., in the same order that the digit columns to the left of the decimal point represent "ones," "tens," "hundreds," "thousands," etc. Thus, we can write 555 as:

$$500 + 50 + 5 = 555$$

and we can write .555 as:

$$5/10 + 5/100 + 5/1000 = 500/1000 + 50/1000 + 5/1000 =$$

$$555/1000$$

In money notation, where the unwritten denominator is 100, the decimal is only written out to two places. Note that .50 is the same as .5. However, it is written as .50 because we refer to it as 50 cents as well as a half-dollar, and also to avoid confusing it with .05. In general, our decimal money notations are read more as hieroglyphics than place-value notations because of how they are referred to verbally and because of our coin system. Thus:

100¢	$1.00	one dollar or dollar
50¢	.50	half dollar, fifty cents

25¢	.25	quarter, twenty-five cents
10¢	.10	dime, ten cents
5¢	.05	nickel, five cents
1¢	.01	cent

Demonstrate how decimals can be converted into decimal fractions, then reduced to proper fractions:

$$.50 = \frac{50}{100} = \frac{1}{2} \qquad\qquad .05 = \frac{5}{100} = \frac{1}{20}$$

$$.25 = \frac{25}{100} = \frac{1}{4} \qquad\qquad .01 = \frac{1}{100}$$

$$.10 = \frac{10}{100} = \frac{1}{10}$$

Converting fractions to decimals. To convert or change a common fraction to a decimal is a very simple and straightforward procedure. It consists simply of dividing the numerator (with zeros annexed) by the denominator and placing a decimal point before the proper figure of the quotient. For example:

$$1/2 \qquad 2\overline{)1.0}^{\,.5} \qquad 1/2 = .5$$
$$\underline{1\ 0}$$

$$1/4 \qquad 4\overline{)3.00}^{\,.75} \qquad 3/4 = .75$$
$$\underline{2\ 8}$$
$$20$$
$$\underline{20}$$

$$1/4 \qquad 4\overline{)1.00}^{\,.25} \qquad 1/4 = .25$$
$$\underline{8}$$
$$20$$
$$\underline{20}$$

Have the pupil read the following amounts:

$.38	$.09	$.65	$1.25	$1.98
$9.65	$12.25	$25.25	$42.01	$99.99
$175.15	$305.02	$548.23	$690.50	$952.33
$1,000.00	$1,025.08	$1,200.50	$5,493.26	$6,004.10
$4,444.44	$9,500.00	$7,320.01	$10,000.00	$13,679.84

Provide exercises in adding, subtracting, multiplying and dividing monetary sums. You can use a shopping list for additions, regular prices vs. sale prices for subtractions, multiple buying for multiplication (if one cost 3.98, how much will 3 cost?) and unit pricing for division (if the price of the item is 3 for $1.00 or 5 for .88, how much will one cost?).

Teach the pupil to read large sums of money in round figures up to one million:

$100	one hundred
$1,000	one thousand
$10,000	ten thousand
$100,000	one hundred thousand
$1,000,000	one million (one thousand thousand)

Step 62: Linear measurement. Explain the following measurements:

1 inch		
12 inches	=	1 foot
3 feet	=	1 yard
5,280 feet	=	1 mile
1,760 yards	=	1 mile

Teach the child to read the following measurements:

1 foot 2 inches	=	1 ft. 2 in.	=	1' 2"
5 yards	=	5 yds.		
20 miles	=	20 mi.		

Teach the pupil to add, subtract, multiply, and divide feet and inches. Note that in subtraction and division we can simplify computation by converting feet into inches by multiplying feet by 12, subtracting or dividing in inches, then converting back into feet and inches for the final answer.

Addition:

$$\begin{array}{rr} 3' & 10'' \\ 4' & 9'' \\ \hline 7' & 19'' \end{array} \quad = 8' \ 7''$$

Subtraction:

$$\begin{array}{rr} 10' & 8'' \\ -\ 2' & 4'' \\ \hline 8' & 4'' \end{array}$$

Subtraction:

$$\begin{array}{rr} 10' & 2'' \\ -\ 3' & 9'' \\ \hline \end{array} \ = \ \begin{array}{r} 122'' \\ -\ 45'' \\ \hline 77'' \end{array} \ = \ \begin{array}{rr} 10' & 2'' \\ -3' & 9'' \\ \hline 6' & 5'' \end{array}$$

Multiplication:

$$\begin{array}{rr} 5' & 3'' \\ \times & 10 \\ \hline 50' & 30'' \end{array} \ = \ 52' \ 6''$$

Division:

$$10' \ 8'' \div 4 \ = \ 4\overline{)128}^{\,32} \ = \ 2' \ 8''$$

Computing with fractions of inches can become complicated, especially in division, where conversion to decimals is usually necessary. If the pupil is up to it, show him how it is done with the following examples:

Addition:

$$\begin{array}{rrr} 6' & 5 & 1/2'' \\ 4' & 10 & 3/4'' \\ \hline 10' & 15 & 5/4'' \end{array} \ = \ 10' \ 16 \ 1/4'' \ =$$

$$11' \ 4 \ 1/4''$$

Subtraction: 6' 5 3/8"
                -2' 4 1/4"
                ─────────────
                 4' 1 1/8"

Subtraction: 6' 2 3/16" = 74 3/16" = 74 3/16" =
                -3' 9 1/4"   -45 1/4"   -45 4/16"
                ─────────────   ──────────   ──────────

                        73 19/16"   6' 2 3/16"
                       -45 4/16" =   -3' 9 1/4"
                       ──────────   ─────────────
                        28 15/16"   2' 4 15/16"

Multiplication: 12' 8 3/4"
                  x   18   = 216' 144" 54/4" =
                  ─────────────

216' 144" 13 1/2"   = 216' 157 1/2"   = 229' 1 1/2"

Division: 38' 1 1/2" ÷ 3   =   457 1/2" ÷ 3   =

                              152.5
                           3)‾457.5‾   = 12' 8 1/2"

Step 63: Liquid measurement. Undoubtedly the pupil will be familiar with our liquid measurement terms. However, he may not know how many pints make a quart, etc. Devise problems in which pints are converted into quarts and quarts into gallons, etc.

```
 pint

2 pints   -   1 quart

4 quarts  -   1 gallon
```

Step 64: Weight. As with liquid measurement, the pupil will be familiar with weight measurement terms. However, teach him the relationship of ounces to pounds and pounds to tons.

```
    ounce

4 ounces      =   quarter-pound

8 ounces      =   half-pound

16 ounces     =   1 pound

2,000 pounds  =   1 ton
```

Step 65: Time. Find out how much the child knows about telling time. Then explain our time system in an organized way. Start with the fact that a day is divided into twenty-four hours, a day representing a full rotation of the earth on its axis. A clock's face is divided into twelve hours, which means that the hour hand circles the clock twice each day, once for the morning hours, once for the afternoon and evening hours. Explain that a.m. is the abbreviation of the Latin word *ante-meridiem,* which means before noon, and that p.m. is the abbreviation of the Latin word *post-meridiem,* meaning after noon. Noon, or the *meridiem,* is the time of day when the sun is highest in the sky. Before noon the sun rises; after noon it starts going down. Before clocks were invented sundials were used to tell the time of day. The sundial is an instrument that indicates time by the position of the shadow of a pointer cast by the sun on the face of a dial marked in hours. At noon, when the sun is directly above, no shadow is cast to the right or left of the pointer.

The clock has two hands—an hour hand (the short hand) and a minute hand (the longer hand). The hour hand circles the clock every twelve hours, the minute hand circles it every sixty minutes or hour. Some clocks have a second-hand which sweeps around the clock each minute, that is, every sixty seconds.

To tell the correct time we must note the position of the two hands. When both hands are at the twelve position, it is either 12 noon or 12 midnight. The clock itself does not tell us whether it is a.m. or p.m. This we determine by our own observation.

The hour hand, of course, tells us what hour it is. The minute hand tells us how far into the hour we are. Since an hour is composed of sixty minutes, when the minute hand is at the figure 3, it is a quarter past the hour; at the figure 6, it is half past the hour; at position 9, it is three-quarters past the hour, or one quarter before the next hour. In terms of minutes, each position on the clock represents 5 minutes. Thus, the figure 3, or one-quarter past the hour, represents 15 minutes. The figure 6 represents 30 minutes past the hour, and the figure 9 represents 15 minutes before the next hour.

Demonstrate clock positions to the pupil by drawing a clock-face on the blackboard and drawing the hour and minute hands in a variety of positions.

Give the pupil practice problems in telling time, and in converting hours into minutes, minutes into seconds, minutes into fractions of hours, and seconds into fractions of minutes. Devise problems in which time must be calculated. For example, if we leave New York at 11 a.m. and arrive in Boston at 3:25 p.m. how long does the trip take?

Explain the four different time zones in the United States: Eastern Standard Time (E.S.T.), Central Standard Time (C.S.T.), Mountain Standard Time (M.S.T.), and Pacific Standard Time (P.S.T.). Each time zone is one hour earlier going from east to west—because it takes the sun one hour to travel 60° on the earth's surface. Thus, if it is 4 p.m. in New York City, it is 3 p.m. in Chicago, 2 p.m. in Denver, and 1 p.m. in Los Angeles. Thus, if you are flying from New York to Chicago, leaving New York at 3 p.m. E.S.T. and arriving at Chicago at 3:30 p.m. C.S.T., how long does the trip take? The correct answer is one and a half hours, not a half hour.

Daylight-saving time is one hour ahead of standard time, generally used in the summer to give an hour more of daylight at the end of the usual working day. Unless the time is designated as daylight-saving time (D.S.T.) it is standard time. Thus, when we enter daylight-saving time we move the clock forward one hour. When we go off daylight-saving time, we move the clock back an hour. We move forward to daylight-saving, back to standard.

After the pupil has mastered an understanding of our domestic time zones, you can take up the time zones in the rest of the world. This can be done by determining the time in the major cities of the world in relation to the time zone in which the pupil lives. Explain that the world is divided into twenty-four standard time zones calculated east and west of a line drawn through Greenwich, England, a borough of London. This line is known as the Prime Meridian (first meridian). In other words, the twenty-four time zones were determined on the basis of their relationship to noon at Greenwich. Naturally, when it is noon at Greenwich, it is midnight on the other side of the globe. At midnight we pass from one day to the next. On the other side of the globe, the prime meridian becomes the 180th meridian.

For the sake of establishing a universal calendar, the nations of the world agreed to accept a line drawn largely along the 180th meridian in the middle of the Pacific as the International Date Line. Thus, although it may be noon on the 180th meridian it will be 11 a.m. Sunday at the next time zone west of the date line and 1 p.m. Saturday at the next time zone east of the date line. Thus, you lose a day when you travel west across the date line, but you gain a day when you travel east across it. This may seem to be a strange phenomenon to those who never travel out of their time zones. But the earth is constantly rotating, and while most of us remain in the same place, we go from one day to the next in the middle of the same night and think nothing of it. On New Year's Eve, at the stroke of midnight, we go from one year to the next. Nothing visible has occurred, but what has occurred in terms of human understanding is so great an event that celebrations take place to commemorate it. New Year's Eve is the best way to prove that mass hysteria can be induced by a set of arbitrary numbers. The reason for this, of course, is that the passing of time has meaning and that the numbers we use to represent the passage of time take on added significance. Thus, numbers like 1776, 1860,

1914, 1939, 1984 become incredibly powerful stimulators of the mind, in that they conjure up events and cataclysms that have left their mark on human history or will do so in the future.

Step 66: The Calendar. Undoubtedly the pupil will know the days of the week and the months of the year. He will know the four seasons. He will probably know that there are seven days in a week and twelve months in a year. But he may not know how many days or weeks there are in a year.

When we ask how many days there are in a year, we are really asking how many times does the earth rotate on its axis as it completes a full circle or revolution around the sun. The earth rotates 365¼ times each year. But since we cannot have a calendar with a quarter-day, we compute the calendar year as having 365 days, a quarter-day short of a full year. Every four years (leap year) we add an extra day. This extra day is tagged on at the end of February which regularly has 28 days but has 29 in leap years. So every four years we make our arithmetic adjustment in our calendar. If you explain the basis of our calendar in this way, the pupil will understand the meaning of leap year as an arithmetic adjustment. He will also understand the difference between the year as a calendar computation and the actual physical year of the earth's movement around the sun.

To remember the number of days each month has, teach the pupil the well known rhyme: Thirty days hath September,/April, June and November/All the rest have thirty-one/Except February alone,/Which has four and twenty-four/Till leap year brings it one day more.

There are fifty-two weeks and one day in the year, with an extra day in leap years. Ten years make a decade, a hundred years make a century. The years in the 1900's are in the twentieth century. To explain this, show how the years 1 through 100 were the first century, the years 101 through 200 were the second century, etc.

Our present calendar system starts with the birth of Christ, so that the year 1 A.D. means 1 year after the birth of Christ, while 1 B.C. means 1 year before the birth of Christ. Have the pupil compute such problems as the number of years between 3500 B.C. and 1970.

The significance of the calendar is not only that we use it to give our everyday lives a sense of order and continuity, but also to keep track of our history which is crowded with events and people. The calendar reveals a great deal about man's basic nature, his need to fit the order of his life to the order of the physical universe, his need to devise tools with which to aid memory and keep records, his need to live a regulated, nonchaotic existence in which he can plan the future.

The calendar also represents a considerable human achievement in terms of solar-system observance. It was the first practical result of man's astronomical studies in which he could relate the seasonal changes on earth to the changes taking place in the heavens. In those days it was assumed that the earth was stationary but that everything in the heavens moved around it. By recording all these movements and observing their regular recurrence man was able to predict certain future conditions and plan accordingly. The calendar became the primary tool for planning. It is one of the best tools man has ever devised to help him control his environment and plan ahead. It should be noted that all astrological forecasting is based on the calendar in relation to the movements of heavenly bodies. While man has devised more scientific and accurate ways of forecasting the future, astrology remains a popular way to predict the unpredictable.

Teach the child to read dates and to make his own calendar. Everyone's birthday is an important calendar date. Have the pupil relate his own birthday to important world events. Also devise problems using dates; for example, computing the 250th anniversary of the signing of the Declaration of Independence or the age of George Washington if he were alive today. Teach him to make a chronological chart of events, to chart his own program of activities for the coming year. This will show the child how to use the calendar in planning ahead.

In teaching the four seasons, explain the phenomenon of the equinox, that is, the two days each year in which both day and night are of equal length. They occur on the first day of autumn and the first day of spring when the sun's rays are vertical to the earth. The first is called the autumnal equinox and occurs about September 23, the second is called the vernal equinox and occurs about March 21. You can use this lesson on the calendar as a means of stimulating the pupil's interest in the solar system and how mathematics is used to understand the relationship of one heavenly body to another.

Step 67: Intermediary Arithmetic. We have covered all of the arithmetic skills a child is expected to learn in the primary and elementary grades. Some children, obviously, will learn faster than others. The slower children will require explanations in the simplest, most elementary form and will need to have these explanations frequently repeated, with variations in the approach and in the nature of the illustrative examples. The brighter pupils will see reasons, grasp concepts, and understand processes more quickly. But once the child has firmly mastered the material in this course of instruction he can move on to arithmetic on the intermediary levels. What follows is an outline on how to expand the skills already learned.

Addition: The pupil should learn to add longer columns of ' numbers with a variety of digits, making sure that the right digit is added in the right column. He should perfect his skill in carrying, regardless of how many digits there are in the numbers added.

Subtraction: Here the child should develop his equal adding or borrowing skill in subtractions with numbers of three, four, five, six or more digits.

Multiplication: The pupil should be taught to multiply with both larger multiplicands and larger multipliers. The first step is to teach him to multiply two-digit multiplicands with two-digit multipliers, as in the following example, without carrying:

a.   43
          22
          ——

b. Multiply the multiplicand with the "ones" digit of the multiplier.

          43
          22
          ——
          86

c. Multiply the multiplicand with the "tens" digit of the multiplier, placing the first written digit—the "ones" digit—of the partial product directly under the "tens" digit of the multiplier. The reason why we must indent the partial product so that it falls directly under the "tens" digit in the multiplier is because we are actually multiplying the multiplicand by 20 not 2, since the 2 in the "tens" column represents multiples of ten in our place-value system. However, we accomplish the same thing more simply by multiplying the multiplicand by 2, not 20, and indenting the partial product so that it falls directly under the "tens" digit of the multiplier.

```
 43
 22
 ‾‾
 86
86
‾‾‾
```

d. Add the two partial products for the final product.

```
 4 3
 2 2
 ‾‾‾
 8 6
8 6
‾‾‾‾
9 4 6
```

The next example requires carrying.

a.　69
　　23
　　‾‾

b. Multiply the multiplicand with the "ones" digit of the multiplier.

```
    2
  6 9
  2 3
 ‾‾‾‾
2 0 7
```

c. Multiply the multiplicand with the "tens" digit of the multiplier, indenting the partial product as shown in the previous example. Write the carried digit above the previously carried digit distinctly enough to avoid confusing them.

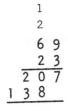

```
    1
    2
   6 9
   2 3
  ─────
  2 0 7
1 3 8
─────────
```

d. Add the two partial products to get the final product.

```
   6 9
   2 3
  ─────
  2 0 7
1 3 8
─────────
1 5 8 7
```

In the next step we multiply three-digit multiplicands with two-digit multipliers, first without carrying, then with carrying:

```
                      2 3
                      3 4
   1 2 3            2 6 8
     2 1              4 5
  ───────         ─────────
   1 2 3          1 3 4 0
 2 4 6            1 0 7 2
 ─────────      ───────────
 2 5 8 3        1 2 0 6 0
```

In the next step we multiply three-digit multiplicands with three-digit multipliers, first without carrying, to demonstrate the process more simply, then with carrying. Note the indention of the "tens" and "hundreds" partial products consistent with place-value notation. You can demonstrate the validity of this method by multiplying 231 by 3, 20, and 100 and adding the three products together.

```
   2 3 1
   1 2 3
  ───────
   6 9 3
 4 6 2
2 3 1
─────────────
2 8 4 1 3
```

When carrying is required in multiplying with each digit of the multiplier, be sure to have the pupil write the "carries" clearly and separately in their own lines to avoid confusion.

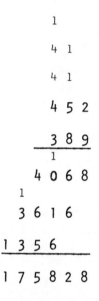

In the next steps, we multiply four-, five-, and six-digit multiplicands by three-, four-, and five-digit multipliers

Multipliers ending with zeros. When the multiplier is 10, 100, 1,000, etc., the product is obtained by adding the number of zeros in the multiplier to the multiplicand. For example:

$$4,342 \times 10 = 43,420$$

$$396 \times 1000 = 396,000$$

$$42,437 \times 100 = 4,243,700$$

Other examples of multipliers ending with zeros:

a.
```
      345        or          345
      250                    250
    17250                  17250
    690                    690
    86250                  86250
```

b.
```
      345        or          345
      200                    200
    69000                  69000
```

c.
```
          4 5 6 8      or        4 5 6 8
          3 4 0 0                3 4 0 0
    1 8 2 7 2 0 0          1 8 2 7 2 0 0
  1 3 7 0 4              1 3 7 0 4
  1 5,5 3 1,2 0 0        1 5,5 3 1,2 0 0
```

d.
```
          4 5 6 8      or        4 5 6 8
          6 0 0 0                6 0 0 0
    2 7,4 0 8,0 0 0        2 7,4 0 8,0 0 0
```

Checking multiplication. Multiplication can be checked by interchanging the multiplicand and multiplier and comparing products, which should be identical.

Division: Developing the ability to divide with two or more digit divisors requires developing considerable numerical judgment. This judgment consists of the ability to mentally estimate how many times a divisor can go into a dividend and the successive digits in the quotient. Such numerical judgment can only be developed with a great deal of practice. Such practice will enable a pupil to see, for example, that 22 goes into 90 four times with a remainder of 2. If the divisor is 27 and the dividend 96, the pupil will estimate the quotient by thinking of 30 into 90. His final answer will be a quotient of 3 with a remainder of 15. Here is how these problems appear on paper:

$$
\begin{array}{r} 4 \\ 22\overline{)90} \\ 88 \\ \hline 2 \end{array}
\qquad
\begin{array}{r} 3 \\ 27\overline{)96} \\ 81 \\ \hline 15 \end{array}
$$

In developing the ability to divide with larger divisors, first give the pupil exercises with two-digit divisors and two-digit dividends, then two-digit divisors with three-, four-, five-, and six-digit dividends.

Next, advance to three-digit divisors with three-, four-, five-, six-, and seven-digit dividends. From there, provide exercises with four-digit divisors and appropriate dividends. Once the pupil has mastered the skills learned in solving these problems, he should have no trouble dividing any size dividend with any size divisor.

Examples:

Two-digit divisor with a three-digit dividend.

a.
$$58\overline{)849}$$

b.
$$
\begin{array}{r} 1 \\ 58\overline{)849} \\ 58 \\ \hline 26 \end{array}
$$

c. Bring down 9. Estimate 58 into 269 as 50 into 250.

$$
\begin{array}{r} 15 \\ 58\overline{)849} \\ 58 \\ \hline 269 \\ 290 \end{array}
$$

d. 5 is too large. Try 4.

$$\begin{array}{r} 14 \\ 58\overline{)849} \\ \underline{58} \\ 269 \\ \underline{232} \\ 37 \end{array}$$

e. Final answer is quotient of 14 with remainder of 37.

Note how numerical judgment only provides us with an estimate. The final correct answer is arrived at by trying different numbers. It is like trying on different sizes of shoes to see which one will fit.

Provide sufficient exercises to help the pupil develop numerical judgment.

Two-digit divisor with a four-digit dividend:

a.
$$39\overline{)8754}$$

b.
$$\begin{array}{r} 2 \\ 39\overline{)8754} \\ \underline{78} \\ 9 \end{array}$$

c. Bring down 5. 39 goes into 95 twice.

$$\begin{array}{r} 22 \\ 39\overline{)8754} \\ \underline{78} \\ 95 \\ \underline{78} \\ 17 \end{array}$$

d. Bring down 4. 39 goes into 174 five times?

```
         225
    39)8754
       78
       95
       78
      174
      195
```

e. Five is too large. Try 4.

```
         224
    39)8754
       78
       95
       78
      174
      156
       18
```

Two-digit divisor with a four-digit dividend in which the divisor is larger than the first two digits of the dividend:

a.
```
    86)6387
```

b. Since 86 goes into 63 less than one time, we must divide 638 by 86. Our numerical judgment suggests that we try 7.

```
          7
    86)6387
      602
       36
```

c. Bring down 7. 86 goes into 367 four times?

```
        74
   86)6387
      602
      367
      344
       23
```

d. Correct answer: quotient of 74, remainder 23.

Two-digit divisor with five-digit dividend:

a.
```
   92)62430
```

b.
```
          6
   92)62430
      552
       72
```

c.
```
         67
   92)62430
      552
      723
      644
       79
```

d.
```
        678
   92)62430
      552
      723
      644
      790
      736
       54
```

Two-digit divisor with a six-digit dividend:

a.
$$48\overline{)328,407}$$

b.
$$\begin{array}{r} 6 \\ 48\overline{)328,407} \\ 288 \\ \hline 40 \end{array}$$

c.
$$\begin{array}{r} 6,8 \\ 48\overline{)328,407} \\ 288 \\ \hline 404 \\ 384 \\ \hline 20 \end{array}$$

d.
$$\begin{array}{r} 6,84 \\ 48\overline{)328,407} \\ 288 \\ \hline 404 \\ 384 \\ \hline 200 \\ 192 \\ \hline 8 \end{array}$$

e.
$$\begin{array}{r} 6,841 \\ 48\overline{)328,407} \\ 288 \\ \hline 404 \\ 384 \\ \hline 200 \\ 192 \\ \hline 87 \\ 48 \\ \hline 39 \end{array}$$

Three-digit divisor with a four-digit dividend:

a.
$$609 \overline{)8661}$$

b.
$$
\begin{array}{r}
1 \\
609 \overline{)8661} \\
\underline{609} \\
257
\end{array}
$$

c.
$$
\begin{array}{r}
14 \\
609 \overline{)8661} \\
\underline{609} \\
2571 \\
\underline{2436} \\
135
\end{array}
$$

Three-digit divisor with a five-digit dividend:

a.
$$589 \overline{)25890}$$

b.
$$
\begin{array}{r}
4 \\
589 \overline{)25890} \\
\underline{2356} \\
233
\end{array}
$$

c.
$$
\begin{array}{r}
43 \\
589 \overline{)25890} \\
\underline{2356} \\
2330 \\
\underline{1767} \\
563
\end{array}
$$

Three-digit divisor with a six-digit dividend:

a.
$$357\overline{)892,600}$$

b.
$$\begin{array}{r} 2 \\ 357\overline{)892,600} \\ \underline{714} \\ 178 \end{array}$$

c.
$$\begin{array}{r} 2,5 \\ 357\overline{)892,600} \\ \underline{714} \\ 1786 \\ \underline{1785} \\ 1 \end{array}$$

d.
$$\begin{array}{r} 2,500 \\ 357\overline{)892,600} \\ \underline{714} \\ 1786 \\ \underline{1785} \\ 100 \end{array}$$

Three-digit divisor with a seven-digit dividend:

a.
$$920\overline{)5,780,325}$$

b.
$$\begin{array}{r} 6, \\ 920\overline{)5,780,325} \\ \underline{5\ 520} \\ 260 \end{array}$$

c.
```
          6,2
920)5,780,325
    5 520
      2603
      1840
       763
```

d.
```
          6,28
920)5,780,325
    5 520
      2603
      1840
       7632
       7360
        272
```

e.
```
          6,283
920)5,780,325
    5 520
      2603
      1840
       7632
       7360
        2725
        2760
```

f. Three is too large. Try 2.

```
          6,282
920)5,780,325
    5 520
      2603
      1840
       7632
       7360
        2725
        1840
         885
```

Notice all the skills required to perform long division: division, multiplication, higher decade additions with the multiplication "carries," and subtraction with equal adding or "borrowing." Long division, in fact gives the pupil lots of practice in most of the arithmetic skills he has learned. However, it is essential to see where the pupil is strongest and weakest in his use of these skills. In this way his weak points can be strengthened by remedial drills and exercises.

SEQUENCE OF INSTRUCTION